The Early Mode
A Facsimile Librar

Series II

Printed Writings 1641–1700: Part 4

Volume 6

Eleanor Davies, Writings 1647–1652

The Early Modern Englishwoman: A Facsimile Library of Essential Works

Series II

Printed Writings 1641–1700: Part 4

Volume 6

Eleanor Davies, Writings 1647–1652

Selected and Introduced by
Teresa Feroli

General Editors
Betty S. Travitsky and Anne Lake Prescott

Routledge
Taylor & Francis Group
LONDON AND NEW YORK

The image reproduced on the title page and on the cover is from the frontispiece portrait in *Poems. By the Most Deservedly Admired Mrs. Katherine Philips* (1667). Reproduced by permission of the Folger Shakespeare Library, Washington DC.

First published in paperback 2024

First published 2011 by Ashgate Publishing

Published 2016 by Routledge
4 Park Square, Milton Park, Abingdon, Oxon OX14 4RN

and by Routledge
605 Third Avenue, New York, NY 10158

Routledge is an imprint of the Taylor & Francis Group, an informa business

British Library Cataloguing-in-Publication Data
Douglas, Eleanor, Lady, d. 1652.
Eleanor Davis, writings 1647–1652. — (The early modern Englishwoman. Series II, Printed writings, 1641–1700, part 4 ; v. 6)
1. Prophecies.
I. Title II. Series III. Feroli, Teresa.
828.4'09–dc22

Library of Congress Control Number: 2010938057

ISBN: 978-0-7546-6228-0 (hbk)
ISBN: 978-1-03-291804-4 (pbk)
ISBN: 978-1-315-25684-9 (ebk)

DOI: 10.4324/9781315256849

CONTENTS

PREFACE
BY THE GENERAL EDITORS

Until very recently, scholars of the early modern period have assumed that there were no Judith Shakespeares in early modern England. Much of the energy of the current generation of scholars has been devoted to constructing a history of early modern England that takes into account what women actually wrote, what women actually read, and what women actually did. In so doing, contemporary scholars have revised the traditional representation of early modern women as constructed both in their own time and in ours. The study of early modern women has thus become one of the most important – indeed perhaps the most important – means for the rewriting of early modern history.

The Early Modern Englishwoman: A Facsimile Library of Essential Works is one of the developments of this energetic reappraisal of the period. As the names on our advisory board and our list of editors testify, it has been the beneficiary of scholarship in the field, and we hope it will also be an essential part of that scholarship's continuing momentum.

The Early Modern Englishwoman is designed to make available a comprehensive and focused collection of writings in English from 1500 to 1750, both by women and for and about them. The three series of *Printed Writings* (*1500–1640*, *1641–1700*, and *1701–1750*) provide a comprehensive if not entirely complete collection of the separately published writings by women. In reprinting these writings we intend to remedy one of the major obstacles to the advancement of feminist criticism of the early modern period, namely the limited availability of the very texts upon which the field is based. The volumes in the facsimile library reproduce carefully chosen copies of these texts, incorporating significant variants (usually in the appendices). Each text is preceded by a short introduction providing an overview of the life and work of a writer along with a survey of important scholarship. These works, we strongly believe, deserve a large readership – of historians, literary critics, feminist critics, and non-specialist readers.

The Early Modern Englishwoman also includes separate facsimile series of *Essential Works for the Study of Early Modern Women* and of *Manuscript Writings*. These facsimile series are complemented by *The Early Modern Englishwoman 1500–1750: Contemporary Editions*. Also under our general editorship, this series includes both old-spelling and modernized editions of works by and about women and gender in early modern England.

New York City
2011

INTRODUCTORY NOTE

[A complement to Teresa Feroli's facsimile edition of Eleanor Davies' pre-1640 texts (Ashgate, 2000), this pair of volumes contains 60 texts by Lady Eleanor, selected from the corpus of 66 printed between 1641 and 1652 because they are highly representative and in reproducible condition. Because many of these texts are heavily annotated, Dr Feroli has provided copious transcriptions of the annotations, as well as helpful transcriptions of hard-to-read and occasionally crossed-out passages, to assist her readers. This high number of texts has led us to three departures from our usual practice, each made to assist readers in using the volumes. First, we have included modern page numbers at the foot of each page. Second, we have numbered the texts in the Table of Contents, and each reference in this Introductory Note to a text included in the volume is followed ***[in square brackets and in bold font]*** *by the number of that text as designated in the Table of Contents. Extracts are identified by the page number of the original. Finally, Wing numbers, where they exist, have been supplied in the Textual Notes, rather than as a block at the head of the References. Following Lady Eleanor's biographer Esther Cope, Dr. Feroli refers to Eleanor Davies as 'Lady Eleanor' throughout. The decision to use 'Davies' as Lady Eleanor's surname follows recent scholarship. Readers should note, however, that Wing lists her surname as 'Douglas', as do many libraries, archives and earlier scholarly articles. – The General Editors]*

Eleanor Davies: (1590–1652)

A daughter of George Touchet, Baron Audeley, and his wife Lucy, Lady Eleanor Davies spent her early years in an aristocratic family with dwindling economic resources. In 1609 her father arranged her marriage to the poet and prominent barrister Sir John Davies in an exchange of aristocratic ties for money. She bore three children, only one of whom, Lucy, survived into adulthood. John Davies died in 1626, and in 1627 Lady Eleanor married the professional soldier Sir Archibald Douglas. Douglas died in 1644.

In 1625, Lady Eleanor's life took a dramatic turn when, by her account in 1641, a 'Heavenly voice' told her: 'There is Ninteene yeares and a halfe to the day of Judgement, and you as the meek Virgin' (**[1]** p. 14). That same year, 1625, she published her first treatise, *A Warning to the Dragon*, initiating her controversial career as a writer of prophetic tracts. Between 1641 and 1652 she produced some 66 of them out of a corpus of 69 treatises. As a group, these tracts focus on a complex of personal and political events that Lady Eleanor thought indicated the fast approach of the 'last days' foretold by the biblical prophets Daniel and John of Patmos. Three key personal events informed her writings during this period: her tribulations as a prophet, her struggles to regain inherited properties after being widowed, and her outrage over the execution in 1631 of her brother Mervin, Earl of Castlehaven, on charges of rape and sodomy. Believing that the course of the English Civil Wars showed that the world was nearing its last days, she emphasized three political developments in particular: the rise of Parliament and the New Model Army, the execution of the powerful William Laud, Archbishop of Canterbury (one of her brother's judges), and the defeat and execution of Charles I.

A striking feature of Lady Eleanor's writing is her use of the Bible to gauge the cosmic significance of events, great and small, taking place in her nation and in her personal life. While to modern readers her claims for the apocalyptic significance of her own sufferings may seem outlandish, her approach to Scripture and to the apocalyptic books in particular is in harmony with that of many religious radicals in her age who used typological interpretations of Scripture to verify their calculations concerning the imminent arrival of the last days. Such claims on Lady Eleanor's part, in my opinion, attest not to a narcissistic desire for self-promotion but to her fervent belief that she was called by God directly to warn the people of her nation of the impending Day of Judgement.

The years between 1625 and 1641 were difficult for Lady Eleanor. Neither her two husbands nor the king received her prophecies well. Soon after she first published in 1625, John Davies burned her prophetic writings. Lady Eleanor told him 'within three years to expect the mortal blow' (**[20]** p.15), and he died shortly afterwards, in 1626. Her second husband, Douglas, likewise burned her books, and Lady Eleanor cryptically predicted that 'worse then death should befal' (**[20]** p. 23) him – he apparently lost his wits in 1631, and until he died in 1644 lived apart from his wife under the care of family members. In 1633, after Lady Eleanor travelled to Amsterdam to publish three treatises for English distribution, the Commission for Ecclesiastical Causes, at the prompting of Charles, sanctioned her. The Commission found her guilty 'of unlawful printing & publishing of books' (**[36]** p. 11), for which she spent two years in the Gatehouse prison. In late 1636 or early 1637, she was jailed again – this time in Bedlam – for literally occupying the bishop's throne at the Cathedral of Litchfield, declaring herself 'primate and metropolitan', and defacing the Cathedral's tapestries.

Writings 1641–46: The End of the Old Order and the Advent of New Jerusalem

In terms of Lady Eleanor's prophetic career, the years between 1641 and 1646 were productive and triumphant. She published with greater ease, thanks to the Long Parliament's suspension of censorship regulations in 1641, and spent no time in jail for her activities as a prophet, although she was imprisoned in July of 1646 for unpaid debts. She witnessed the execution in January of 1645 of a personal enemy, Archbishop Laud, asserting that the timing fit her prediction of the last days' approach, a prediction strengthened, in her view, by the New Model Army's defeat of Charles later that year.

The Lady Eleanor, Her Appeale To The High Covrt of Parliament **[1]** appeared at a turning point in England's political situation and marked a shift in the author's prophetic career. Lady Eleanor directed the *Appeale* to Parliament, rather than to members of the royal family, calling attention to its increased power. Her text also shows that she had codified her prophetic identity, for the first time claiming her prophetic mission as originating in a call from a 'Heavenly voice' (p. 14) telling her to expect the last days in the aforementioned nineteen and a half years. She would reproduce this vocation narrative in exactly this form in eleven later treatises.

In her next four treatises, Lady Eleanor meditated on Charles's waning fortunes, comparing him to Samson betrayed by a wily woman (in his case his French Catholic wife, Henrietta Maria) and to the doomed king Belshazzar in the Book of Daniel. Her *Samsons Fall* **[2]**, presented to Parliament and published in January of 1643, thus describes Charles as a new Samson. Appended to this is *To ... Parliament* **[2** and **3]** in which she offers to restore Charles to himself, in the sense of his true nature as one who is 'fearefull of the Lords coming' (**[3]** p. 3), and to the service of Parliament. Her *Samsons Legacie* **[3]**, prefaced by *To the Most Honorable*, expands on the comparison of Charles to Samson and offers more commentary on life in England during the first Civil War (1642–46); in particular she upbraids Laud, here likened to the Beast prophesied in Revelation, for destroying her tracts in 1633. *Amend, Amend; Gods Kingdome Is At Hand* **[4]** is a reissue of *Given to the Elector*, originally directed to Charles's nephew, the Elector Palatine, first printed in Amsterdam in 1633, and reprinted in 1648 and 1651 **[34, 57]**. The body of the text is a verse rendering of the story in Daniel 5 of the ill-fated king Belshazzar and of God's monitory handwriting on the wall, but Lady Eleanor opens the 1643 version with an anagram explicitly warning the king that: '*Belchazer*, Be-*Charles*' (p. A2).

Lady Eleanor's last tract of 1643, *The Star to the Wise* **[5]**, integrates the topical references of her earlier treatises, particularly those regarding Charles, into a more comprehensive vision of England as the direct addressee of Revelation and of herself as the prophet chosen to communicate this fact to her nation. She directs the text to Parliament and promises that peace, in the form of the second coming of Christ as portrayed in Revelation, is on the horizon. God conveys this message of hope and redemption, she says, just as he did at the time of Christ's birth: through a woman. She compares her imprisonment in Bethlehem Hospital or 'Bedlam' to Mary's journey to bear Christ in a Bethlehem 'Barn' (p. 11).

Lady Eleanor's tracts of 1644 continued to alert her readers to the imminent end of time, but now in a more considered and scholarly way. This is most evident in her Latin tract *Prophetia de die* (late 1644; not reproduced here because of the poor quality of the unique copy in Trinity College, Dublin). But it is also the case in *The Restitvtion Of Reprobates* **[6]**, in which she cites the early Christian but heterodox theologian Origen to buttress her belief in an infinitely merciful God who does not damn sinners forever. She supports her case with a catalogue of related scriptural passages, and closes with the hope that her 'WORDES' (p. 30) will bring comfort to those in Hell. *Apocalypsis Jesu Christi* **[7]** addresses the religious leaders gathered at Westminster to work out a new religious settlement. This tract predicts that Laud, who had been imprisoned since 1640 in the Tower of London, will ultimately be 'cast out of heaven' (p. 32) and reminds the Westminster Assembly that the author has delivered many accurate prognostications. *Her Blessing To Her Beloved Daughter* **[8]** is a meditation on motherhood in the life of her nation that pits Charles's French Queen, Henrietta Maria, the 'occasion of this LANDS *deep* CONSVMPTION' (p. 17), against Lady Eleanor, a type of the woman clothed with the sun in Revelation 12 who reveals 'the truth of the Resurrection time' (p. 35). She tells the tract's addressee, her daughter Lucy, that because she has been her 'mothers Copartner' and 'sole support', she can look forward to '*endlesse Joy, life eternall*' (p. 38).

In January of 1645, Archbishop Laud was executed on charges of treason (at the prompting of the Scots who sought to advance a Presbyterian model of church government). Lady Eleanor's response was both personal and political: she saw Laud's death as God's justice for his role in her brother's 1631 execution and in her own 1633 trial and imprisonment. More broadly, she saw Laud's death as coinciding with the Day of Judgement that she had predicted after her call in 1625. *The Word Of God, To The Citie of London* **[9]** focuses primarily on the death of her brother, linking it to those of Laud in 1645 and of Thomas Wentworth, Earl of Strafford – one of Charles's principal advisers – in 1641, so as to assert that time's end approaches. Her broadside *As not unknowne* **[10]** again pronounces on Laud's death, claiming that it is the fruition of her prophecy, and that he is justly punished for having suppressed her writings in 1633. To drive this point home, she attaches some legal documents from the proceedings against her. In *The Brides Preparation* **[11]** Lady Eleanor uses some imagery from Revelation that she correlates with current events. She continues in *Great Brittains Visitation* **[12]** to emphasize the imminence of the last days: Revelation 7 indicates that when 1644 is complete, 'disolution comes quickly' (p. 26). Laud's political stances, she continues, had engendered the chaos that made this imminent. She takes a similarly assertive stand on this matter in *For Whitsontyds Last Feast* **[13]**. As her title suggests, she believes that the Whitsunday (Pentecost) of 1645 is the last, and that this is fitting because 'the second *Comming* of the *holy Ghost*' (p. 5) will arrive, as Peter (by way of Joel) proclaims at the first Pentecost, just before the Last Judgement (Acts 2: 17–21, 33; Joel 2: 28–32). *The* [*Second*] *Co*[*ming*] **[14]** again projects the end of 1645 as the time of the Last Judgement, but her emphasis shifts to a denunciation of those 'witts or Scoffers' who make 'sport' of 'those tydings of the great Day' (p. 17).

A tonal shift from urgent insistence on the approaching end of time to more reflective theological statements is apparent with the publication of *Of Errors Ioyned with Gods Word* **[15]**. This tract, addressed to Parliament, attempts to correct some errors Lady Eleanor has detected in King James's interpretation of Revelation. (Here, she may be referring to his *A Paraphrase Upon the Revelation of the Apostle S. John* that appears in his *Workes* of 1616.) In November of 1645, Lady Eleanor reissued her *Prayer* **[16]** of 1644. There is no extant copy of the original 1644 tract, published after a significant Royalist military victory. This event appears to have prompted Lady Eleanor to drop her usual mode of mapping the predictions in Daniel and Revelation onto England's political situation and instead to implore God's 'pardon and forgiveness' (p. 4) for her unworthy people. She also published in 1645 a translation of her 1644 *Prophetia de die, Prophesie of the Last Day* **[17]**. In this text, of which only a fragment remains, she proclaims that the last days are coming soon, as can be seen in such signs as the 'raging & roaring' of Satan evident in '*the madnesse of the World*' (p. 8). (She also published *I am the first and the last* in 1645; extant copies are in poor condition and so are not included here.)

Lady Eleanor's first published tract of 1646, *For the blessed Feast Of Easter* **[18]**, celebrates the 1645 defeat of the Royalist army by the, in her view, blessed New Model Army. In a text published less than two months later, *The Day of Ivdgements Modell* **[19]**, she returns to the imminence of the Last Judgement. In a series of typological interpretations of Revelation 7 and 14, she is excited even further by the parallels to her own times. Her last three treatises of 1646 represent the full array of her self-reflexive, theological, and topical modes of discourse. *The Lady Eleanor Her Appeal* **[20]** (distinct from *Her Appeale* of 1641), directs its remarks to Thomas May, Secretary of the Parliament, and recounts her experiences as a prophet as well as her relationship with George Carr, a boy she encountered and housed just prior to her own calling, who possessed uncanny powers of prediction. Her *Je Le Tien* **[21]** is her second work on the general redemption of the damned at the Second Coming. In it she rehearses many of the arguments from *The Restitvtion of Reprobates* **[6]** but inserts a criticism of contemporary Anglicanism's relative neglect of the Book of Revelation. Lady Eleanor's final tract of 1646, *The Revelation Interpreted* **[22]**, portrays Buckingham, Laud and Charles as figures straight out of Revelation whose existence points to 'the Last day at hand' (p. 12). Earlier in her career, Lady Eleanor had gained notoriety for predicting the 1628 assassination of Charles's most trusted advisor, Buckingham, and in this tract she continues to denounce the now deceased former Admiral of the Navy as the beast that emerges from the sea.

Writings 1647–52: Political Upheaval and Personal Reflection

In July of 1646, Lady Eleanor was imprisoned for debts related to printers' fees, and she appears to have remained in the Gatehouse through the spring of 1647. Undeterred, she published several treatises in 1647. The first, her aptly titled *The Gatehouse Salutation* **[23]**, written in verse, promises that at the Second Coming there will be 'no more pain, prison, strife' (p. 6). She tacitly refers to her imprisonment again in her third treatise on Christ's salvation of the damned, *The Mystery of General Redemption* **[24]**, when she mentions the 'worlds general pardon' (p. 4) and when she denounces the 'illegal constructions' (p. 28) that have kept people from belief in God's infinite mercy. When she produced her *Ezekiel the Prophet* **[25]**, in April of 1647, she appears still to have been in prison, and in this text she meditates on a visionary experience she had in 1634 while in the Gatehouse. At that time, she insists, 'the Holy Ghost' (p. 4) visited her in her cell for an hour, leaving behind the scent of ambergris. It is not clear whether she was still in prison when she took up her meditation on Ezekiel for the second time in 1647, in *Ezekiel, Cap.2.* **[26]**. As Esther Cope observes, this tract emphasizes the prophet's encounter with a 'rebellious nation' (*Handmaid*, p. 133).

Whether Lady Eleanor was in prison in August of 1647 when she produced *The Excommunication out of Paradice* **[27]** is also unclear, but this is the first in a series of tracts addressing the situation of Charles, now held captive by the Army. Directing her treatise to Cromwell, she claims that Charles will soon be '*brought to judgement*' (p. 16). When she took up her pen again to write in early spring of 1648, she found herself once more in prison, this time at the King's Bench. Her *Reader, The heavy hour at hand* **[28]** proclaims, as the title suggests, the approaching end of the world. In *Wherefore to prove the thing* **[29]** (also issued in 1648 under the title *And without proving what we say*), Lady Eleanor meditates on her legal struggles to retain her rights to the manor at Pirton (bought for her by Davies as her jointure) and on the hapless king. When she regains her property, she says, Charles's plight may improve. Her *Writ of Restitution* **[30]** again laments her legal struggles, extending her discourse about property so as to assert the redemption of the damned. Those who fail to recognize Christ's sacrifice as 'Restitution' seek, in her view, to disinherit the Son of God.

With the start of the second Civil War in the spring of 1648, Lady Eleanor turned from her property to her role as a prophet. In *Apocalyps, Chap. 11* **[31]** she announces that the ill treatment of her books since 1633 is a sure sign of the Apocalypse. Once more, in *The Lady Eleanor Her Remonstrance* **[33]**, she notes England's failure to heed her warnings and warns of the approaching Last Judgement. *Of the generall Great Days Approach* **[32]** addresses Sir Thomas Fairfax, the commander-in-chief of the New Model Army, informing him that biblical evidence and contemporary events point to Great Britain as the addressee of John's message in Revelation. In the same month, September, Lady Eleanor reissued her 1633 tract *Given to the Elector Prince Charles of the Rhyne* **[34]**. The later edition includes a brief address to the reader, printed comments in the margin, and two closing stanzas dated September 1648. These last remind Charles that the tract's addressee, his nephew the German Prince Charles, has been imprisoned and so too, since 1645, has he.

Charles and his execution on 30 January 1649 are the focus of Lady Eleanor's first four treatises of that year. The first, *Her Appeal from the Court to the Camp* **[35]**, appears to have been written during Charles's trial. She directs it to Fairfax and advises him of both the legitimacy of her prophetic career and the illegitimacy of Charles's reign. *The Blasphemous Charge Against Her* **[36]** uses the occasion of Charles's trial to revisit her own trial of 1633. The text consists of a letter to the imprisoned king, urging him to seek her forgiveness, and a set of documents related to her trial. (The Folger Library's copy omits the prefatory letter to Charles and instead indicates that he has been executed.) Her next tract, *The Crying Charge* **[37]**, is a companion piece to *The Blasphemous Charge*. Directed to the court presiding over Charles's trial, it accuses the king of sanctioning her brother's execution and includes a copy of Castlehaven's declaration of fealty to the Church of England on the scaffold. In *The New Jerusalem At Hand* **[38]**, Lady Eleanor extends her preoccupation with questions of inheritance to the situation of Charles's children, disinherited by his death, and to the claim to the throne of Lady Eleanor's now deceased second husband Douglas who, she insists, was in fact King James's first son, a claim she deems further legitimated by his possession of the prophetic gifts that he demonstrated in a letter to the London clergyman, Dr James Sibbald; she reproduces a copy of this letter as evidence. (Douglas had made an apparently specious assertion that he was the son of James and the daughter of James's tutor, Sir Peter Young.)

By the second half of 1649, the execution of Charles appears to have lost its immediacy for Lady Eleanor, as she incorporates this event into a broader vision of an England nearing the end of time. In June, she reissued her *Prayer* of 1644 with *A Prayer or Letter for the Peoples Conversion* **[39]**. This latter tract reviews the events since the publication of her 1644 *Prayer* and argues that the English people have committed real 'Treason' by '*Shuting*' (p. 10) out God. With *Sions Lamentation* **[40]**, written to mourn the loss of her oldest grandson, Henry Hastings, Lady Eleanor returns to her career-long interest in explicating the cosmological significance of events in her personal life. She sees the death of this young man, only nineteen and about to marry, as a 'warning piece of those very perilous dayes stoln upon us' (p. 2). (An identical version of this tract held at the University of Illinois and lacking the title page is sometimes referred to as *Zach. 12.* because it begins with an epigraph from Zechariah 12:10.) In August, the Commonwealth printer Robert Ibbitson published yet another version of her 1633 *Given to the Elector* under the title *Strange and Wonderfull Prophecies* **[41]**. As Esther Cope observes, this tract testifies to the increased public interest in Lady Eleanor's predictions in the aftermath of Charles's execution. It contains a series of non-authorial printed glosses that link points in her prophecy to specific events associated with Charles's death. *Strange and Wonderfull* is unique in Lady Eleanor's canon for containing the editorial hand of a person other than herself. (In addition to Ibbitson, the only other printer known to have been involved with the production of her tracts is Thomas Paine.) Lady Eleanor subsidized the printing of all of her tracts; Cope surmises that as a result many are of poor quality.

The importance of prophecy itself is the subject of her tract on education, *For the Right Noble Sir Balthazar Gerbier* **[42]**. Gerbier had proposed to open an academy for the sons of noble families, and Lady Eleanor urges him to include the Bible in the curriculum so that his students, like Lady Eleanor herself, can promulgate the typological readings of Scripture that draw connections between contemporary events and those in the Bible which herald the arrival of the last days. In October 1649, in *For the Most Honorable States* **[43]**, she again published advice, this time to the Council of State, which had taken the reins of government. Reviewing episodes in Amos, Mark and Luke that describe the casting out of devils from those they had possessed, she comments on the need to cast out such devils as Laud and Charles from the nation. She continues to reflect on the reign of Charles in a new edition of a tract first published in 1644, *A Sign* **[44]**. (No copies of the 1644 version survive.) Here she compares King James with Hezekiah and Charles with Manasseh, faulting Charles for adopting idolatrous religious practices. She also proposes a new projected date for the end of time – 1655 – although she would not refer to this date in subsequent treatises. Historical reflection again takes centre stage in *The Everlasting Gospel* **[45]** of December 1649. Here, Lady Eleanor recounts her prophetic career, comparing, in one notable instance, her flight to Holland to publish her 1633 tracts to the Virgin Mary's flight to Egypt to escape Herod's massacre of newborn children. Embracing her literal role as mother, rather than her metaphorical one, she closed out 1649 by publishing her daughter Lucy's answer to a theological question about the Trinity, *The New Proclamation in Answer* **[46]**.

In her six treatises of 1650, Lady Eleanor continues in the more reflective vein she espoused in the second half of 1649, but with diminished emphasis on Charles. She meditates on some key concerns that characterized her career up to this point – prophecy as not limited to biblical times but continuing in her own age, the imminence of the last days, and her struggles to regain her inherited property – while introducing the claim that her authority as a prophet transcends that of Parliament. In addition, her criticism of England's politics now focuses on general trends – frequently, her times' 'backslidden' condition – rather than on specific events or individuals. In *The Bill of Excommunication* **[48]**, she attempts to re-establish the sanctity of religious life in England by proposing that the Sabbath move from Sunday – a day she now associates with desecrations such as sports – to Monday. As a prophet, she argues, she is more qualified than church or state officials to make this decision. She uses the death of Fairfax's father from a festered toe to assert in her *Arraignment* **[47]** that God's power is greater than that of the Army. In *The Appearance or Presence of the Son of Man* **[49]**, she adopts an air of resignation about her travails over her property – Heaven is, after all, her true jointure – and then remarks that, coincidentally, a fire broke out in London in 1650 just when she was cast out of her estate at Englesfield.

She found herself in prison in September of 1650, in her words, at Queen's Bench (which probably means Upper Bench) when she produced *Before the Lords Second Coming* **[50]**, a text that invokes the rhetoric of 'Freedoms and Liberties' (p. 5) and 'Tolleration or Liberty of Conscience' (p. 13) to underscore the failure of those in power to recognize theirs as an age of prophecy. Her *Elijah the Tishbite's Supplication* **[51]** of October calls upon God to make his presence known and insists that the number 50, as in 1650, points to a 'Blow' (p. 7). The significance of the number 50 reappears in *Her Jubilees Appeal* **[52]**, a tract noting that a bad end had come in 1650 to one John Stawell who, like James, had set aside his 'first wife' for a second. Lady Eleanor, of course, had maintained for some time that her deceased second husband Douglas was the son of James's 'first wife' and thus the true heir to the throne.

In the penultimate year of Lady Eleanor's career, 1651, she produced seven texts that embrace her standard autobiographical and theological concerns and that demonstrate an increased emphasis on historical reflection and on the superiority of heavenly to earthly authority. Throughout her career Lady Eleanor had attributed great significance to anagrams; like other radical visionaries of her age, she saw them, in Clement Hawes's words, as articulating a 'sense of the total immanence of God in language' (Hawes, p. 60). Toward this end, she frequently used her maiden name, Eleanor Audeley, to create the anagram: 'Reveale O Daniel' as testimony to the legitimacy of her prophetic vocation. In *Hells Destruction* **[53]**, her meditation on the circumstances of her 1646 imprisonment in Woodstreet Compter on charges of failing to pay her printer Thomas Paine, she illustrates another perspective on the supreme significance of language. She finds fault with the arrest warrant that identified her as '*Eleanor* Lady *Davers*' (p. 6) and turns to the Bible to demonstrate the importance of accurate naming. Another earlier imprisonment, this time that of 1633, played a role in her next treatise, *Of Times and Seasons* **[54]**, helping to establish her main point: heavenly power surpasses earthly. In sending her to prison in the Gatehouse, Laud did not exercise control but merely enacted the prophecy in Revelation 12 regarding the Serpent and the Woman clothed with the sun (of whom Lady Eleanor is a type).

The Woman's triumph over the Serpent is the theme of *The Serpents Excommunication* **[55]**. The title page shows what is apparently a strangely shaped Ash branch, and the tract, written in verse, refers repeatedly to imagery associated with trees including, notably, Eden's Tree of Life. Picking up on the arboreal theme, one 'M: Tuke', whose praise of Lady Eleanor is appended to the tract, describes her prophecies as a '*Rod*' (p. 7). [Tuke identifies himself as her kinsman, and stylistic markers suggest that he was the minister Edward Tuke who wrote *Jehovah Jireh Merito Audiens, praeco Evangelicus, An Angell from Heaven, OR An Ambassadour for Christ* (1642) and *The Souls Turnkey, OR, A Spiritual File For Any Prisoner lockt up in the Dungeon and Chains of Sinne and Satan* (1656). Tuke may well have been the only male to commend Lady Eleanor's prophetic writings in print.] At the end of October, Lady Eleanor returned to the topical concerns characteristic of her tracts of the 1640s when in her *Benediction* **[56]** she praises Oliver Cromwell for his defeat of Charles II and the Scots at the Battle of Worcester in September of 1651. By substituting an 'h' for the 'c' in his surname, she transforms O CROMWELL into the anagram: HOWL ROME. In 1651 she also reissued new editions of earlier tracts; her *Given to the Elector* **[34]** and her *Blasphemous Charge* **[36]**. She reissued these bound together as *Given to the Elector* appended by T*he Dragons Blasphemous Charge against Her* **[57]**. The 1651 version of *Given to the Elector* contains new marginal comments, including a reference to another female prophet of the day, Grace Carey, and closes with a synopsis of events between 1633, when Lady Eleanor issued the first version of her text, and the 1649 execution of the King. Likewise, the 1651 *Dragons Blasphemous Charge* presents a set of printed comments in the margins, some of which duplicate Lady Eleanor's handwritten comments in the margins of the Folger Library's copy of her 1649 *Blasphemous Charge*.

In December of 1651, Lady Eleanor found herself in jail yet again, this time in the Fleet and for reasons she does not specify in her writings, and it was there that she produced what she regarded as her magnum opus, *The Restitution of Prophecy* **[58]**. Its interest derives not from its chief purpose – to urge watchfulness in the face of Christ's imminent return – but rather from its encyclopaedic compendium of cosmic and mundane as well as public and private concerns, including Henrietta-Maria's Catholicism; Queen Mary's bloody and Queen Elizabeth's glorious reigns; the trial and execution of her brother; Sir Kenelm Digby's poisoning of his wife Venetia Stanley; General Fairfax's response to one of Lady Eleanor's tracts; the crimes and executions of Laud and Charles I; and wool as a good defence against cold weather. She organizes this jumble of topics according to the three apocalyptic parables in Matthew 25, and so her text falls into three sections under the rubrics the ten wise and foolish virgins; the talents; and the separation of sheep from goats. Despite her efforts to structure her tract, *Restitution* remains a text teeming with images that Lady Eleanor does not fully explain. In many ways, her text embodies the chaos of an age that is, in Lady Eleanor's view, dissolute and thus ready for the Second Coming.

Lady Eleanor died in July of 1652 (of unknown causes), her two treatises published in the spring of that year having summarized the theological and autobiographical reflections that had characterized her prophetic career. Her *Tobits Book* **[59]**, published as a 'Lesson … for Lent' (title page), examines the apocryphal Book of Tobit to encourage readers to recognize that suffering is always followed by redemption. She effectively combines her belief in the redemption of the damned with her belief in the impending Second Coming so as to assert that although hers is a condemned generation, God will afford it the magnificence of the New Jerusalem. Attesting to Lady Eleanor's independence from both the established Church and the radical sects, hers is the only extended commentary on Tobit printed in those years, perhaps because more militant Protestants opposed its publication in the canonical Bible. Her final tract, *Bethlehem Signifying The House of Bread: or War* **[60]**, passionately defends Lady Eleanor's destruction of some of the tapestries at Litchfield Cathedral in 1636, one of the acts that had led to her imprisonment in Bedlam. The tract presents a rather melancholy reflection on her strenuous efforts to reveal the truth to a generation determined to bury it. Her daughter Lucy captured Lady Eleanor's extraordinary devotion to her prophetic vocation in the epitaph she prepared for her mother: 'In a woman's body a man's spirit, In most adverse circumstances a serene mind, In a wicked age unshaken piety and uprightness … Nay she was full of God to which fulness Neither a smiling world could have added, Nor from it a frowning world have taken away' (Quoted in *Handmaid*, p. 162).

References

Cope, Esther S. (1992), *Handmaid of the Holy Spirit: Dame Eleanor Davies, Never So Mad a Ladie*, Ann Arbor: University of Michigan Press

_____, ed. (1995), *Prophetic Writings of Lady Eleanor Davies*, New York: Oxford University Press

Feroli, Teresa (2006), *Political Speaking Justified: Women Prophets of the English Revolution*, Newark: University of Delaware Press

_____ (1994), 'The Sexual Politics of Mourning in the Prophecies of Eleanor Davies', *Criticism* 36: 359–82

_____ (1994), 'Sodomy and Female Authority: The Castlehaven Scandal and Lady Eleanor's *The Restitution of Prophecy* (1651)', *Women's Studies* 24: 31–49

Hawes, Clement (1997), *Mania and Literary Style: The Rhetoric of Enthusiasm from the Ranters to Christopher Smart*, Cambridge: Cambridge University Press

Hindle, C.J. (1936), 'A Bibliography of the Printed Pamphlets and Broadsides of Lady Eleanor Douglas the Seventeenth-Century Prophetess', *Edinburgh Bibliographical Society Transactions* 1.1: 65–98

Mack, Phyllis (1992), *Visionary Women: Ecstatic Prophecy in Seventeenth-Century England*, Berkeley: University of California Press

Matchinske, Megan (1993), 'Holy Hatred: Formations of the Gendered Subject in English Apocalyptic Writing, 1625–51', *English Literary History* 60: 349–77

_____ (1998), *Writing, Gender and State in Early Modern England: Identity Formation and the English Subject*, Cambridge: Cambridge University Press

Nelson, Beth (1985), 'Lady Elinor Davies: The Prophet as Publisher', *Women's Studies International Forum* 8: 403–9

Pickard, Richard (1996), 'Anagrams *etc*. The Interpretive Dilemmas of Lady Eleanor Douglas', *Renaissance and Reformation* 20 (3): 5–22

Porter, Roy (1994), 'The Prophetic Body: Lady Eleanor Davies and the meanings of madness', *Women's Writing* 1.1: 51–63

Smith, Nigel (1989), *Perfection Proclaimed: Language and Literature in English Radical Religion, 1640–1660*, Oxford: Clarendon Press

Spencer, Theodore (1938), 'The History of an Unfortunate Lady', *Harvard Studies and Notes in Philology and Literature* 20: 43–59

Watt, Diane (1997), 'Alpha and Omega: Eleanor Davies, Civil War Prophet', *Secretaries of God: Women Prophets in Late Medieval and Early Modern England*, Cambridge: D.S. Brewer, 118–54

TERESA FEROLI

23. The Gatehouse Salutation (1647; Wing D1991A) is reprinted, by permission of Harvard University's Houghton Library, from the clear copy held at the Houghton (shelfmark EC65.D7455.B652t). In identifying the date of publication as 1647 rather than 1646 as on the title page, we are following the Gregorian calendar rather than the Julian one then in use; for Lady Eleanor and the English printers the new year began on March 25. The text block of the original measures 195 × 140 mm; the facsimile has had to be reduced here to fit this book's text area.

Hard-to-read words:

3.17	what restless eyes those day and
6.20	record at last; he that is other-

THE
Gatehouſe Salutation
From the Lady
ELEANOR.

Revelat. cap. 4.

Serving for *Weſtminſters* Cathedral, their old Service.

And Courts of *Weſtminſter*, thoſe Elders ſitting, *&c.*

February, 1646.

Printed in the Year 1646.

Revel. cap. 4.

Post hæc vidi, & ecce ostium apertum in Cœlo, &c.

New PSALM or SONG;

The CONTENTS.

THe Holy Ghost first knocks, so high extold, shews the end come; by New writ witnessed and Old; in whose Kalender the time set out, a week expired of Centuries thereabout; VVhen as Twenty four from *Normand* Race sprung, cast their Crowns down, Times hour-glasse (as 'twere) run.

So opend the aforesaid gate or door, what winged Beasts be those four, what restlesse eyes those day and

A 2 night;

night; The first ruff a Lyon like: The other smooth as a Calfs skin soft: The fourth an Eagle flying aloft: Midst them one visag'd as a MAN; which knot unloose he who can: what eyes these before and behinde, *Holy, Holy, &c.* all of one minde; *Which was, which is, which is to come,* say, *Glory to Father, Spirit, Son.* Inthroned, powther'd within whose Robe, in right hand whose the Starry Globe, the likenesse of the Iudgment Day, as Resurrection robes display.

Benedicite omnia opera.

The four Beasts, *&c.*

Bethlems Manger sometime the Throne, as its describ'd, where she did grone; a Feather-bed cald otherwise, some Dormix curtains wrought with eyes;

eyes ; their work both ſides alike doth ſhew, full of holes, beſides all eaten ſo ; A Rug and Blankets thereon laid, a woful priſoner, the aforeſaid, whoſe companions tedious hours, no better Church then priſoners towers : As Elders white arrayed ſo ſhine, Four and twenty firſt crownd of time : Seaſons four, alſo with Feaſt days, crowns reſign, aloud him praiſe, all proclaiming Eternity, away with tyrant Time they cry.

All Bleſsing, Power, Honor, ſay, to him dedicate a third day ; worſhip no Throne but his alone, beſides whom King nor Prieſts is none : Like as with twain that covered their face, other twain with flying apace, their feet covered alſo with twain, Time paſt, preſent, and futures reign.

So

So Tabernacles three let us make, one for *Moses*, *Christs*, and *Elias* sake; as for those that adore the Beast, no Sabbath have, day nor nights rest.

Lo Moonday she coelestial virgin Bride, as *Behold, I make all things new, Gates wide, new Earth*, &c. *Jerusalems* peaceable rest, Spouse of the Sun, our splendant new Moons feast, Monethly, as the golden Tree of life like renders its fruit, no more pain, prison, strife: As spar'd a million of *Belial* Sons, better then touch one of those sacred ones: O kisse this precious Altar Coal, purges division, makes ye whole.

Away with former fashions old and past: New Lights appear, new Song record at last; he that is otherwise

wiſe at his peril, as he that righteous is, be he ſo ſtill.

So Gates and Priſon Doors be no
more ſhut,
The King of Glory comes, your
ſouls lift up.

Farewell.

To the Tune of *Magnificat.*

F I N I S.

---

24. *The Mystery Of General Redemption* (1647; Wing D1996A) is reprinted, by permission of the Folger Shakespeare Library, from the clear copy held at the Folger (shelfmark D1996A bd. w. D2010). The text block of the original measures 140 × 90 mm.

Hard-to-read words:

12.20	whence say they is no Re-
13.18	*sians*
14.7	*infolding*
16.20	of
17.3	reverse
31.3	*rara Avis*,
32.2	brethren
32.5	pieces
32.9	*and*

THE MYSTERY OF *General Redemption.*

By the Lady *ELEANOR.*

---

1 Pet. 1.13. *Wherefore gird up the loyns of your mindes, &c. and hope to the end, for the grace that is to be brought unto you at the revelation of Jesus Christ.*

Printed in the Year, 1647.

The Mystery of general Redemption.

AND the Grave and Hell, one and the ſame word ſerving for both in the Native Tongue or Language, as obſerved both by Prophets and Apoſtles, between which, and the word Sepulchre or Monuments, diſtinguiſhes and puts a difference: So that doubtleſs of the Reſurrection may as well doubt, as out of Hell believe or hold is no redemption; whereof the Prophet *Hoſea* thus, who affirms, 13. *I will ranſom thee out of Hell*; confirmed by that, *Cor.* 15. *O Death, where is thy ſting? O Hell, where is thy victory, &c.* in

A the

the first place to our Saviors soul not left in Hell, applyed, nor his body in the earth to see corruption, according to the Psalm; But every one in his order, instanced as by the fruits of the earth: Touching which word its extent unto the Devil, the mystery not unknown; to *Saul* foreshewd he and his sons to morrow to be with him; a taste or token whereof had then by his falling all along, as shews was sore afraid, *&c.* provided for him against the next day.

And according to the Scriptures, for proving the affirmative, The worlds general pardon, kept till last, like the good wine; This place for one, of *Adam*, the figure of him to come, saying thus, *Wherefore, as by one man sin entred into the world, and death*

death by sin; and so deathpassed upon allmen, &c. Therefore as by the offence of one, &c. so by the righteousness of one, &c. Rom. 5. came upon all men, &c. and he one able to distinguish between the general and special, *Cor.5.* argues, in short, the same point; *And if all were dead, then dyed he for all:* And to *Timothy, God the Savior of All, especially of them that believe, who gave himself a ransom for all, a propitiation for our sins, not only, but for the whole worlds sins.* And so muchfor these who by reason of the Law and several Statutes, have incurred such penalties and forfeitures to the whole world, therefore that sends forth these; *That as in Adam all dyed, so in Christ all are made alive,* according to *Cor. 15.* and his

own

own promiſe, *If I be lifted up, I ſhall draw all men to me*; anſwerable to the angels firſt ſalute, *Behold, tidings of great joy to all people*; and the cryers Voyce, *Behold the Lamb of God that taketh away the ſins of the world.*

Concluding not ſome, but All, the whole degenerate maſs of Angels and Men, pardoned that partake of the pit where no water is, or taſte the ſecond Death too, from whoſe bleſſedneſs (to wit) in the firſt reſurrection, who have their part, it detracts not, but is beyond meaſure an addition, to whō they but as the numerous commō ſort in compariſon.

Laſtly to free this Larges from any tax that may befal in reſpect of ſuch ample expreſsions.

Behold elſe where in penning

it,

it, how cautious the same Apostle to the letter, saying, *Now Abrabraham and his seed, &c.* he saith, *Not seeds*, of many, but as of one; *And to thy seed*: and again, *Behold, I shew you a mystery, we shall not all sleep, but we shall all be changed* (Thess.) And in every thing so) Hebrews, *For in that he put all things under his feet, he left nothing that is not put under: but that he by the grace of God, should taste death for every man*: as, *O the height and depth of his Grace, for whom in his appointed time nothing is too difficult.*

And again, for a farther manifestation of his strictnes this way, *Brethren, if it be but a mans covenant, yet if it be confirmed, no man disanulleth or addeth thereto*: and yet this consolation,

solation of ours, how it is endeavored to be hidden from us amongst the good seed, by tares sowed, by this blinde or envious age, bear witness, to whom the word *Age* such an unwelcom Guest how perverted, in that Thanksgiving Psalm, its golden burthen, *For his mercy endures for an Age*? Englished, *For his mercy endures for Ever*; which upon their words taken or believed, signifies without end reiterated so.

And lo, throughout the New Testament, this passes for current, *Heb. By whom the worlds were made*, when the truth of it, *By whom the Ages were made*, viz. *Secula*: Likewise in *Jude* closed with these words, *To whom, &c. In all Ages; And now, and in all Ages of Ages, Amen*: By our

Doctors

Doctors concluded or curtaild, *To whom, &c. for ever, Amen*: of which falſe Brethrens Doctrine and doings more dangerous to the Truth, then the practice of open enemies: Heretofore moreover thus, *Apocal.* he ſaying, *I am he, &c. and behold, am alive for Ages of ages*, Amen; *and have the Keys of Death & Hell*: By whom (as though thoſe Keys at their command) rendred, *For evermore, Amen*, at fartheſt ſignifying but Ages and farther, or from henceforth. Again, (*Revelation* the 14.) *Et fumus, &c. aſcendet in ſecula ſeculorum*, from age to age, from day to day; alluding in their being tormented without intermiſſion, and reſtleſs, to mettals refined thoſe ſulpherous ſmokes, yet who

B con-

continue the old Antichriſtian note, of extending theſe to a perpetuity or unlimitd eſtate, being *finit*, taking upon them, above him, taken up into the third Heaven; *Paul* preſsing no farther then *What if God willing to ſhew his wrath, &c.* indured with long ſuffering, &c. And why not then, *What if God unwilling* as when *Moſes* deſired to behold all his glory) *to make known all his mercy*; or if pleaſed to ſhadow it under a term, not infinite, but determinable, lawful ſhal it be therfore for them, when it was unlawful for the Apoſtle to utter the things he heard: Thus *to take away without warrant*, whoſe laſt charge *to beware of it, Rev.* 22. leſt partake *of thoſe Plagues*, which were they to endure but a moment, enough

enough to break in two the ſtrongeſt heart, or to diſtract: yet but as a Dream compar'd with the days of Heaven, although ſuch horror to continue a thouſand *Methuſalahs* ages, and thus by ſuch Addition continued of *EVER* and ſometime *NEVER*, groaning under the burthen of miſunderſtanding for ſo many ages; not the word Age alone (as manifeſt) but this going for currant alſo, *The Fire that never ſhalbe quencht*. And *the worm*, &c. *Not onely alluding to Sodoms wilde fire, but by the inſuing bidden to have ſalt in themſelves: Alſo, to remember Lots wife, ſo faithleſs, worthy to be made an example, commended unto them.*

VVhereas the *Greek* and *Hebrew*

both agreeing (*Mar.* 9. *Isaiah* 66.) *Where the fire is not quenched, and the worm dyeth not*; *Ignis non extinguitur*, from one new Moon to another, or from Sabbath to Sabbath; unmindful of *Pauls* unable *to contain himself*, *O the depth of the Riches both of the Wisdom and Knowledge of God, how unsearchable, who hath known his minde? &c.*

So that either some design, like those Brethren who sometime upon a doubtful speech cast out by our Savior, presently gave out, *That that Disciple should not dye*: because replied, *What if I will he tarry till I come*; though in that it opposes the article of our Lords descending, &c. a thing of more dangerous consequence; whence say they is no Redemption:

demption: by whom those torments were undergone; so sure as that wine and gaul prepared for him, mixt like Hope and Despair; witness that outcry *Psal.* 88. *O Lord my salvation, I have cryed day and night, I am so fast in prison I cannot get out: why abhorrest thou my soul? I have stretched out my hands unto thee, &c.* True it is, *Isa.* 26. once have been true to the sence this far in the Margin thus, Heb. *Rock of ages*: translated, *The everlasting strength*; which word by way of terror sometime used, by them not having the Spirit, extend it to their *Non plus ultra*, now like the Decree of the *Medes* and *Persians*, though shewed to be erroneous, neverthelesss irrevocable, who bring us forth *Hercules* for *Samson*,

Ovid

Ovid for *David*, and *Seneca* before *Paul*, &c.

VVhereas *the Kingdom of GOD speaking better things*, then ſuch ſtraight paſſages teſtifying, *In my Fathers houſe are many Manſions*, *one myſtery infolding another*, as *Ezekiels* viſion, *A fire in the midſt of the cloud*. And, *put the fire, lightning*, &c. ſo, *wheel within wheel*: Thoſe Cherubims their intricate work, incloſing the Mercy-ſeat, *of whoſe Kingdom ſhews there is no end*; *and they worthy to be heirs thereof*; *promiſed to be equal with the Angels*, *ſhall dye no more*, (Luke 20.)

And, *Pſal*. *No end of his years*, *from everlaſting to everlaſting*: Heb. *indiſſolvable*, *paſſes not from one to another*, *&c*. different from the King-

dom

dom of Darkneſs, or like the Beaſts *Dan.* 7. declaring *a prolonging of life was given unto them, for a time and ſeaſons*; whoſe dominion taken away, or authority, as *Jude* gives to underſtand of thoſe *angels, reſerved in everlaſting chains under darkneſs, unto the judgement of the great day*, againſt whom, namely the Devil, *the angel Michael durſt not bring railing accuſation*, only *The Lord the rebuke thee*, was to conſider them, who had no more but ſo much belief, as ſerved to deprive them of HOPE under ſuch reſtraint.

So with his ſecret Providence proceeding, the common Salvation hidden, like that Grace beſtowed on the *Gentiles*, ſo long waited for, alike

alike held impoſsible, what if he, after *Joſephs* reſerved way, as he toward his untoward Brethren before made himſelf known who kept them in hold, queſtioned both for ſpies and theft; but correſpondent to his ſilence ſhe when running & crying after him, at length as though but loſt her labor; anſwered her, *was not but to the loſt ſheep ſent of the houſe of Iſrael*; yet overcame him, obtained her ſuit, the *Gentiles* fore-run, deriving her title from *Canaan*, ſhewing *Dogs ought not periſh*.

Concluding the Prince of Peace; his Mercy ſeems rackt up in aſhes of Deſpair, as it far'd with them ſo many days in ſuch jeopardy that ſaw neither ſun nor ſtars, for his ſervant *Pauls* cauſe; not a hair of their heads

periſhing;

perishing; came safe every one to land (*Acts*) much more for his own sake, will never reverse his own judgement against Law for any to do; having spoken it, Namely, for the womans seed to vanquish the Serpents power; and of such triumph to come, *His leading captivity captive*, to reduce every one to their former liberty: as what special blessing otherwise such a numerous generation promised *Abraham*, much like that the Apostle speaks of himself, else *man of all creatures most miserable, were Redemption but for a handful*, as though *All souls are not his* (*Ezek.*) whom *Moses* calls, *The God of the Spirits of all Flesh*.

VVhose last these, *Woman, behold thy son, figur'd in Adam and the Ser-*

C pent

pent both ; who then to his mo: her made his first word good ; finishing with *Father forgive them every one.*

Then mercy extending to thousands wi: hout number , exceeds so far his hate, *but unto the third and fourth generation*; accordingly who came into the world, made to wait four thousand years near , embraces no less then as wide as east from the west, &c. So far be it from him, for our first Parents first offence surprised in state of Innocency, to lay it all upon their Progeny , as they better able to discharge this obligation, kept on foot still, when those two debtors because had nothing to pay, frankly both forgiven , both contrary to the New and old Law , the childrens teeth for the fathers default set on edge;

edge; whereof the Lord ſaid, there was no more occaſion to uſe any ſuch harſh proverb, &c. (*Ezek.*) who may be merciful as he pleaſes, rather then unjuſt in the leaſt.

Making ſuch preſidents of no force (the day of Iudgements figure) intolerable ſinful *Sodom* for ſo few their ſakes which had been pardond, preſt *Shall not the Judge of all the earth do right?* or *ſhall the moſt high be implacable againſt Duſt and Aſhes, to contend with a Worm, an earthen veſſel?* *O from him far be it.*

And ſo, *Doſt thou well to be angry Jonas*, pleads himſelf, the cauſe, how children ought not for the Parents to ſuffer, contradicts *Moſes* Law, in regard of it, which that King, the children of the Murtherers of his

C 2 father,

father, put them not to death(*Kings* 2.) ſo *Ninevehs* to be drownd in forgetfulneſs neither, in tender conſideration of a world of Infants pardond all; the whole *worlds* figure *Jonas* being his, ſhewing *Summum jus, ſumma injuria, all as knowing not what they do* without ſpecial grace, as all doing they know not what.

And thus much concerning that principle, not of more Antiquity then Truth, *That every thing returns to the place from whence it came*: ſo then, *if Duſt thou art, to Duſt return.*

Much more in point of mercy, where goodneſs ſo immenſe to reduce the ſame, as behold ſaw every thing very good at the firſt,&c. *Gen.*

Laſtly, to breath the breath of Life

Life into theſe ſtrait paſſages: *Judas* called, *The Son of Perdition*, granted *good for that man he had never been born*, yet extends not to deprive him of happineſs in that he had a being, though unborn; as *Job* for example, notwithſtanding *blames the knees that prevented him*, which concerns at all not his conception, or the time of life, though beſtows imprications alike, on *the night wherein he was conceived*, as upon his Nativity, to be blotted out of the Kalender, yet unto annihilation extends not, harbors no ſuch vain wiſh, *Job* 3.

Alſo he on the left hand, that thief, by ſaying to the other, *This day be thou with me, &c.* a limited day, implies another day for him, (*Hebr.*) that

that author but after his order ſhew-ing, in that hee ſaith anew, *He hath made the firſt void*, in ſpeaking of the Covenant, as in another place of in-terring in the *Reſt*; a certain day in-ſiſts thereon at large.

So again for that ſin, forgiven nei-ther here, nor in the other world, but puniſhed in both: *He that ſpeaks a-gainſt the holy Ghoſt, or the holy Breath or Breathings, but ſhall be in danger, &c.* Firſt, who knows how many worlds are to come; as *Peter* ſpeak-ing of that before the Deluge, calls it, *The world that THEN WAS.*

And for the word *Danger* what it imports who knows not (to wit) a poſsibility of eſcape.

Beſides his pointing to *Peter* and *Judas*, The fall of the one through frailty,

frailty, as *Adam*; the other of arrogancy, as the Devil: likewise ſhews who oppoſes the holy Spirit (in the original) *Breathings*, or *holy wind*: He that ſeeks to ſtop that breath, a mill-ſtone a fitter ornament for him; better firſt had been his own Executioner: *In thoſe days ſuppos'd though or held preſumption, to expect gifts of ſuch high nature.*

And ſo for correcting the ſeverity of this Parable too, ſhewing *Of a fixt ſpace between them two* (*Luk*.16.) no other then a prefixt ſpace of time, termed by them a fixt Gulf impaſſible, otherwiſe in reſpect of place but unneceſſary, which moves not to ſay fixt, more proper for Times perpetual motion; where moreover touching the type of his finger dipt, &c.

&c. as points to *Hagar* who had her eyes opened, ſaw a well of water, calling it, *Thou God ſeeſt me*; The truth of it, The Myſtery of Redemption out of Hell, to be clearly ſet forth foreſhews, and from *Abraham* calling him Son alſo, and he him father, thus but a line of Mercy craving; from this *Lazarus* no ordinary Beggar; as thoſe Allegorical Ulcers, or wounds, but anſwerable to that of *Abrahams* boſom; likewiſe that Rich man, one in ſome eminent Office, calling Brothers, who it ſeems dyed of a Fever, or elſe ſome one craving a pardon for his life; one in *ſome eminent Office, both by his Robe and Calling, them his five Brethren.*

The ſum of it in part, who ſo performs not without compulſion pe-

nance

nance here, makes it good there: And thus making no long dwelling or commentaries on evident things. As for the word *Chasma* (or a *Gulf*) a Learned author, though upon an other occasion borrowing this figurative word, hereupon applies it thus; *A Chasma, or void space of time, in the mention of some inter reign: GOODWIN by name.*

And as suppos'd not to be avoided of *a purgatory appointed for the Saints after this life, being both Birds of a feather*; briefly thus, founded on this and the like places, *Verily thou shalt not come forth thence, till paid the utmost mite*: The verity of it, *a certain moment, or signifying till the last minute expired, as the godly become here Exiles in this world, so on the other side till*

D *Gods*

Gods wrath appeased, they excluded his presence under Excommunication.

VVhich Article of the Chriſtian Faith famous *ORIGEN* underſtood well, of whom the worſt they could ſay was, *That when he wrote well, as he went before all men, ſo no man did worſe when he wrote ill*; from whoſe judgement other Fathers erring, were inforced to erect a Purgatory, being faln between this *Sylla* and *Charybdis*.

VVhereto a word adding Exhortative from the parable preceding (*Luke* 15.) *of his unnatural preferring a Calf before his own Brother, would not be drawn to ſee him. And thoſe Laborers poſſeſt with a like ſpirit of Envie*: Of ſuch evil aſpect mutining and grudging that nothing at all to damage

damage them, like that cutthroat for another ſerv'd in the ſame kinde, *without compaſſion on his fellow ſervant, points to priſon, &c.*

A Leſſon for his Diſciples not unſeaſonable, void of ſpleen neither againſt the other twain; a diſeaſe reigning in *Eſaus* world: *Jonas* was entred into it, about a ſtraw matter as angry, by whom a goard more taken into conſideration, then a City of great and ſmall; concerning which uncharitableneſs in the higheſt degree, and unchriſtian belief thus to judge: *Lo that parable of the day of judgements ſentence, where behold charged with nothing beſides, rewarded with* Lex talionis, *Goye, &c.* (*Mat.* 25.) *in that ye did it not to the leaſt, &c.* ſometime my ſad companions,

D 2 thoſe

those heavie prisoners, when *sweat those clods of blood, in no small measure in that Garden or orchard, encountring no inferior Temptations.*

Concluding with this, a Remedy for all Diseases, *The end at hand, even Time aged,* 1647. *stoln away, attaind to* Noahs *days*; so that no great danger in *leaving the door open, or for dismissing the guard,* hitherto fortified under pretence of withstanding presumption, with illegal constructions and terrification of that uncharitable nature: wherfore pray'd, away with such sinister suspition any longer in defence of it, being arrived the port; as *Behold the appointed time of the Son of mans coming: The Ancient of days holding the Seven Stars in his right hand, of no small moment a mysterie, if*

his

his word to be taken or believed (*Apoc.* 1.) before whose Throne *the Dagons of the Earth now prostrate*; even Tyrant time also resigning all his rights and priviledges with them; agreeable with that Rule, *When ceaseth the the cause of the Law, then ceaseth the Law it self also*: of which Time, namely the end, *Enoch the seventh from Adam* (as by *Jude* foreshewed) he being a figure of it prophesied, *was not, God took him*, after had fulfilled *three hundred threescore and five years*, according to the days of the year, walked here no longer: The first prophet foreseeing their hard speeches, accompanied with hardness of belief, whom the Lord will convince howsoever, who *like Kore and his companions, not having the spirit*,

rit, despise Prophesie not onely, but take upon them to contradict the express VVord: shewing that the first fruits and root be holy, also the branches and whole lump. So that in stead of his Spirit, the last of the old prophets, and the first of the new: *John the Baptist,* upon them have *Balaams* spirit, witness *Timothy, He a ransom for all,* as *O Hell, I will be thy destruction, &c.* In due time to be testified; and *John, a propitiation for the whole world,* as instanced afore, and proved: The which maintaind by them to be the whole for the part, spoke by a figure, say they, like that of *All Jury went out to John*, and his decree *Cesars, that went forth from all the world to be taxt* (Luk. &c.) where the one spoken after

after the vulgar way, the other in high strain of Kings.

But this *rara Avis*, one Swallow makes no Summer; rather making choice to be abrupt then farther prolix, supposing ye will imitate the cruel Soldiers, resolved to kill the prisoners, or be worse then their captain, (*Acts* 27.) or more inexorable then his furious Majesty of great *Babylon*, revoking his hasty sentence or lowd Proclamations, beyond expectation all of them, when saved by *Daniel* the prophet, so preserved with his companions, &c. with whom, *Blessed bee the Lords Name, A seculo & usque in seculum, & ipse mutat tempora & ætates*, (Dan.2.21.) Leaving them to swim for their Lives, or at least will not

gain-

gainsay a possibility of escape for these Captive brethren, whom *Abraham* refuses not the stile of *Sons*, shall present these not unlike the broken boards or pieces of the ship for the present. To which passages or New song, the end of which, *Behold I make all things new: Let every creature in Heaven and Earth, and Sea, and under the Earth, say* Amen.

FINIS.

---

25. *Ezekiel The Prophet Explained as follows* (1647; Wing D1988A) is reprinted, by permission of the Folger Shakespeare Library, from the unique copy held at the Folger (shelfmark D1988.5 bd. w. D2010). This copy contains a handwritten note that may be in Lady Eleanor's hand. The text block of the original measures 140 × 87 mm. This text lacks a title page.

Hard-to-read words:

1.4	His writ servd of Rebellion lamentation Mourning and woe [transcription]
1.6	Labyrinth
4.10	house
6.11	*Cause thy belly to*

E Z E K I E L

THE

PROPHET

Explained as follows.

His .uvit Serud of Rebellion Lamentation Mourning and Woe

SO many having attempted the ſtraits or paſſages of this Labyrinth and loſt their labor who went about it, could not but drop a word, have thought it not amiſſe or unſeaſonable, as wiſe as they are that miſſed their mark, a taſte or touch to give them, of the tree of Life, otherwiſe cald the myſtery of Times and Seaſons, reſerved for the laſt time, this Sacramental little Rowl, with ſuch a ſolemn proteſtation bound touch-

A ing

ing times being no longer, which precious Manna, the Prophet *Ezekiel* and *John* the Evangelist both tasted of, not longed for a little (*Acts* 11)

But hastning on *Cap.* 1. now in the Thirtieth year, &c. *And I looked, and behold a Whirl-wind came out of the North, a great cloud, &c.* where those winged living creatures four, &c. represented by the Tabernacle; also the Lamp, &c. as it were those Curtains, every one of one measure joyned one to another with so many loops or eyes, and rings above so high, besides their running side-ways, like those swift creatures who went on their sides when they ran, their displayed wings sending forth such a noise, of a spherical work, &c.

And

And so much for these Curtains of his Pavilion, typifying the four Evangelists agreeing in one, said to kisse or touch, &c.

VVhereof *Apocalyps* the Fourth thus, of the aforesaid four Beasts, and the Lightning proceeding out of the Throne, shews first of the Lamp; *And there were Seven Lamps of fire, which are the Seven Spirits of God, &c.* Cap. 5. *The Seven Spirits and Seven Eyes sent forth into all the Earth*, as their Characters ☉ ☾ read through the world.

So to shew the truth of it, even the full Moon described its palenesse in the Saphir-like Firmament, and no other likened to the Amber, and Fire its brightnesse, when this con-

A 2 ception

ception or gift of the holy Ghoſt, &c.

Giving withal to underſtand, received or rejecting it, notwithſtanding how Propheſie ceaſed not, nor the Spirit (as the world would have it) totally is quenched; But the VVrit or Label of this little ſealed Rowl being firſt ſerved on them, cald a houſe of Rebellion, or a rebellious houſe ſo often; afterwards to be ſerved again, reſerved even for our days, as if any be pleaſed to obſerve, directed to our ſeventeenth Century, by the ſlain Lamb, Redemptions figure, *Cap.* 5. having ſeven Horns, and as many EYES; alſo witneſſe the grand Iury, thoſe Twenty four Crowned Elders, ſo many times mentioned, and

and as ſhewing ſince the Conqueſt Four and twenty Crowned, ſo Seven hundred years ago thereabout.

And thus going on when this ſacred *Writ* to be ſerved, how it came to paſſe; how diſtaſteful to them, *hony in the mouth*; *bitter in the belly*; compared to a womans travel, or as fares with Officers earning a Fee venture their lives upon Arreſts, even the ſum of this Viſion reſtleſſe Priſons deſcription, clouded under the glory of the Tabernacle, ſets forth a Chamber-Bedſted and appurtenances, the Gatehouſe priſon, in the year of Redemption, 1634. *September* 24. full Moon the everlaſting Lamp, priſoners fire and candle, who from the Angel ſent thither the Holy Ghoſt, that by the

ſpace

ſpace of an hour, the Bed his throne reſted thereon, from his mouth for a farewel received a ſalute; and for another farewel, that had on his right hand an Amber glove, left ſuch an odoriferous ſcent when he was gone, all oyled with Ambergreece, the ſpirit thereof proceeding from the Leather, ſo far beyond expreſsion, as it were inviſible food, like when as ſaid, *Cauſe thy belly to eat, and fill thy bowels*, the hand being ſent to him with the Rowl or Book ſpread, *&c.* a Holy, holy, holy day, by whom obſerved ever ſince.

And for Lamentations, Mourning and VVoe, ſuch cryed up and down: So much for this time cryed unto, *O Wheel, cap.* 10. beſides pro-

proclaims winged Times reign includes years, containing the ſour Seaſons, Moneths, VVeeks, Days and Hours, not returning reſtleſſe time, with the Clock wheel its motion, likewiſe Rings out the Abbey Bells, thoſe mounted wheels, *Verſe* 18. *Verſe* 19. like theſe living creatures likened to burniſhed Braſſe, with their aſcending and deſcending; and for the dreadful Rings ſo much, &c. *Cap.* 1. *ver.* 18. that were ſo high, their ſound or noiſe like great waters, the Voice of the Almighty coming from Heaven, as it were: And ſo farther for that ſpacious round VVindow, the glaſſe its curious work compared to the *Beril* of a Sea-green colour, as the dreadful Chriſtaline Heaven all with one

voice,

voice proclaim the dreadful Iudgement day reveald at hand, to a City most rebellious.

Given under the hands of those *Cherubs*, under their wings that had hands, with that hand sent, &c. seals and signifies it, rings out Times farewel: And for the word of the Lord expresly so much. *Rev.* 1. *Write the things which thou hast seen, and the things which are, and the things which shall be hereafter.*

April 2. 1647.

Eleanor.

F I N I S.

26. *Ezekiel, Cap. 2* (1647; Wing D1988) is reprinted, by permission of the Folger Shakespeare Library, from the copy held at the Folger (shelfmark D1988 bd. w. D2010). This copy contains a few handwritten notes that may be in Lady Eleanor's hand. The text block of the original measures 140 × 90 mm. This text lacks a title page.

Hard-to-read words and handwritten annotations:

1.1	His writ Servs of Rebellion Lamentation Mourning & woe April 2. 1647. [transcription]
1.10–16	though then others he no more timorous, neverthelesse by such several admonitions given him, doubtless intendeth (no other, or no lesse) then captivity lead captive, attended with innumerable chariots: The Lord of Hosts marching on the wing'd winds
5:19	proclaims
8.2–4	or to the House of Austria [transcription]
9.15	*his coming*
9.16	*us*;
9.20	*me, as appears* by that
11.1–3	him from its motion, a voice of a great rushing, to remember him; again another warning, as a
11.14–16	Serving for the present feasts distraction [transcription]
12.17	or ran, returned
12.19	contradiction easily recō-
12.20	their recoiling
14.1	*be the glory of the Lord*, from
14.2–3	to wit, in the Church; sufficienty manifest
14.11	faces and hands
14.12	and what living
14.14	when those went these went,
14.15	those stood these stood
14.17	besides Ringers no strange creatures
14.19	informing
14.20	their plumits and weights drawn
15.20	one withall,
17.1	none such
17.2	*shuts*
17.9–10	Hierglipical
21.9-10	to call them
21.20	same.
24.15–16	*an Item to both*

12

Ezekiel, Cap. 2.

His writ Serue of Rebellion Lamentation Mourning & woe April 2. 1647.

WHereas this Vision, stiled *The appearance of the likenes of the glory of the Lord*: whereby as appears then a warning-piece of great *Babylons* preparation, reports some greater judgement of more moment or importance then their Captivity: above all his fellow brethren the Prophets, though then others he no more timorous; neverthelesse by such several admonitions given him, doubtless intendeth (no other, or no lesse) then captivity lead captive, attended with innumerable chariots: The Lord of Hosts marching on the wing'd winds,

A much

much rather then the King of *Assyria* his Army: The great days Alarm sufficiently visible.

And so of these vigilant living creatures in this Vision, This watchmans Looking-glass, the first visag'd like a Man looking upward, another a Lyons voice, the third the laborious Ox, the fourth for speed to an Eagles swiftness likened; whose faces every way besides full of eyes before and behinde, other motion none but straight forward, requisite; in Prophets those watchmen or seers especially, who bend their course that way, the future the mark they shoot at: And having had such a full view of this glorious Vision, every one so many faces, fell on his face, by a voice commanded, *Stand upon thy feet* (to wit)

wit) *I am the Resurrections voice*, unlike that of the tempter, *If thou be the Son of God, cast thy self down:* And where the Devil threw him down, when the evil spirit cast out, thus stood up instantly, gives him withall to understand (*Verse*) I ordain thee one of the order of *Prophets*, my Spirit I have appointed to to enter into thee, and *Jure Divino*, no lesse, at all points armd with his commission, he with a writ of Rebellion to serve them, saith, *I send thee to a rebellious Nation*, Cap, 2. *that have rebelled against me: And they, whether they will hear or forbear*, who stop the ear like the deaf Adar, *I send thee unto them, say thou thus, Thus saith the Lord, whether they hearken or refrain, chuse them, for they a rebellious house, yet*

A 2 *shall*

shall they know there hath been a Prophet amongst them, verse 5. And thou, be not daunted or dismaid howsoever they look, of their looks be not afraid, though they a rebellious house, leave that to him, the Holy Ghost who will not be so answered, protesting though *Noah*, *Daniel* and *Job* were present, they should but save themselves.

And line upon line, even the Lords own words again and again expresly, what can be said more plain; then thou shalt speak these my words unto them notwithstanding as aforesaid, whether they will hear or forbear, for they are most rebellious: *But thou, hear what I say, Be not rebellious like that rebellious house*, weigh not their favor nor frowns, let them know

know they have been visited, give them warning howsoever, *Open thy mouth, eat what I give thee; standing on thy feet receive it*, the Resurrection tidings, and as expresly commanded, so to a tittle observed; of which Angelical food, the Evangelist *John* communicated even the little Book opened, &c. where heard such a noise of Trumpets, an Angel the cryer, stood roaring like a Lyon, so many Thunders uttering their voices; as Drums, a Cryers voice too; he in the Isle of *Patmos*, in that Desart, crying, *He that hath an Ear, let him hear what the Spirit saith to the Churches, Rev. cap.* 2. *&c.* besides, *Fighting against the Holy Spirit*; forewarning all to beware, proclaims the Iudge of quick and dead his coming

ming;and both of theſe agreeing thus in the ſad condition of the time, as it were, not to be awakened, bidden in another place, *Son of man, ſigh with breaking of thy loins, ſmite thy hands, &c.* an end, the end is come upon the four corners of the earth (or land, as ſignifies both) now the end; an e-vil, an only evil, behold is come: *Thus ſaith the Lord,* Cap. 7. *An end is come, it watcheth for thee, behold it is come,* as it were, all is accompliſhed, the day of Iudgements forerunner is come, ſmothered although by our Over-ſeers, faſt aſleep for all, as in this Ci-ty of late, ſome ſleepers (characters of the cariage of the time) women, never the like, awakened not not by the pains of their travel, but as faln aſleep many days before, ſo con-

tinued

tinued ſtil ſleeping, whileſt in the bed theBabe choked,&c. Another whoſe Arm lay broyliug on the fire (lately gone into the Hoſpital) ſhe in the mean while aſleep.

Furthermore for whoſe commiſsion before this Prophets being diſmiſſed, thus much without aggravation or augmentation he, unto ſuch an unexpected Banquet invited, being not ſent faſting away, of Lamentations, Mourning and VVoe ſpread before him.

Cap. 3.

Moreover ſaying, having cauſed him to eat, bidden freely to fill himſelf, &c. *I ſend thee not to the Cotages unto Day-laborers, thoſe of a rude ſpeech,*

ſpeech , them of thick or great lips ; ſurely had I ſent thee unto them they would have hearkned unto thee , and have anſwered.

or to the House of Austria.

And with motives and admonitions ſuch , this Meſſenger of his prepared ; and this no news , of a Prophet to be leaſt honored where beſt known ; for the moſt part there diſhonored moſt : Even theſe the Lords gracious warning , his words expreſly ſhall go on with them.

Saying , *Go, get thee to the houſe, ſpeak with my words unto them : who hardly will hearken to thee,* receive thy teſtimony, whom neither peſtilence, the like unheard of ; the ſword, Brother againſt Brother , Children againſt their Father, Famine, evil Spirits grown familiar acquaintance , as though

though Satan now faln from Heaven : And thus mixt new and old like a Scribe in both instructed, &c. proceeding with the Commission saying farther, for as steel they be of a stiff forehead; But thy face I have made strong against their faces, and thy forehead against their foreheads, as an *Adamant*.

Harder then flint, embrace or salute them not; shake off the dust of their houses, go not amongst them, who say in their hearts, *He delays his coming*, or, *We will not have this man to reign over us*; as though of some other nation, we know not what he says, moreover *Bring them forth, and slay them before me*, as appears by that Prophetical Parable,

B rable,

rable, when as supposed the Kingdom of God immediately to appear, as it were, even, *Mine eye shall not pity them, though they cry aloud, I will not hear them &c.*

And therefore that will by no means incline or hearken to thee, with none of them communicate, for all their looks, see thou be not weak or daunted, though they a rebellious house, *verse 9.* receive and take it into thine heart, and hear it with thine ears, *For all my words shalt thou speak unto them, &c.* Look, see thou forbear them not, having a watchmans care, speak unto them, and tell them, *Thus saith the Lord,* &c. (*ver.* 11.)

Verse, who then taken up in the Spirit, shews how he heard behinde him

him from its motion, a voice of a great rushing, to remember him) again another warning, as a clock its Alarm before it strikes (cap. 1.) likened to the voice or speech of an Host, those Alarms, or unto the noise of great waters their rushing, and the like; as compared to the Almighty voice, coming from Heaven: Their wings and wheels one within another, &c. Thus what before he saw, now his ears witnesse bears of it.

Much like as when all they were sitting or assembled, Penticost when fully come, *Acts* 2. which filled the House where they were, suddenly such a sound, a rushing of a mighty wind from Heaven.

Serveing for the present feasts (distractio

When *Elias* like, also this Pro-

B 2 phet

phet ascends, lifted up the King of Glory his fiery chariots from above sent down, drawn by the aforesaid living creatures four; swift as the wind, with their two joynd wings on this side, and on that side sparkling, likened to burnished brass, and burning coals of a brightness unspeakable, yet not flying, but went or ran: even the workmanship of clocks and watches with their christal covers, so dreadfully exprest; besides the shadow on Dials (these the emblem of Prophets) not to go backward in the least degree, all their motion strait forward, who when they went or ran, returned not, although in another place shews they returned; a contradiction easily reconciled: from their running likened to the

the Heavens perpetual motion, in a moment through as a flash of lightning, retire at the King of Glory his appearance or presence, Verse 17. They return'd not when they went, &c.

And of this sacred essence; each grain or dram requisit to weigh it, annexed to a charge thus given upon life and death; whether they will, or will not: as afore declared; much more every fathom and quarter, to sound of this deep: a calling to discharge of more consequence then his voyages: or any Belman or VVatchman, shewing what hour of the night, and what past: But let that pass, moreover whose charge, thus (verse 12.) where heard that voice *Blessed be ke the glory of the Lord,* from this place, to wit, in the Church, sufficiency manifest where the Suns Tabernacle; the clock stands, shadowed under the Tabernacle, as from the head to the sole of the foot drawn, the Cherubins by witnesses appearing more then one, shews they had round feet: according to the Hebrew, and strait with faces and hands stretched upward, and what living creatures these, not deemed difficult to discern, adding when those went these went when those stood, these stood, plain enough to be understood: besides Ringers no strange creatures; these having under their wings the form of a mans hand; informing clocks their plumms and weights drawn up

those

those, feet too : together with Ringers, their posture stretching their loins, standing on their toes, as by the soles of their feet, &c. the length of which easie to be taken, unto calves feet likened, to wit, Neats leather their shooes, or Calves leather, each exprest, as this Prophet portray could, we understand.

And so far for *Aarons* Bells, these their rushing heard into the utter court: Bells a glory, wherein we surpasse other Nations.

Besides this for another, (*cap.* 9.) where those six men standing, beside the brazen Altar: Amongst whom one with a writers inckhorn by his side: among the wheels, the Sexton or Clerk that keeps it in order: He for one withall, & shewing,

ing, he reported had the matter as he was commanded or ordered to do, in the next place as refers to the Rolls Office, its six Clerks, those reports of theirs by the said Roll or VVrit, that woful lamentation, &c. likewise certifies with the inck-horn, that slaughter weapon too wit) the penknife, to beware of cutting mens throats therewith, such doings, &c.

Cap. 10. Thus running over the words of it, from the beginning of the Book to the end, as the Alphabet the literal sence, he that runs may read it, hidden although from Rabbies, Fathers & Modern both, taken with that admiration into consideration, giving thanks to his Father, *that had made of his great*

counsel:

none such (17)

Counsel: He that shuts and no man opens; opens and no man shuts: Behold the little book seald with the Seven-stars; which book holds in his right hand, no man worthy, or so wise, for all their libraries, so much as to behold the out side of it; they held at such distance, no looking within the shadow of those Hierglipical Cherubin Curtains, *The Spirit and the Brides bed*, thereof to touch a loop, so much edge or selvedg, like the scattered bones out of hope, *cap.* 37. Though here brought bone to bone, as it were, *Live O obstruse Oracle*; containing the living creatures, namely, The Holy Ghosts Heralds, betokening not only this terrestrial Tabernacles clothing of rags, covered with

C vermin

vermin for vermillion, celestial forthwith exchanged, with the whole Creations Restitution, figured forth; the renewed estate of men and Angels, each in its order.

But even engines of VVar, the great dreadful days likeness, as in his hearing (*cap.10.*) *O wheel*, cried unto, where he between the wheels, the man in linnen, & match made of linnen, pointing there to great Ordnance, even gives fire to them; beware the brass Piece loud enough, cried whose motions strait forward, whether the head looked, mounted on their beril coloured wheels, all put into a colour, compared to the Almighty thundering voice, when he speaks, plainly spoken, what a noise

noiſe utters when their monſtrous ſhot diſcharged, compaſſed with no little ſmokes and fire, as the appearance of the glory of God, &c. their terror repreſented by the cloud in the day time, and the fiery pillar by night; theſe living creatures likewiſe in the Brazen ſerpents likeneſs, when bitten in that maner, whoſe ſouls ſo much loathed the Manna, could not digeſt ſuch light meat (*Num.* 21.)

Though ſtill all but light, how perſpicuous ſoever; nevertheleſs with the Prophets laſt inſtructions, ſhall proceed to give a taſte of it; where ſhewd him the forefront of the houſe eaſtward, all the form of the houſe charged to obſerve it; to be brief, Church-Reformation de-

C 2 mon-

monſtrates, *cap.*46. with its Chambers, inner Chambers, and outer Courts, namely, the ſeveral Courts of Iuſtice likewiſe to be reformed; as by ſuch exact dimenſions for a rule given, with the Temple and inner Temple, every corner ſurveyed, as of late diſordered Coledges, called Temples in this City, repaired too, ſet forth in this Map of *Iſralites* days: The holy waters anſwering thereto, like one deep calling to another, tokens of no inferior conſequence, when at ſo low an Ebb, iſſuing from the threſhold that became an ocean for fiſhers, exceeding many from *Eng.* to *Engl.* &c. not to be circumſcribed within ſo narrow limits, reſerved to a larger table.

Have

Have only ſounded the trumpet, here given the word, *O houſe bear, Thus ſaith the Lord, &c. for they a Rebellious, &c. for their ſtanding in contempt, ſerved the ſubpena*: Thus hard and ſlow of hearing, removed the pillow from their elbows: of ſome paſſages and tokens, touching the woful preſent given a touch to call them from the foreruners of his coming, what an over-turning goes before it, whoſe voice as the ſound of many waters, even the floods voice. *Noahs* days 1700. VVhen as repented him he made man, as in this preſent century appears, un paralleld for ſuch ſurpaſsing ſins and judgements.

But going on with the words of his commiſsion to perfect the ſame.

Cap. 3.

*Cap.*3. *Verse.* 2. 6. *Thoushalt not go amongst them, &c. for they a Rebellious house*; a multiplyed phrase after the maner of clerks, in drawing bills or books; the aforesaid *as it were*, the word *book* authorised otherwise, called a bill of divorce, as thus stiled the book of *Ezekiel* the Prophet, signifying both book and bill.

Cap. 12. *verse* 2. thus inlarged, *Thou dwellest in the midst of a Rebellious house* (Verse 3.) *For they a Rebellious house: though they a Rebellious house, &c. And hath not the Rebellious house said unto thee, &c. concluding the matter thus, For in your days, O Rebellious will I say the word, and perform it saith the Lord,* Verse 25. Acts 13. *Therefore beware, lest that fall upon you: behold ye despisers, and*

wonder

wonder and perish ye, for I do a work in your days, which ye shall not believe, though one declare it unto you.

VVhere last of all, because if the cause should depend beyond what was expected, before ripe for a hearing (Thus) a cloud about breadth of a hand appears, *Verse* 27. *Thus saith the Lord, He that heareth, let him hear; and he that forbeareth* (to put in his answer) *let him forbear*: for they, &c. alters both mood and number, hereby shewing what though some be dumb or willful, yet he at least, let him open his mouth, and not with one voice, *Shut him out whilest he made stand at the door knocking, making as they asleep were*, bears witness, Revelations 22. he that is unjust, let him be unjust still, and he that is filthy

thy, &c. and come saith the Spirit and the Bride (revealing before the glorious Throne, our appearing immediate) and let him without delay answer that heareth, and say come, &c.

The Grace of our Lord, &c.
Ezek. cap. 3.

Postscript.

Least that come to pass, *Friend, how camest thou in hither, not having a Wedding garment? and he was speechless &c. without his robe of Parliament, without doubt (in adding thereto) many called, but few chosen, an Item to both Houses. Mat. 22.*

F I N I S.

27. *The Excommunication Out Of Paradice* (1647; Wing D1987) is reprinted, by permission of the Folger Shakespeare Library, from the clear copy held at the Folger (shelfmark D1987 bd. w. D2010). This copy contains a few handwritten notes that may be in Lady Eleanor's hand. The text block of the original measures 140 × 92 mm.

Hard-to-read words and handwritten annotations:

title page	[bottom] in the same Hower this given to the House with Her owne Hand. not only a woemans Brains beaten out. By the Abey ... *&c.* But ... serveing for the present feasts distraction [transcription]
Av.1–3	Anagr. O crowmel Howl Rome [transcription]
Av.5	name [transcription]
Av.6	*vied*
4.7	*believeth*
4.12	*believest*
5.1	not
9.18	amounts the Grigean
10.20	*Portsmouth*
11.17	Revenue
11.18	pounds
12.10-12	with His wounded ... Head K: C: Heald others *&c.* [transcription]
12.11	[two 'x' marks; transcription]
13.3–4	as it were the others up [crossed out]
13.6	pretending [transcription]
13.6–12	That sea monster or Dolphin. Ludovitius 666 And [illegible word] surname Joh: Bap [transcription]
13.7	French K [original printed 'K' transformed into 'R' by hand; transcription]
15.17	*both*
16.1–9	*succeeding those three*
16.6	*being taken*
16.7	*Resurrection*
16.13	*are not incapable of* ['*are*' and '*in*' crossed out]

THE
Excommunication
OUT OF
PARADICE.

By the Lady *Eleanor*.

GEN. 3.

So he drove out the MAN.

Printed in the Year 1647.

in the same Hower they given to ye House
wth Her owne Hand. Not only a Woemans
Braing beaten out By the Abey Doore &
[illegible]

To the Honorable, *Oliver Cromwel*, Esq; Lieutenant-General, &c.

Noble Sir,

(Anagr: O: cromwel Howl Rome

*Y*OUR *own high merit not onely, but that renowned Family of your* (*envied a little not,*) *Lord* Cromvvel *Earl of* Essex, *such a Benefactor or Pillar of Church, begets this boldness in her to salute you, though farther to be acquainted have not the honor; but so much honoring them or their memory, through whose clemency or zeal, when the Faith lay at stake, we enjoy'd the Scriptures first in the vulgar or mother tongue, which began with the Commandments and Lords Prayer, &c. She saying nothing but according to the Scriptures; whereof thus,*

August, 1647.

Being your humble Servant, &c.

The Excommunication out of Paradice,

By the Lady *Eleanor.*

THe Ark, Baptiſms expreſs figure (*Pet.* 3.) No ſuch cuſtom admits in Church, of thoſe knowing not *good from evil,* to be Baptized; witneſs at mans eſtate all of them ſaved by water: where his three Sons, though married all, *yet had one born unto them till after the flood,* Noah *that according to all the Lord commanded, ſo did he.*

Neither after our Lords example, of obedience giving to underſtand, *As my Father gave me commandment, ſo I do*; he at full age arrived: The Dove when as deſcended, or abode on him,

A 2 who

who began then to be about thirty of Age, thrice ten : Certainly had a great thing been commanded, as they replyed, *Naaman bidden, Go and wash in Jordan, &c.* How much rather this imposed, *But go ye and preach ; He that believeth and is baptized, shall be saved* (vers.) according *who went forth and preach'd every where*; where thus (ver.) *Both men and women were Baptized* : As the Eunuch for another, *If thou believest with all thine heart, thou mayest be Baptized* : So he whose Father and Mother answering, *He is of age, ask him* ; and again, *Therefore said his Parents, He is of age, &c.* (Ioh.9.) He bidden, *Go and wash,* as much to say, God-fathers and God-mothers needless.

The Church past non-age, hath need

need of milk no longer, ſuch meat not belonging to Babes: Now (to ſearch the Scriptures) the wedding Garment expected from none ſuch under age; witneſs Marriage honored with his firſt Miracle; of *the good wine till laſt reſerv'd*, himſelf the bleſſed Bridegroom watch'd ſo long for.

And *He that deſpiſed Moſes Law* (Heb.10.) *if dyed without mercy; what incur they that offer deſpite thus unto the Spirit of Grace?* alledging, becauſe of Children brought unto him, *and ſetting one in the midſt of them, ſaying, Who ſhall offend ſuch one of theſe little ones, &c.* and *laying his hands on other*; and *except ye receive the kingdom of God as a little childe*, therefore the perſons of men and women are excepted: whereas of another ſort in truth ſignifie

Babes

Babes and Sucklings, of whom said, *I thank thee, O Father, that hast revealed these things unto such and such,* hidden from the learned ; whose weak Objections these, of *Little children to come unto me, for of such is the kingdom of heaven* ; onely spoken after a comparative way, as afore shewed, little for their purpose : who produce Circumcision, appointed for Males, to uphold this Antichristian custom in times of Ignorance, through subtilty crept into the Church, with the Serpent (as it were) yea, hath God said, *Ye shall not, &c.* the very forbidden fruit untimely tasted, as the Common prayer book partly confesses, in old time ; but at *Easter* and *Whitsontide* administred, which custom, say they, out of use, cannot well for many considerations

be

be restored, &c. without mentioning so much as one in behalf of their mock-Baptism, founded on Circumcision of Infants, a character not to be blotted out in the flesh, that impression even verifying the *Sows returning to the mire, and the Dog gone back, &c.* as accompanied vvith a point of more concernment then *Joroboams* prefering to the priesthood the inferior sort, or his offering incense, those Mother Midwives *Joan Baptists* suffered to take that office upon them, because of *Ziporahs* circumcising her Son.

So turn ye to that warning piece (*Apocal.*13.) of the Antichristian Beast *whose desperate wound was healed*; and the false Prophets description, and see upon what foundation both State and Church stauds in the last days (vers.)

And

And I stood upon the Sea, and I saw a beast rise up out of the sea, having seven Heads and ten Horns, crowned, &c. expresly, bears date the present seventeenth Century, even the British beast also armed at all points, from *Brute* its Name derived; where *Europia* (as it vvere) carried into the Sea: Besides *Cesars* adored Image, not to be drowned in forgetfulness, and tribute money from strangers, vvounded sorest of all by *Brutus*, he of his ovvn begetting foretold of the fatal *Ides* of *March*; by vvhom the year vvas set according to the Sun, Three hundred sixty six days, corrected the Kalender, vvhose Names lives to this day both of them, *Julius Cesar*, the Moneth of *JULY* named after it. As for the Man of Sin, the other Beast his coming out of the

the earth, horned like the Lamb, but a Dragons voyce, the tythes (to wit) or fruits of those Rams, no few sirnamed, *Pope Innocent, he that runs may read it*; whose feigned Miracles, with Cross and Crucifix adored, like that of Gold, *whose height sixty cubits, and breadth six* (Dan.3.) and thus running over the Number of his Name *666* namely, *Julius Cesar* and *August*, whose numeral letters *V i c L v v v i* about the fortieth year of which Reign (*Augustus*) who reigned 55 years and odde Moneths; *the Lamb of God came into the world*, aged 36: *in the fifteenth of Tiberius reign* (Luke, &c.) so that the aforesaid the 55 years and six Months, to Moneths *666* amounts the Grigean Account put into the reckoning; since which Empires rising (1600

B com-

compleat)as low declined; & whether or no our Britiſh Goat the Leopards ſpotted or pothered robe (verſ.) be not as *Eſaus* voyce from *Jacobs* to be diſcerned, or the Lambs from the Dragons language, even paralleld with the ten perſecutions, theſe days of ours the ten horns ſubſcribes it; one Iſle calling unto another, *Patmos* Iſle unto *Great Britains*, and *this great beaſt followed ſo, and admired of all the world*; ſaid to *riſe up out of the ſea*; begins not too with that Founder of the Spaniſh Faction, *George* Duke of *Buckingham*, of the Order of Saint *George*, Maſter of the Horſe, Admiral of the Seas, as by the Names of Ships, the one a *Leopard*, the *Lyon* another, the *Bear*, *&c.* he with a Butchers knife ſlain at *Portſmouth* in the Montth of Auguſt 1628.

1628. having continued from 1625. March, beyond expectation; ten years that was a Minion to the former. And so much for *his three years and an half*, (ver.) together with the time exprest of his continuing how long, who went away from his Parliament (1641. *Jan.*) until *Nazebies* victory (1645. *June*) vvhere the Dragons great Authority personates, S. *George* the patron of that Order; as count the number of his Name also, Viscount *Vvilers* (*V i c L v v v i*) or *666.* wanting no open mouth, if standers by to be credited, his last words heard at *Portsmouth*, at whose dispose not onely high Offices, but the Crown Revenue, Six hundred thousand pounds and more *per annum*, the weight of *Solomons* Gold (2 *Chro.9.*) *666* Talents aluding therto.

VVhere

VVhere the treaſurerſhip the other Beaſt that *came up out of the earth*, ſpake as the dragon, not a true word as much to ſay, of late in the Clergies cuſtody, as by the horns of the Lamb ſignified the two Archbiſhopricks bought and ſold with the reſt.

And as the ſtory of 88 the Spaniſh Armado's defeat, witneſs in this catalogue, the Hangings of the the Houſe of Peers, bordered about with ſo many Heads and Names, as it were (*v.*) *I ſtood upon the ſand of the Sea, and I ſaw a Beaſt riſe up, &c. with all thoſe crowns*, &c. alſo in the Houſe of Commons, thoſe pieces of Tapiſtry, of Fruitage and Flowers, all in their pots coming out of the earth about *666* ſometime in number; and ſo much touching that Allegory of their riſing

up,

ſet between pillars, referred to the beholders, Hangings ſometime belonging to the Abbey, ~~as it were the others up~~, and that ſpake, &c (verſ.xi.) the influence of the ten Horns, pretending to the French R. for another, with no inferior mouth 1610. mortally wounded, whoſe Faction revived by the Cardinal, lives and breathes to this day by his skill, ſuch the mutable condition of all, *Behold, as he ſtood upon the ſand*, though ſaid, *Who is able to make war with the Beaſt?* As *Eſſex* behold too Viſcount *Hereford* ſuch another, from Heralds myſtery deriving that appellation, as the Stag or red Deer bearing it for his Creſt; and ſo count again, *Numerus ejus ſex centi ſexaginta ſex, Rev.* of whoſe riſing from the generation of the *Walters*: *Walter Devorex*

That sea monster or Dolphin

Infdoring 666:

As manage surname Joh: Bap

vorex begetting *Walter*: and *Walter Dev. Walter* and *Walter*, *&c.* ſome ſix one after another of that Name.

Not without his ſevenfold Blaſphemous Titles, ſuperſcribed one as deeply intereſſed in the Horns as any other, in the Forehead ſigned with the Horn; that married was in the year *1606.* at the years of *16. 1636.* who father'd a ſon; and the year *1646.* Sept. *16.* aged *56.* in the ſixt year of the Parliament was ſtricken in the head by an an Apoplexy, that blow inviſible too, whoſe Father, aged *36.* that was beheaded, plotted by *Walter Rawley*, when as the Adored Image of the Beaſt, with thoſe coat arms ſo adornd, as though he had been alive followed of all: In S. *John Baptiſt* Chappel interr'd for the *Walters* ſake, the laſt of his name of *Eſſex.*

Laſtly,

Laſtly, in theſe troubleſome Seas toſſed Kings of the North and South, *French* and *Spaniſh*, ſuch dutiful ſons of *Rome*, the horns ten pointing that way not onely from *Cornu & Corona*, as *Carolus* derived, ten in number, four of the Race of *Charls the Great*, and ſix of the Houſe of *Auſtria*; but from *Henry* the fourth of *Lancaſter* Houſe, unto *Henry* the Eight, and his progeny ten even Crowned; whereof the prophet *Daniel* thus, cap. 7. v. 23. of theſe devouring Tyrants, treading dovvn Laws, &c. *And another ſhall riſe after them, diverſe from the firſt* (to wit) of another nation, *before whom three fell, by whom changed bo h the Name of the Kingdom, and their Liberties, &c.* no other then *Great Brit.* Scotiſh-horn, ſpeaking with ſuch a lawleſs mouth, ſuc-

succeeding those three without issue, Edw. 6. Mar. *and* Eliz. *of whose time and times and half, or three yeers and half, the truth shewed afore of it, from the most supreme mystery that of times and seasons, signifying how long from his unhappy departure from his Parliament, until his being taken* 1645, *and outed,* &c. *of whom the last news, his Resurrection or rising out of the sea, brought to judgement; so hitherto the end of the matter, as* Daniel 7, &c. *onely these,* Let him that is filthy, be so still, and he that is holy also, &c. and he that is athirst, take the water of life freely, *which children and Infants are not capable of, are free without it, cannot thirst or long for what they never knew,* the Spirit and the Bride saying, Come, and if any man thirst, &c. out of his belly (*he that believeth*) shall flow rivers of living water, (Joh.) *proclaimed that great day, of it so much.*

FINIS.

28. *Reader, The heavy hour at hand* (1648; Wing D2005A) is reprinted, by permission of the Folger Shakespeare Library, from the unique copy held at the Folger (shelfmark D2005.5 bd. w. D2010). The text block of the original measures 135 × 86 mm. This text lacks a title page.

Hard-to-read words:

1.17	*of which Ambassage, shewing Israel being cut off, as*
2.3	*sinful Kingdoms,*
2.7	*Hosts*
2.8–9	*roaring as a Lyon*
2. 10	*four corners*
2. 11	in
2.12	*whether*
2.13	*came to pass*
2.14	*Kings*
2.16	*his word*
2.17	*captives;*
2.19–24	*to accompany this warning piece of the* Turkish Armado's *preparation, added a sign, as* Isaiah *sometime gave one of the* Suns going back so many degrees retiring, *before their captivity at*
3.1	*given of the*
3.2	Three half
3.12	*guardians*
3.13	*assigned*
3.18	*much*
3.19	*new sign*
3. 21	*traying*
3:22	*Engines,*
3.23	*execution; and*
3.24	*in those*
4.1	*shadowed under*
4.2	Tabernacles

READER,

THe heavy hour at hand, *that it should not* as a Thief surprize us in the night, Babylons *scattering whirl-wind our final or utter blow*; *or lest should say*, There had not a Prophet been amongst them, *could not refrain giving thee warning, though like* rolling the restles stone, *prove but* labor in vain.

Where Line upon Line, *no vain repetition, Stiles them* A house of Rebellion, *and* Most Rebellious, *Cap. ver. &c. Nay (as it were) had been sent to the house of* Austria *their Churches, replyed*, Had long ere this in sack-cloth and ashes; *or to a People of* a deep lip, *of* another language, *&c. The first-fruits of which Ambassage, shewing Israel being cut off, as by* Ezekiel *tasted of*, watchman over the rebellious house of Israel, *made to* eat the roll or writ, Lamentation, Mourning *and*

A Woe,

Woe, *superscribed within and without*; *so by all signs and tokens without doubt served on our three sinful Kingdoms, home charged with open Rebellion, neither hearkning to the Prophet bidden,* stamp with the foot, smite with the fist, with the breaking of thy loyns sigh, *their musick but made and song, The Lord of Hosts when uttering his thundring voyce, roaring as a Lyon, the tokens of his coming, an end come on the four corners of the earth, ready to fall asleep,* or sitting in the seat of scorners, *All their elbows grown to the pillows, they and their fathers.*

And so farther informing whether silent or otherwise, as it came to pass in the fifth year of such a Kings captivity accomplished (Ezekiel Cap. 1.) *the hand of the Lord when upon him, his word coming expresly to him, saw the great Vision of God, he amongst the captives; Also from this place, the Kings Bench Prison amongst this Society, give to understand; to accompany this warning piece of the* Turkish Armado's *preparation, added a sign, as* Isaiah *sometime,* [illegible] ny degrees retiring, *before their* [illegible]

hand

hand foreshewed then; Another gi[illegible] Moon, *from his giving the* Three [illegible] Moons, *whose Army harbors at* Argier, *attending* Sions *being delivered up into his possession:* *These* Islands *three to be under his lash of Jurisdiction, drawn from which premises these, for his Crest or Coat-Arms who gives the* Half Moon, *not far off his house called* Sion, *committed to whom three prisoner Princes, one of no inferior estate, under* Babylons Bashaws, *typifying even our estate, those* Mahometans *our guardians, the third Earldom of this Realm, assigned thereby to* Algernon *Earl of* Northumberland *by Name, sometime Admiral of the Seas, paralleld with that Northern scourge,* The Assyrian Army, *how given up into his protection the houses of the Lord.*

And so much (Reader) *for this flight of ours, and this new sign of the* New Moon *going before it, where cannot pass over* Ezekiels *portraying our Cities siege shewed by those battering rams or brazen Engines, so to the life their swift doing execution; and dreadful wheels motion and thundring voyce, in those living creatures (as sha-*

[illegible] *under the* Seraphin work of the Tabernacles Curtains, *the Lord of Hoſts Pavillion, each loop of which not without a Myſtery, as obſervable* Fifty in one curtain, and fifty in the other, (Exod. 26.) *containing the myſtery of winged time, the midſt of the Century, even directed to, joyned like thoſe Cherubin wings of theirs.*

And of this your day drawing near, whoſe ſilver and gold the ſtumbling block, Author of unhappineſs all, as he unto all the people of Judah, *ſaying from ſuch a year of the King of* Judah, *even unto this day; that is, the Three and twenty year* (Jer. cap. 25.) *Alſo the word of the Lord have I ſpoken unto you, riſing early, but, &c.*

1 6 4 8. 23. of the preſent Reign.

F I N I S.

29. *Wherefore to prove the thing* (1648; Wing D2017) is reprinted, by permission of the Folger Shakespeare Library, from the clear copy held at the Folger (shelfmark D2017 bd. w. D2010). This text sometimes appears under the title *And without proving what we say* (Wing D1968). The text block of the original measures 145 × 92 mm. This text lacks a title page. Page 1 is misnumbered 3.

Hard-to-read words:

[1].1	thing
[1].11–12	*Et hi tres unum*
2.1–6	third answerable to the Holy Ghosts slow operation, *PROPHESY* for a time ceased, or like that saying of theirs, *Have not so much as heard whether any Holy Ghost*, &c. to whose Ministery
2.17–18	throw … Ioynture, …years
2.19	dows Estate
2.20	trivial incumbrances sifted forth:
4.3	place
5.1–3	since, a cup whereof himself since hath drunk the dregs, cannot deny it, This is the business that sleeps not.
6.1–3	about their neck a meeter ornament what weight not unknown.Yet for making atonement in that case,
6.8	three
6.9–10	Captivity
6.14	his own seeking hapned.
6.15	good
6.18	in him
7.1–3	to this pacification such an adversary, wherein the general good also a copartner with this
7.6	misprision hath
7.9	*Amoveas Manus*
7.12	Restauration, first
7.15–18	star both; … star born …*How art thou faln, &c.* first of that Name, King *Charls*, and last
8.1–3	whose hands the Lord vouchsafes to accept satisfaction none, declared as afore, which cost him his life, eaten
8.8	to whom not unknown mercy af
8.12	possession

WHerefore to prove the thing, otherwiſe as good as nothing what we ſay; but like ſaying and doing, which are two: concerning wch of more conſequence then ſuppoſed, even of thoſe three witneſſes in earth, what power indued withal, in relation to the three in the high Court of heaven (*Joh*, &c.) they ſtiled Iudges of the Earth (to wit) the grave and prudent Barons of Exchequer; *Et hi tres unum*, &c. Mr. Baron *Trevare*, the *Ancient of days* in his likeneſs; The ſecond like the Son of man, the azure clouds mixt his Foot-Carpet; The

A third

third anſwerable to the Holy Ghoſts ſlow operation; *PROPHESY* for a time ceaſed, or like that ſaying of theirs, *Have not ſo much as heard whether any Holy Ghoſt*, &c. to whoſe Miniſtery committed the Myſtery of Times and Seaſons, by all the world derided, &c. ſeveral days before whom this troubleſom tryal appearing of the Manor & Rectory of *Pyreton*, by what indirect courſes & ways taken, thereto the King intitled, by jugling Projectors plots, an old Outlawry revived, cauſed hereby to ſtretch it ſelf out by their breathing into it, &c. to overthrow a lawful Purchaſe and Ioynture, after injoyed ſo many years, waiting their opportunity, the widows Eſtate to cut it off, by ſuch trivial incumbrances ſifted forth: the

the very Image of the Beast, *Revel.* 13. by the Great-Seal fac'd forth, onely paying His Majesty about a Mark yearly; a costly purchase therein by his own officer for one born out.

Not unlike that dispute about *Moses* body, between the Archangel and the other, reported by *Jude*, this Law point debated so often in open Court by the advantage taken of her imprisonment, got into possession, so passing from this to the Judges charge for repairing this breach, appointed to stand in the gap, hereby to take off the Lords heavy hand from him, namely the King, by conjuring this Spirit down, raised up in his Name, the three kingdoms suffering for it, no less then for the sin against the holy Ghost comitted, added thereto, forgi-

A 2 ven

ven neither in this world nor the o-ther; witneſs the Archbiſhop for one, gone to his proper place from Tower-hil: and yet deliverd not for all ſo long in travel the aforeſaid Kingdoms, ſuch diſtraction witneſs continuing in Eccleſiaſtical and Civil affairs both.

No ordinary offence or treſpaſs for, but with a high hand, as not un-known to himſelf: That for her co-ming unto him not without manife-ſtation of a Commiſsion in that caſe: To give him a taſte of his judgement at hand, no leſs then the hand writing (*Dan.* 5.) ſerved on him in his galle-ry; immediately by a reference under his hand bearing date, 1633. *Octob.* &c. *Whitehal*, committed for that cauſe the ſpace of two years a cloſe priſoner in the Gatehouſe, &c. ſtript of all ever

ſince,

since, a cup whereof himself since hath drunk the dregs, cannot deny it, This is the business, that sleeps not.

Howsoever he faln asleep, like them bidden to sleep on, &c. she though then, and since armd with no few sad tokens of that kinde come to pass on others no obscure ones.

VVith this for another observation, her Ioynture the Manor of *Englefield* whilest she in the Gatehouse, bought by the Marques of *Winchester*, how his of *Basing*, such an Example not the like, unluckey *Babel* Towers, how costly to widows and fatherless, now made to kiss the ground.

All put upon his rekoning, in the Isle of *Wight*, and impeached of treason in this kinde; as *Whitebals* desolation too: no light thing; shewed about

about their neck a meeter ornament what weight not unknown. Yet for making atonement in that caſe, for his Majeſties folly, now this ſuffices; like as when *JOBS* captivity ſaid to return, was appointed to pray for his three friends: So on the other ſide, the aforeſaid Iudges three to make his peace, to turn his Captivity away, fallen ſo low as hard to judge, whether expoſed to the dunghil, or the dungeons Slavery the greater or better Eſtate, unhappily by his own ſeeking hapned.

Nor his Name wiped out of this Record, once that a good Confeſſion made, afterward makes as bad an end lifting up the heel, as much as in him lay, like *Balaam, loving the wages of unrighteouſneſs*; his own Solicitor General,

neral, to this pacification such an adversary, wherein the general good also a copartner with this, of the widows cause which the Lord defends, and stands up for it.

In which, if any misprision hath been since their judgement irreversable, may if they please, appoint the *Amoveas Manus* to be renewed, &c. And with this belief concluding, *Behold, I make all things new*, including *Lucifers* Restauration, first and last of that Name, when the times of refreshing comes, morning and evening star both; (and his own Badge the star born; its Motto too, *How art thou faln, &c.* first of that Name, King *Charls*; and last of great Britains Kings, counsold by her his *Eve*, or *CHAVAH*, also *Adams* figure, from whose

whoſe hands the Lord vouchſafes to accept ſatisfaction: none, declared as afore, which coſt him his life, eaten by a Lyon, he ſent to cry, *O Altar*, &c. charged neither to eat bread, nor water to drink there, that kings arm which reſtored (*Kin*.13.) ſo then learnd Iudges, to whom not unknown mercy afterward, as well as *judgement begins at home*; your charge the ſubſtance or ſum of it, when *Zions* widow reſtor'd ſetled in her poſſeſsion, which makes ways for others, by your means, orders a mitigation for his diſcharge; ſo faſt in the Sea (as it were) about his neck a milſtone, &c. every one in his order, even *Sodoms* inlargement, before the return of *Capernaums* Captivity. *Endleſs praiſe be to whom aſcribed.*

Anno 1643.

F I N I S.

30. *The Writ of Restitution* (1648; Wing D2019) is reprinted, by permission of the Folger Shakespeare Library, from the copy held at the Folger (shelfmark D2019 bd. w. D2010). This copy contains some handwritten notes and corrections that may be in Lady Eleanor's hand. The text block of the original measures 145 × 92 mm. Page 5 is misnumbered 6.

Hard-to-read words and handwritten annotations:

title page	largely illegible handwriting; some fragments include: 'to excuse him though had no [illegibile word] yet Had no Examples to forebide it,' 'referd to the Kings mercy as outlawryes to kepe us from contempt of ye Lawe not to mine utterly illegible word] posterity *&c.*' and 'for many these giving (Mark 24 ... Sinn no more ... to keep Him ... more Awe.' [transcription]
1	*A Signe* [transcription]
1.6	Prince
1.12–13	*Maynard*
2.1	Before whow [sic] this day, the day of
2.3	Error
2.8–15	given for a signe unto you afore hand [transcription]
2.9	a signe [transcription]
2.9	to bee [transcription]
2.12	said [transcription]
2.9–10	timely; these men yet each discharged and
2.13	*saved*
3.1	*made by him,*
3.3	*of dust return to dust,*
3.11–17	judgment other fathers erring, forced were to erect a Purgatory for Saints, that *Babel* edifice of theirs; of whom the aforesaid ancient father, the worst they could say of him was, *As he did worst of any when he wrote ill, so exceeded all men when he did well.*
3.19	Case
3.20	where the fiery adversary
4.1	pressing
4.8	outed
4.11	appearing
4.15	Solicitor
6.1–2	gthning which, another writ, a *Writ of Restitution* produced, brought in
6.5–6	as let happen to the enemie of *General Restitution,* sent to that parable of
6.8	*neads*
6.18	state or stile of a high Sheriff
7.3	*I: Rand*
7.12	Trinity term
7.17	presaging
7.20	wer the third person
10.1	erroneous
10.3	late that affirm

THE

Writ of Restitution:

By the Lady

ELEANOR.

PSAL. &c.

Be wise now therefore, O ye Kings; Be learned ye that are Iudges of the earth.

ACTS 3. 21.

Whom the Heaven must receive, till the times of Restitution of all things which God hath spoken by the mouth of all his Prophets since the world began.

Printed in the Year 1648.

THE

Writ of Restitution:

...till the times of
Restitution of all things which God hath spoken
by the mouth of all his Prophets since the
world began.

Printed in the Year 1648.

A Signe

THE

VVrit of Restitution:

BY

The Lady *ELEANOR.*

AND now in this his cause, *the Iudge of all the earth, Prince of the Kings of the earth*, a case wherein all concerned; these are to pray three, who here sit in his place Iudges: Give me leave to speak, and shew you a mystery, from this writ *Amoveas manus*, defended by the happy Mr. *Maynard*, notwithstanding opposed by Mr. Solicitor, with S. *John, not knowing what Spirit he's of.* or sign

A2 Be-

Before whom this day, the day of Iudgements figure, ſhewing by rea-ſon of a writ of Error, not executable, three ſtand charged with contempt of the Court, pleading *Ignorance*, notwithſtanding the aforeſaid *Amove-as manus* writ being executed (as it were) the *forbidden fruit* taſted un-timely, theſe men yet each diſ-charged and acquitted: as let it nei-ther be reputed impoſsible, how much oppoſed ſoever by others, for *All to be ſaved at laſt, when the utmoſt mite or mi-nute ſatisfied* or expired; the worſt of reprobates not excepted, in his time whoſe immenſe mercy inſcrutable: this is the argument, Againſt whom no writ of Error feiſible either or poſ-ſible.

Who ſaw every thing very good at firſt made

made by him, reduced to be no doubt to the same estate, as holds good from that *of dust return to dust*, every thing to the place from whence it came; fain Angels and men restored every one, not left a hoof, &c. or lost of that kinde bearing his Image.

Of which general deliverance well understood to be an Article of the Christian Faith, famous *Origen*, from whose judgement other fathers erring, forced were to erect a Purgatory for Saints, that *Babel* edifice of theirs; of whom the aforesaid ancient father, the worst they could say of him was, *As he did worst of any when he wrote ill, so exceeded all men when he did well.*

And so proceeding with this reported Case of this days Hearing, where the fiery adversary upon their

A 2 surfurmisings, pressing for a present sentence, before the accused, heard or answering, charg'd, that although moved in open Court such a writ, the *Amoveas manus* to be respited ; and accordingly a *Supersedis* issued out, delivered to the Sheriff then in being; the Tenants neverthelesse outed of possession by the now under-Sheriff of that county about three moneths ago : whereupon he cald and appearing, demanded of whom, how those doors came to be opened, denied not what he had done by vertue of such a sealed writ, by such a Solicitor brought to him as for other writs concerning them, pleads *Ignorance* ; One *Pomfred* by name, (*alias Pomum*) surprized in state of inocency, like her *first in the transgression* ; (for pursuing which Allegory thus)

thus) ſhewing one *Maſsingal* cald, pleading ignorāce too as the man lay-ing the fault on *Eve*; he (ſome three years ſince in that Office) onely had a *SuperJedis*, of what validity now he knows not; for other writ, none came to his hand.

Alſo *Jo:Rand* Solicitor cald, he ap-pears, no yong Fox, not to be foold with pocket Errors, refers to the Iud-ges, whether year after year that writ like to be of much force, brought be-force ſuch and ſuch Officers; namely the Treaſurer, &c. when as in being none ſuch, or like to be: And ſo this the Epilogue or end of it, their ſtale Errors being quaſht; the writ ſtands good for taking off or removing his Majeſties unhealing hands, his Te-nants caſhier'd; moreover for ſtren-

gthning

gaining which, another writ, a *Writ of Restitution* produced, brought in COURT, stops the Lyons mouthes, forced to put up their pipes, as let it happen to the enemie of *General Restitution*, sent to that parable of *the unnatural elder Brother towards his own flesh and blood*, Luke, and *murmuring laborers, because their fellows made partakers with them*; endless unmercifulnes thereof to bid others beware.

And here to make an end with what penance imposed on those three for a presumption of that nature; these a touch of it: The under Sheriff *Pomfred*, somewhat of a low pitch, he never to aspire or take upon him the state or stile of a high Sheriff; the other sometime in the same imployment or Office, *Massingal* to return

turn to his domestick function or calling deserting former dainties. The honest poor Solicit. *J. Rand* as for him unto other Solicitors an example his lot, besides to pinch himself with hard and thin fare, never to attempt the Kings Solicitors place, or St. *John* to be cald like the wandring Iew.

And so farther, no jesting matter neither of mean consequence, where like Twins, this finished tedious Law Suit in Trinity term; and Gods word both sympathizing or joyned in wedlock, like the blessed Virgin and just *Joseph* Cousins, though abruptly in brevities behalf handled or penn'd, presaging without doubt, maugre the old Serpents plotting with his smooth outside, through the holy Ghosts power the third person in Trinity, long

B silent

ſilent though, or vaild under a cloud as it were, will immediately decide our Church-Differences, of ſuch troubleſom Times the cauſe; which Lord haſten, and teach them to diſcern the time better.

And ſo haſtning on, ſhewing from hence how all ſhut up under ignorance, know not what they do; the man undone by the woman, aleaging for himſelf, ſuſpected not, ſhe unto him given, the Author to be of his ruine, having warning of it given him never; The woman on the other ſide again, The Serpents intents had ſhe known, ſhe had not been over-reacht by ſuch his falſeneſs & flattery, to the overthrow of her and hers, ſo many: The Serpent his excuſe, he came but to try her for his part, what would befal

fal was above his reach, foresawit not; no more then the old Prophet, that by means of him a Lyon by the *way* should tear his fellow Prophet: Or that such a mass of corrupted mankinde should succeed to perish, since the words to them twain being, *Touch it not lest ye dye*, importing but in danger of death.

And thus since all Original sin the root pardoned in that last prayer, *Father, forgive them, &c.* sealed with his own Blood on the Tree, Restitution of course follows, who can forbid it, or shew why the taking off, or removing of his heavy hand should not be an *Article of our Belief*, seeing this Son of *Adam* his administrator discharges all Debts from the beginning of the world to the end, which by by that erroneous Opinion, Mother of Errors, they go about to annihilate that affirm, *Out of Hell is no Redemption*; who is able, having *Ages of Ages* (Rev. 1.) *even from the worlds beginning, the keys of Hell and Death*, to turn this *water into wine*; and where he hath given a being, to cause such judgements to be for the best, the onely Clay to regain the eye-sight, howsoever Excommunicated this Truth by envious times; of *Esau's* race, endeavoring to disinherit and strip the Son of God, *who gave himself a Ransom*, not for some, but *for All*; *All made alive in him: Forgive them, Father, &c.* as shewed afore, under ignorance concluded.

FINIS.

31. *Apocalyps, Chap. 11* (1648; Wing D1969) is reprinted, by permission of the Folger Shakespeare Library, from the clear copy held at the Folger (shelfmark D1969 bd. w. D2010). This copy contains a handwritten note that may be in Lady Eleanor's hand. The text block of the original measures 140 × 92 mm. This text lacks a title page.

Hard-to-read words and handwritten annotations:

1.5-9	=where neither the gifte of prophecie [remaining words illegible: transcription]
8.18	yon
8.19	prohi
8.21	*I*, I, &c.

APOCALYPS,

Chap. 11.

Its accompliſhment ſhewed from the Lady *ELEANOR*.

THus Reader in a word to thee, what the unſealed words of this Propheſie imports; VVe even in the ſame Eſtate with them, called well Spiritually hardned *Egypt*, and ſinful *Sodoms* great City (pointing expreſly to the Spiritual calling in the laſt days what incurable Blindeneſs Arrogancy begets: Here impeached of the ſin againſt the Holy Ghoſt, guilty of the blood of theſe his ſacred Ambaſſadors ſlain by them: the Prophet *Daniel* and *John*, no inferior prophets, their Books being interpreted by the ſame Spirit they wrote, and theſe Imprinted at *Holland, Anno* 1633. immediately ſeized on, ſhrowded in a looſe ſheet of paper: their embalmd bodies about Doctors Commons, the good hour waiting for of their reſurrection wounded in that barbarous manner, aſſaulted by mercileſs, deſperate men, unto a ſenceleſs, ſaltleſs age ſent; bidden, *Remember her looking back, Lots faithleſs Wife*, who neither diſcern the time, know not the voyce of the prophets, enemies to the Churches deliverance (*Micah* 4.) promiſed, at laſt, the downfal of her foes, come upon themſelves have fulfilled it: By filling the meaſure up, reaching to Heaven: an account but current heretofore, never compleat till now the holy Ghoſt in ſuch manner blaſphemed: The invincible truth tearm'd madneſs, nefs, the Prophets Teftimony as extant on Record, and publifhed, fentenced deteftable, as if any thing were too hard for the *Lord* in his appointed time: whofe dead bodies trodden underfoot daily, or fwept out like weekly Occurrences, thofe truths; and proceeding with the bruitifh fact committed on thefe facred VVitneffes, or Ambaffadors arived what their entertainment; though not ignorant what power extraordinary indued with: wonders of the higheft kinde at their word, waters turn'd into blood, VVar forefhewed, Heaven fhut, and the like, fmite the Earth with plagues as often as they fpeak the word, yet thefe rafh wretches fuch a vexation their prefence, clad in Sackcloth, &c. gratifie with prefents making merry,

A 2 as

as the maner by ſtoping one anothers mouths, to make up the Breach; triumphing over their corps ſlain by the Beaſt coming out of the ſmoking pit or Abyſs, as appears, making VVar with them, with his furious Train, armed at all points this Britiſh beaſt.

Not a little wilde concerned in it, becauſe ſhewed in this maner: *He muſt be killed* (verſe) which harms them, touches a leaf of the Tree of Life, a violent death, whoſe doom be he whatſoever, *verſ.5. cap.*11.

And though ſince ſee it true, viſible as their unexpected Reſurrection and Aſcenſion, beheld by their very Enemies, eye witneſs of it: Gentlemen no leſs ſlighted, then by thoſe impious perſons inſenced at their Teſtimony, ſuppoſed ſuch an impoſsibility

in

in thoſe profane feaſting days, adored by his riotous Lords, Courted by his Concubines, with *Belſhazzar*, born under a like malevolent Planet: And though needleſs any farther ſhewing, concerning in the laſt time, the laſt days approach to be revealed out of the Prophet *Daniel* and the *Apocalyps*, one a Phenix of great *Babylon*, the other an Eagle, his flight from *Patmos* Iſle, of times tyranical Reign cut off, and his caſhiered Generation; ſuffering for which glad tidings murthered by wretched caytiffs (verſ.) confirmed both by their Reſurrection and Aſcending: & whoſe ſcaled writs reſerved for the end, not opened to be till then or ſerved. Notwithſtanding of Times myſtery thus, his being bidden, *Ariſe and meaſure the Temple*;

after

after the ſeven thunders voyces utter-ed, proclaiming of a certain in what century, ſworn in his wrath, Times being no longer; He forbidden to meaſure the Court,leave it out,given to the Gentiles; of whoſe treading under foot 42 moneths the City, as follows, ſignified by the *Temple of God*, the year of God howabout 1642.from his leaving the High Court, &c. unto *Nazebies* blow given him, juſt three years and a half, even from *Jan.* 1641. unto *Anno Dom*.1644. compleat, that Aſcenſions feaſt and cities ſolemn thankſgiving. And thus as the heavens one contained in another, under that great victory obtained, ſhadowed out the general day of Iudgement not far off; whereat the holy prophets and Elders not more rejoycing, then

tho

the ireful Nations inraged; like those so many thousand prisoners brought up, &c. filling every place like Hell, likened to that great Earthquake 1645. after the aforesaid feast, when a List returned with Names, &c. ver. *a remnant onely escaping, giving glory to God*, or took their flight, as shewed (v.13.) all pointing to the present century; as moreover 7000 slain by the cities fall, the tenth part of it in the same hour, &c. confirm'd by the divided number of Seven, *a time and times and half* (or part.) And so much for measuring out of these times of division never such; and the third wo said *to come quickly*, shewing the other two are past: what signs and woful tokens visited with (to wit) monstrous levied Taxes devouring yong and old, and Engines of war those pieces in a moment destroying,

men

men by Sea and Land innumerable, as though Hell let loose, the Devils short, &c. And for these in special, let so much suffice of Heaven opened, or the Temple of GOD, &c.) with the two *Candlesticks, and two Olive-Trees anointed* ones, passing over the General, what war hath bin waged against the Old and New Testament, and two Sacraments, the sum of it, *oyl in their lamps*, or watchful; &c. including your *Holland* Ambassadors welcom, & that the Cedar if not spared, or the root, let the Firtree beware, the branches must not be too bold; between whom (the King & Bishops in hot blood) to judge referd to those two divided brethren, one returning a cross answer, the yonger as free of his fair language, prohibits deferring to give God the glory, or going about to deceive him, with *H*, &c.

FINIS.

32. *Of the general Great Days Approach* (1648; Wing D1999A) is a collation of two imperfect copies (both, alas, lacking pages 9 and 10) held at and reprinted by permission of the Folger Shakespeare Library (both at shelfmark D1999.5 bd. w. D2010). This copy has some handwritten notes that may be in Lady Eleanor's hand. The text block of the original measures 140 × 86 mm. Page 17 is misnumbered as 10.

Hard-to-read words and handwritten annotations:

5.10	the [transcription]
5.10	y^{r} [transcription]
5.12	*bylon*
6.17	dead
8.1	full ripeness
8.3	either *Cesar* slain
8.6	with his monthday
8.8	bleeding commiseration
8.9	never too soon in shortening
8.12	expression
8.13	ceeding
8.17	his Father) to whom
11.16	curring,
12.4–11	The Breast plate Blew [remaining words illegible: transcription]
13.4	(144)
13.5	And Ezekiel All seeing wisedom [transcription]
13.10	sort, as a
13.11	some open
13.16	*the ending*
14.1	*claims at hand*
14.5	(as it were) the Suns
14.14	Isle
14.15	Committed [transcription]
16.1	apparition beheld
16.7	strument two
16.10	And so for his voyce as the sound
16.13	*ah*
16.16	*in his*
16.19–20	'A' followed by raised 'O' and '*&c.*' [transcription]
[10].1	belongs to the time
[10].14	extinct
[10].20	*right*
18.1	with his age, &c.
18.9	midst of those Centinels
18.10	solitary
18.12	*furnace*
18.14	*was*
18.20	*mation of the age* (*Mat.* 28) … as
19.3	sent before the last
19.6	as [transcription]
19. 10	tury
19.11	and
19.12	So [transcription]
19.14	when [transcription]
19.16	= fire & sworde [transcription]
19.17	for such a peacable Age … like the Angels…its strength [transcription]
20.1–17	aforehand then the years of scarcity the former when brought forth by handfuls, where *Joseph* the prisoner so advanced, surely more to looke after then *tything of Rue and Rosemary*; *or great tythes either*; Howsoever by the Day of Judgments passed over; From moreover, who wrote to a Lady that loving Epistle, so *He that hath an ear, &c.* (even which accompanies the times general Out cryes, and News cryed) let him give ear to the truth of his presence and company will enjoy, *who stands without and knocks*; *freely offers to sup, &c. to sit in his Throne with him.*

19

Of the general Great DAYS APPROACH.

To His Excellency Sir Thomas Fairfax *General.*

FROM

The Lady *Eleanor Da:* & *Do.*

PSAL.

The Lord reigneth, let the earth rejoyce; Let the great Isles be glad thereof.

Printed in the Year 1648.

A. & O.

F*Rom him which is, and was, and is to come, the alone peace-maker*, his Majesty expresly these the Revelation, by his Handmaid interpreted:

Shewing, that as the word of the Lord, that *Manna*, came in the wilderness to him, sent afore from God, he first of his Name, last of the old Prophets, and first of the new; So to his servant *John* again in the Isle of *Patmos*, sent unto the Gentiles, to whom by way of Characters and other sacred Tokens, signified the express time of the Lords return,

A 2 the

the myſtery unfolded: of which as follows; Cap. 1.

Who on this wiſe, with no ſlender charge, *Bleſſed is he that reads, and they that hear the words of this Prophesie, and keep the things written therein; for the time is at hand* (Verſe) And with precious time to be ſhort, that returns not, the happy Reader which would a taſte of this Angelical food have, miniſtred to *Iohn* by the Angel, whoſe Name ſignifies both the Grace of God, and the Year of Grace, as *Ioann Anno, &c.* by theſe ſhall underſtand, that the Goſpels progreſs or pilgrimage tis to be paced out, by *Noahs* days, or like his few and evil, *Iacobs*; which attained not to thoſe of his predeceſſors: as by this

ac-

account of the *Goſpels* coming ſhort of the former, both before the Law and under, fulfilling ſeventeen Centuries, like his ſeventeen years ſojourning in Egypt, before ended the tedious days of his laborious life, Sevenſcore and ſeven years, his Ladder reaching from Earth to Heaven.

And thus with expedition of ye Churches captivity in ſpiritual *Babylon* finiſhed; *Iohn*, with theſe joyful Tidings the Time at hand, *ſalutes the ſeven Churches, Grace and Peace unto you, from him which is, and which was, and which is to come; and from the ſeven Spirits before the Throne*, beſides the familiar Voyces of Time alſo, perſonating the Holy Spirits gift; even his watchful ſer-

vants

vants day and night, these next to eternity, about to take their leave, remember their service to the churches, especially sabbath days, where inclusive Times whole family, with the Anniversary day Easter; the Resurrections feast, the year when begins and ends, those spiritual, &c. VVho all with one voyce and consent cry down Times person, no more allegiance due, or adored with superstitious Ceremonies longer:

From voyces to good tokens, all to the same end and effect, *vers.* And from Iesus Christ the faithful witness, &c. the first begotten of the dead: The prince of the Kings of the earth that loved us, and washed us from our sins in his own blood; the Lamb of God, &c. a Bathe
able

able to contain certainly the whole world, even from *Iudas Iſcariot* that Traytor in grain, to the Red old Dragon, to preſent them in their primitive eſtate in his appointed time, in whom we live, move, and have our being every one: where points to the cuſtom of former ages of the Church, their adminiſtring about Eaſter, Baptiſm, and the Lords Supper.

VVhich ſeven weeks for ſpiritual exerciſe how imployed before the Holy days, too well known: And the Holy Spirit made their open paſtime too, ſuch a gift beſtowed upon them, poſſeſt with *Sodom* blindeneſs reigning ſuch.

Neverthe leſs, with the words of this propheſie, This tree of Life

come

come to his full ripeness; going on shewing a greater Potentate then either *Cæsar* slain, who set the year, arriv'd at their sun-setting that Monarchy: or then *C. R.* Defender, &c. with his month day 27 about *Easter*, and priests in his presence, in whom bleeding commiseration none such, never too soon in shortening such Reigns hereby as shadow'd out.

And so proceeding with another expression of his much love, exceeding *Solomons* to the queen of the South; which could but ask and have; (*vers.*) and hath made us Kings and Priests (unto God and his Father) to whom be power and dominion to ages of ages, *Amen*; in the Churches old age, as much to say, Princes every one & Preachers

no

God and the Father , *&c.*

VVhereof *Eden* that parted River that became four Heads a figure, where in those three Gold very good; The *Onyx-stone*, and the unknown *Bdellium*, the *Manna* likened to it, compar'd to a round white seed, whence comes doubtless our *Orient Pearl*, that queen of *Egypts* for one, as well bestowed upon a Swine, the *Gentiles* Emblem; how it fares with them even to this day in holy things.

And the whole sacred current flowing this way of Old and New concurring, as the Tabernacle for example, shews *wrought with blue, purple and crimson*, in which *the Table, the Shew-bread, and the Candlesticks*, those Memorials also the significant *Ark four-ſquare*, containing *the Tables of the Law, the pot of Manna, and the budding Rod*: of the four winds, who may doubt too, unknown whence they are: And the fourth part of the VVorld, becauſe but three formerly, or with doubting *Thomas*, &c.

As witneſs this, *Trinity in Unity* (*Exodus the* 3.) ſay, *The Lord God of your Fathers, the God of Abraham, and the God of Iſaac, and the God of Jacob, &c. This is my memorial to all generations*; four ſeveral times repeated, to beware of going leſs, no vain repitition from the Lords own mouth, a Leſſon to his firſt Ambaſſador *Moſes*, bare footed, before the thorny Buſh, the fiery Throne, the fourfold *Alelujah*

voyces,

voyces, saying, *Amen, Revel.* with that four-square virgin City, unfolding as much, said to have *the glory of God*, measured (144) her reign.

So now to return home to the matter of his coming in his cloudy chariot, thus advertised, *verse. Behold, he cometh with clouds, &c. Even so, Amen*: to the greater sort, as a thief in the night welcom, or some open enemy, even wounded by *Jew* and *Gentile* both.

Of his Name, sacred every title; thus, *I am A. and O. the beginning and the ending, saith the Lord, which is, and which was, and which is to come; the Almighty, where the truth of it: the burthen of the word of the Lord the acceptable year proclaims*

claims at hand, witnesd to be with the Scriptures, the Original Languages as pointed unto manifests, the old & New, where the first begins the last ends (as it were the Suns rising of the one, the others setting, like *Antipodes* the *Hebrew* and *Greek*; and so of the Old-year end, married to New-years day.

And as here by his ovvn Example recommended, *Iohn our brother and companion*; what patience requisite in a Prophet, shews he to the Isle of *Patmos* confined, scituated in the *Egean sea* by that Tyrant, &c.

Committed

So a Revolution vvithal as the Noon-day visible, and the Stars in the firmament, directed to this Isles three, *from him which is, was, and is to come*; the very voyce of the present

ſent Reign, the firſt of his name, &c. even this kingdom, where began the Reformation, (as it were) by ſeveral languages or ways to them reveal-ed, his ſecond coming.

And theſe the ſum of the bleſſed words of this propheſie, the day of Judgements ſummons to *Great Bri-tain* foreſhewed.

Shewing upon the Lords-day how it came to paſs a great voyce of a trumpet behinde him heard, me-ditating it may be how long to the Reſurrection, or about the meaning of thoſe, *What if I will he tarry till I come?* anſwered by the Reſurrections alarm appears, ſaying, *I am Alpha and Omega, the firſt and the laſt; and what thou ſeeſt, write in a book, &c.* at which turned about that dreadful

ap-

apparition beheld, one in the likenes of the Son of man, a very book at all points, as it were in fine paper gilded, bound and claſps: the flaming Eyes ſome combuſtable ſtuff declares; not onely but the ſharp inſtrument two edged coming out of his mouth, the cutting or opening of the leaves.

And ſo for his voyce as the ſound of many waters, even the floods voyce lifted up, as the days of *Noah*, the coming of the Son of man, the evening of time come, *the ſeven golden Candleſticks, and the ſeven ſtars in his right hand*, by whoſe influence *Iohn* revived, dead afore, unanimouſly the ſame Viſion the Prophet *Daniel* ſaw, ſaying, *a thing was revealed, but the time was long* (as it were)

4°: 1600 &c:

were) Belongs to the time of the end to be understood, as referr'd to those one and twenty prophetical days, when withstood so long by the *Persian* prince, *Dan*. 10. it being thereabout since *Cyrus*, so many hundred years since this Secret revealed to him. And thus much for the BOOK and its Contents, with his Commission signed and sealed with those mystical letters, and stars seven, to remember the Church to stand on their guard and be watchful; those lights almost extinct, Bishops about 27. in the first place.

A piece drawn *in the Ancient of days likeness; a Robe girt (as it were) spurs and sword, an ireful aspect, answerable to his confused voyce, a rod in his right hand, or scepter,* indued with

C such

such power, with his age, &c. the least touch; his watchword or Motto, vers. *I am the first and the last; I am he that was dead, and am alive to ages of ages, and have the keys of Hel and Death*; consisting of variety of expression, sounding the Resurrections Alarm, he standing in the midst of those Centinels, or walking in that solitary place, not the least among the Isles; like *his walking in the fiery furnace, beheld by the King of great Babylon*, at whose command the same *was heated seven times more then afore*; a forerunner of his own judgement of seven times, &c.

And from these significant things, and those his last words, *Behold, I am with you all days, until the consummation of the age* (*Mat.* 28.) as

fol-

follows, shewing the holy Spirit not in power onely visible to all, but in person again sent before the last Day, to some one even a Revolution or return to be of the former; Also of the very time gives to understand from his standing in the midst of so many watch-lights (to wit) about the midst of such Century, to look about us then, with our brother *John*, who turning saw and heard these, presaging too some special judgement being foreshewd when, accompanied for a testimony of it, with no inferior persecution; And the prophesie accomplished accordingly this to be the day of Judgement Herald, verily to all Nations, &c.

Much more to be provided for

after thou the years of scarcity:
the former when brought forth by
handfulls, where *Joseph* the prisoner
so advanced; surely more to look
after their *tithing of Rue and Rose-
mary* so *great tythes* either; How so-
[redacted]
passed over. From moreover, who
wrote to a Lady that loving Epistle, so *He that hath an ear, &c.* (even
which accompanies the universal general Out-crying and New-joyed)
let him give ear to the truth of his
presence and company will enjoy u
*who stands without and knocks, freely
offers to sup, &c. to sit in his Throne
with him*

F I N I S.

33. *The Lady Eleanor Her Remonstrance To Great Britain* (1648; Wing D2006) is reprinted, by permission of The British Library, from one of two surviving but incomplete copies held at The British Library (shelfmark 486.f.27.[3]). The text block of the original measures 155 × 87 mm.

Hard-to-read words:

5.1	as follows
7.1	*Phoenix*
7.3	of *Patmos*
7.12	oblation.
7.15	seald so fast, consisting of *times*
7.18	but *Daniel*
7. 19	seals onely
7.20	*to un*
8.1	*loose*, which no man
8.3	*on, but*
8.6	*praise*
8.9	Key to open the meaning too of
8.14	ther

3

THE LADY ELEANOR HER REMONSTRANCE TO Great Britain.

LAMENT. 1. 8.

She remembreth not her last end; therefore she came down wonderfully.

Printed in the Year, 1648.

THE LADY ELEANOR HER REMONSTRANCE TO Great Britain.

LAMENT. 1. 8.

She remembreth not her last end; therefore she came down wonderfully.

Printed in the Year, 1648.

The Lady *Eleanor* her Remonſtrance to *Great-Britain.*

AND theſe, *My love awakened not till he pleaſe*; as ſhews the Viſions of the man greatly belov'd, *Daniel*, foreſhewed him (*Dan.* 12.) *For thou ſhalt REST, and ſtand in the lot at the end of days*; ſignifying the myſtery of *Time*, the perfection of propheſie not afore to be revealed: And he, ONE loved not a little, *John*, penman of the holy Spirit, who wrote the *Revelation*; both which in one Character expreſsing the Events, forerunners to be of the End, ſo points expreſly to the preſent Seventeenth Century, the multiplied

tiplied number of *Reſt*, witnes good meaſure and preſsd down: Of *Daniels* weeks, and thoſe threefold periods and a half, of ſeven divided, a time and times and half (or part) each fulfilling five hundred years, which extend to the aforeſaid year of Grace; alſo cloſing it with days, a thouſand two hundred and ninety, *Bleſſed is he that comes to a thouſand three hundred five and thirty*, amounting to about ſeven myſtical years, importing ſome freedom or deliverance time then, which thus paced forth by *Daniel*, *JOHN* crowned *with the ſeven ſtars*, obſerves the ſame meaſure commanded to write their myſtery; after revived was by their influence, wherof a taſte to an Age which no ſtorms

A 2 of

of force to awaken, as follows, neither *fiery Serpents, the Pestilence and War*, such as never, nor *word of the Lord*, thereby charmed to be prevailed with, these sleepers of the seventeenth Century: And so much for these visions, dark heretofore, suffices, shewed here when their captivity returns, or their Commission unsealed; And of those melodious notes the meaning also (*Cant.*) *For my head is filled with dew, and my locks with the drops of the night, &c.* of its return the time when come.

So shall pass on from the prefixt time (when) to the discovery of what place and Nation in the latter days to be visited, a people even charged with High Treason by the prophet, *Daniel* (cap. 9.) from the King, Princes

princes and fathers, to our Iudges that have judged us, having all rebelled, their ears (as it were) ſealed up, or their underſtanding blockt up; which *Malachi* the prophet foreſeeing, concludes thus his laſt words, ſhewing before the great and dreadful Day, what fruit the laſt days produce, when viſited ſhall be again; as, lo our doom thoſe with the Curſe threatned, *Behold, I ſend you Elijah the Prophet, and he, &c. leſt I come and ſmite the Earth.*

And thus great Bleſſings and Corrections coupled, as when *a door in Heaven opened,* alſo *opened the Bottomleſs Pit,* Revel. &c. And therefore which *quench the ſpirit, liſten O Iſles*, Great *Britain* to theſe Viſions, ſpeaking to us the

word

word of the Lord, the one a *Phœnix* of great *Babylon*, the other his flight taken from the Isle of *Patmos*, to our western coasts transporting this Altar Coal, like the Suns course setting here, running about to the end of the earth, whereof as insues concerning the Story of the blessed little sealed Book, in the Fathers own dispose, briefly, as the Angel but touched *Daniel*, caused swiftly to fly (*Dan.* 9.) about the evening oblation.

Revelat. Cap. 5.

Touching which aforesaid Virgin Book seald so fast, consisting of *times* and Seasons mystery, like as the secret which none of the wise men of *Babylon*, but *Daniel* could dream of, so those golden seals onely *the Lyon of Davids line prevails to unloose*,

looſe, which no man, we are ſure, *was found worthy, no not to look thereon, but the Lamb*; that it might be fulfilled, *Pſal. Out of the mouth of babes and ſucklings thou haſt perfected praiſe*; as here acclamation ſuch, and extolling the Lamb far and near: And ſo borrowing *Davids* Key to open the meaning too of thoſe *ſeven Eyes and ſeven Horns*, called *The ſeven Spirits of God*, his Ambaſſador ſent forth into all the earth: *Pſal. One day telleth another, and one night certifieth another*; as much to ſay, theſe Characters, ☉☽, *Even praiſe him Sun and Moon*, &c. *Agnus*, ſignifying, *Anno Domini*; ſuch high Hieroglyks this Kalender, the little Book unfolded by: and ſo much for *Johns* much weeping

ing

34. *Given to the Elector Prince Charles of the Rhyne* (1648; Wing D1992) is reprinted, by permission of the Worcester College Library (Oxford University), from the unique copy held at Worcester College (shelfmark AA. 1.12 [1]). The text is apparently an edition of a tract that is no longer extant, first published in 1633. The handwritten comments in this tract resemble the hand of those that appear on the Folger tracts. The text block of the original measures 183 × 140 mm. (N.B. This item has been reduced to fit the available text area.)

Appended to this text is a separate treatise, *To the Kings Most Excellent Majesty: The humble petition of the Lady Eleanor* (Wing D2014A). The latter is not included in this volume but is discussed in greater detail in the textual note for **[10]**.

Handwritten annotations:

title page	for His Excellencie…[remaining words unclear]
6.20	on scaffold
6.23–24	His Head Severed from His Bodie:
7.1	a cave
7.19	[asterisk]
7.23–24	Even…Hall as…Cardinall Wolseys House so…must..
8.9–16	[largely illegible annotations with exception of '*&c.*']
10.1–8	[largely illegible annotations with exception of '*&c.*']
11.11	pride thy neck
12.	[top margin; illegible annotations]
12.21	Shaft

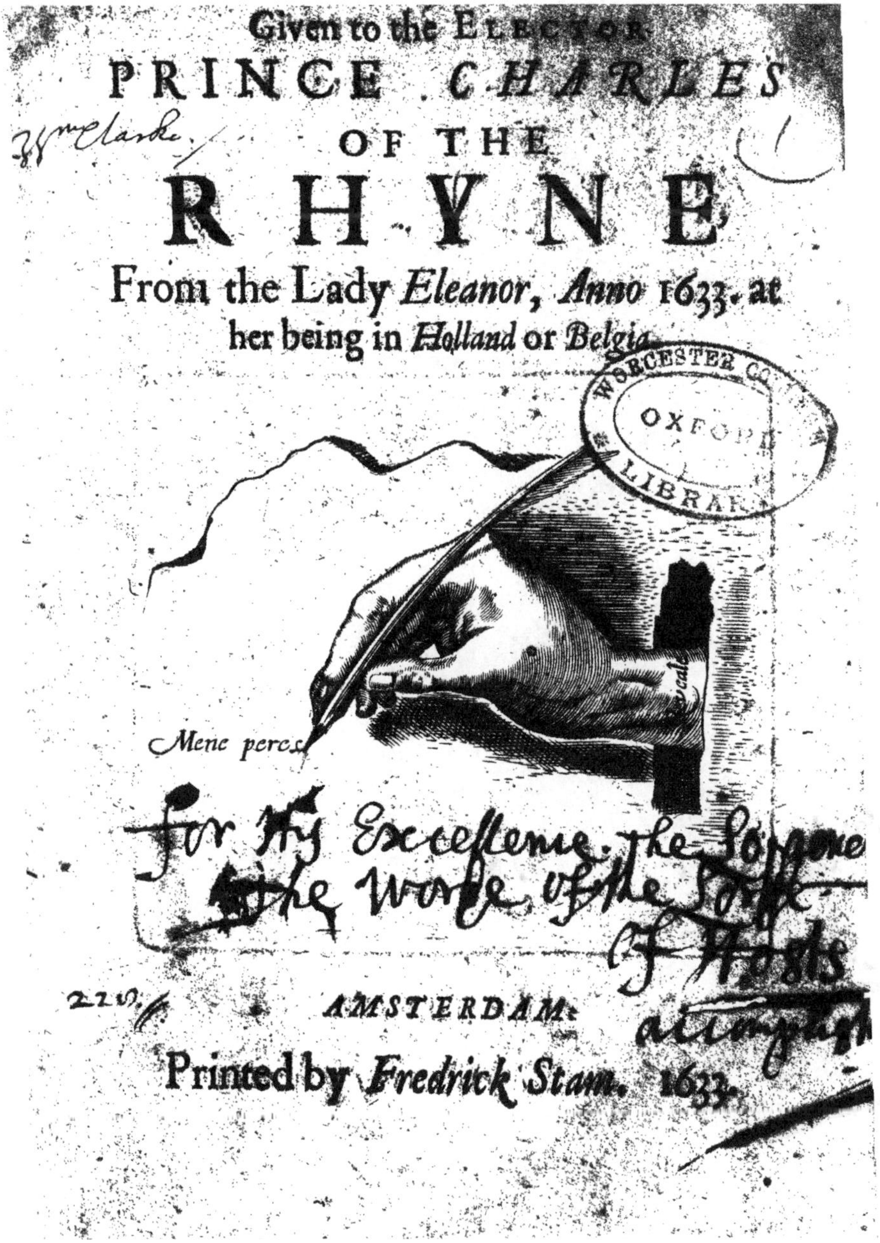

Given to the ELECTOR

PRINCE CHARLES

OF THE

RHYNE

From the Lady *Eleanor*, *Anno* 1633. at her being in *Holland* or *Belgia*.

Mene peres

AMSTERDAM:

Printed by *Fredrick Stam*. 1633.

1648. Reprinted.

To the happy READER.

Whoso readeth, let him understand, &c.
Matth. 24.

L*Ike as in days of* Noah, *foreshews*
when comes the Son of Man,
What posture in, the Church found then
concludes as it began:
Bids thee number by the Floods age,
number the dreadful Day;
Baptisms voyce accords thereto,
no Babe, as much to say.

Ætatis 1600 compleat.

A TABLE,

Shewing what Affinity between Great Babylon and Great Britain, with significant Names.

D*Aniel*, Judgement of God.

Nebuchadnezzar, bewailing of the Kindred.

Belshazzar, without treasure, or a searcher for treasure; he last of the *Caldean* Kings.

Mene, number, &c. *Mene-Laus*, power of the people.

Also *London, Babylon*, confusion signifying; and *Scotland* otherwise called *Caledonia*: *Baby-Charles* bids him beware (whose Anrgr.) *Charles be*: *Belchaser*.

And so from *Nimrods* days unto *Nebuchadnezzars* about 1700 years, the Roman Empires date out, puts into the number.

To

To the Palsgrave of the *RHYNE*, *Charles Prince Elector*:

The Palm of the Hand, *Dan. Cap.* 5.

The Tune to, *Who list a Soldiers life*, &c.

Psal. *I will utter my grave matter on the Harp.*

By the Lady *Eleanor*, *Anno* 1633.

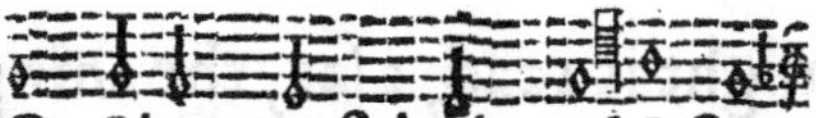

TO *Sion* most belov'd I sing 1.
of *Babylon* a Song,
Concerns you more full well I wot
then ye do think upon.
Belshazzar, lo, behold the King
feasting his thousand Lords;
Phebus and *Mars* prais'd on each string,
every day records.

The Temple Vessels of Gods House 2.
boldly in drank about:
His own ('tis like) were made away,
bids holy things bring out;
Praising of Gold and Brass the gods,
of Iron, Wood and Stone,
See, hear, nor know not, out alas,
praised in Court alone.

As when *Prague* lost, he feasting with Ambassadors was betrayd, &c

A hand

3. A hand appears lo in his ſight,
as he did drink the wine,
Upon the wall againſt the light
it wrote about a line
In preſence of his numerous Peers,
not ſet an hour full,
In loyns nor knees had he no might,
chang'd as a gaſtly skull.

4. Who might it read, alas, the thing,
Belſhazzar loud doth ſhout;
Calls for Magicians all with ſpeed,
came in, as wiſe went out.
Caldeans and Southſayers ſage
the meaning whoſo can
Of *Mene Mene* third Realms Peer
in Scarlet Robe the man.

Which numeral letter of *Mene Tekel Upharſin.* *M U I L.* Entred then (ſnews) into the day even of Iudgement, &c.

5. His Majeſty forgets to Sup,
Nobles aſtoniſh'd all;
Muſicians may their pipes put up,
ſtood gazing on the wall.
The pleaſant wine at length as ſharp,
too late, till thought upon
Diviſion of another ſtrain
unfolds the fingers long.

or Scaffold

His Head ſeverd from his Bodie;

When

When to the Banquetting houſe ſo wide, 6. a cave
where hoſt of Lords did ring,
So wiſely came the graceful Queen,
ſaid, *Ever live, O King.*
Needs trouble, O King, thy thoughts no more,
forthwith ſhall it be read;
Daniel *there is, who heretofore*
like doubts did overſpread.

Could all interpretating ſhew 7.
which profound man ſoon brought,
On whom confer the King needs would
his orders hight unſought.
Needleſs preferments yours reſerve,
Sir, keep your gifts in ſtore;
High Offices let others gain,
there's given too much afore.

Yet unto thee ſhall here make known, 8.
reſolve this Oracle true,
Sure as in thy Banquetting houſe,
where all that comes may view:
The Veſſels of my God are brought,
the palm ſalutes thee know
Herewith; for theſe profan'd by thee Even whi
threatneth the fatal blow. Hall as on
O King,
Cardinall Wollseys House so
church must retur

9\. O King, even thou, the moſt high God
unto thy Grandſire bold,
Caldean Land, a Nation fell
gave them to have and hold.
The Royal Scepter and the Crown
advanc'd whom he would have,
And whom he would he pulled down,
could put to death and ſave :

Caledonians or *Caldeans* ſignifying union mingling or as Devils.

10\. Till walking at the twelve moneths end,
ſubject full Tides to fall ;
Excellent Majeſty how gone,
Court exchang'd for the Stall.
Thy Grandſire on as came to paſs,
at all yet minded not,
As if a feigned Story but
his miſerable lot.

Nebuchadnezzar, a Father and Grandfather both ſignifying, or a Godfather.

11\. Expelled was for words eſcap'd,
memory can ſpeak well,
Hardened in pride, unheard of ſuch,
the wilde Aſs with did dwell :
Sent to the Ox it owner knows,
undreamt of this his doom :
Fowls their appointed time obſerve,
wots not the Night from Noon.

As multitudes grazing at S. James of late.

Who

Whose Heart made equal with the Beast, 12.
driven out with those that Bray;
The Diadem as well fits thee,
Ass, go as much to say.
Until return'd came to himself,
knew him that rules on high,
Over the sons of men appoints
what Office they supply.

During which space, this Assyrian, 13.
what watch kept night and day,
Thus metamorphos'd, over him,
lest makes himself away.
Fields, woods as well ring out, as men
for woe; and Ecchoes call
Mercy this savage King upon,
in holy Temples all.

Bewaild dejected soul, thus faln, 14.
fed now grazing full low,
Whilst they bedew the ground with tears,
discerns not friend from foe.
Earth that of late made seem to dawn
with songs of Triumph high,
Fleeth each wight abas'd as much
among the Herd doth lye.

B By

15. By Star-light for device who gave,
as graven on his Shield,
An Eagle mounted on the Creſt,
a Hart in ſilver field.
Extold again his God as high,
bleſſed him all his days:
Others reputes them as nothing,
alone proclaims his praiſe.

The King of Scots Hart given by *Douglas*, &c.

16. Whoſe ſeven times till ſerved forth,
in vain for reſt to crave;
Whom Devils Legions do poſſeſs,
a Monarch turn'd a Slave.
Depoſed thus, thou kneweſt well,
Belſhazzar, O his Son,
And renown'd ſo deliverance his
voyced by every one.

King & queen of Scots both put to death of late.

17. A day a Trumpet made to ſound
for Generations all;
And with a Feaſt ſolemnized,
that no time might recal:
The memory of ſuch an act,
yet as it had not been,
Thy Favorites who are more this day,
or matched to thy Kin.

1605. November the fifth.

Then

Then they adoring Wood and Stone, 18.
Statutes forſake Divine ;
Meditate carved Statutes on
in Faction do combine
With Enemies of God moſt high,
to thruſt him from his Throne,
And thus haſt lifted up thy ſelf
ſo facile and ſo prone.

How matched with *Arundel* and *Weſton*, &c. his Allies.

Againſt the Lord of Heaven thy King, 19.
not humbling of thy heart,
But ſtiffned haſt with pride thy neck
unto thy future ſmart.
Behold polluting holy things
with Sabbath ſo Divine,
Idolatry and Revels in
that day and night made thine.

Altars again adored.

But he in whoſe hand reſts thy life, 20.
even breathe thy ways all,
Thou haſt not glorified him
ſent this wrote on the wall.
God numbered thy Kingdom hath
ended ; the Hand points here,
In Ballance his weighed thee too,
the ſet hour drawing neer.

21. How light ſoever by thee ſet,
thou as thy weightleſs Gold,
His Image wanting found much more
lighter then can be told.
Parted, divided thine Eſtate,
given to the *Medes* is ;
At Hand, the Hand bids it adieu,
finiſh'd thy Majeſties.

Crowned and married 1625. was defeated 1645. (Trinity feaſt) the Lyons chaſed. Serves alſo for the Eagle put to flight. The Swedes invading the Empire about 1625. and laſtly the Turk.

F I N I S. 1633.

---

1 6 4 8. September.

So filled to the brim the Cup
thy Nephew taſted firſt,
Miſerably that was in France
impriſoned by Lewis the Juſt.
Before it came about to thee
forty five in, to him
When filled up the meaſure had,
twenty five did begin.

O Mene Tekel Upharſin,
{ Anagr. }
Parlement Houſe Kin:
in number about 666.

As eyes a flame of fire reveals
like meaſure for thy pains,
In whoſe right hand the Pen or Shaft
miſſing not Heart and Reins.
From Mene Mene, *doubled twice*
eſtabliſhed even
Parliaments Writs ſtoln too on thee ;
and ſo take leave, Amen,

{Reveale O Daniel.} Anagr. {Eleanor Audeley.}

F I N I S.

35. *Her Appeal From The Court To The Camp* (1649; Wing D1970A) is reprinted, by permission of the Folger Shakespeare Library, from the unique copy held at the Folger (shelfmark D1970.5 bd. w. D2010). The text block of the original measures 150 × 92 mm.

Hard-to-read words:

2.6	*time*
2.14	*name*
4.8	*with*
6.3	*Crowned*
6.5	*nough*
6.9	ONE?
6.12	*knowing*
6.18	*when*
7.2	be?
7.21	*taking* 1000.
8.21	FINIS

HER APPEAL FROM THE COURT TO THE CAMP.

Dan. 12.

Many shall be purified, and made white, and tryed: But the wicked shall do wickedly, and none of the wicked shall understand: But the wise shall understand.

Printed in the yeer 1649.

The Word of the Most High:

To the Lord General, Lord FAIRFAX, From the Lady *Eleanor.*

T*He generality or ſcope of this command touching* Propheſie, *though ceaſed a time, the Church bidden expreſly,* Deſpiſe it not, *but* to try the Spirits, *needleſs to be inſiſted on. Let it ſeem not therefore ſtrange or hard what is here deſired, ſince nothing too hard for him whom ye ſerve,* The Lord of Hoſts, *that you the Commander of the field, prayed* to ſend forth Harveſt-laborers, *to be pleaſed to appoint ſome faithful by name, the truth of theſe things for to examine, no true peace without it, concerning what ſhe hath been a ſufferer ſo many years for;*

no

no less then the burthen of his word to Great Britain (*Anno Dom.*) 1625. *bearing date first of the present Reign, Three and twenty years since; shewing what year in as it were the general Judgment, speaking as through a Trumpet from Heaven: So that the Prophets testimony, the Scriptures which accords therewith, may no longer wait for their resurrection; that have by Antichristian authority been crucified and buried hitherto, like* that golden wedge or tongue, *hidden by him* Achan, *author of so much trouble: Even the Prophet* Daniel, that greatly beloved man; *and John,* whom he loved, that bosom Disciple; *both testifying of great* Britains *visitation at such a time, as from his own mouth also* (Mat.24.) *after such fearful denounced Judgements, the like never afore or again, bidden therefore,* watch, *&c. shews of that blessed* Manna na *their* meat in due ſeaſon, *when to be given them, doubtleſs ſomething to be revealed, a forewarning plain enough.*

As from the Kingdom of Heaven being likened unto thoſe virgins, five wiſe, and five fooliſh, *ſhall ſhew you a mystery, how points to the aforeſaid acceptable year* 1625. *begins with the bleſſed Virgins feaſt (Five and twentieth of the moneth) witneſs when made at midnight* that cry before the Bridegroom; *which as betokens the word of God in ſuch a year ſo to ſuch a Reign directed, that began then; and his marrying with ſuch a one, with the late hour of wedding nights, &c.* (Mat.25.) where the five Talents account given *up, a touch gives of the ſame year too; and for her wiſdom anointed with* her lamp-oyl ſpent *ſo much:* Mary *likewiſe by name much like that, had a name,* She lives, but was dead(*Rev.*3.) brought

brought with her a curse in stead of a blessing, Pestilence, *never such, and Sword* Great Britains *portion; as blessings great set light by, unaccompanied with no smal corrections, where again upon his Prophetical Reply to our Saviour* Christ (*Luke* 14.) Blessed is he that shall eat bread in the kingdom of heaven (*as much to say*) lives to see him reign, his foes put under his feet for ever: *also* Sion, whoso toucheth her, toucheth the apple of his eye, *puts forth this Parable,* A certain man made a great supper, and bade many; and at supper time sent forth his servant, *that intrusted servant, saying,* All things are ready (*to wit*) *the Prophets wait, their visions are awake; when the unworthy wretches with one consent and voyce, all began to make excuse, one this, &c. another* that had married a wife, could not

not come without her leave; *as by* the five yoke of Oxen, *paints too unto his being Crowned and married such a year, in whose room* the maimed bidden, &c. *enough of whose company may be had* (Luke 14.) *in plain English, The careless* Stuart *by name,* justly turned out of Stewardship, what Trust to be repos'd in such a ONE: unto this day not weighing the many Caveats entered, and sacred Statutes, Matt. 24. *Noahs days, knowing not his own house, when hee sees it either:* as, had the goodman of the house known at what hour &c. would not suffred his house to be broken up, *his banqueting house especially,* &c.

And again, like as in days of old what doings, vvhen the Son of man is revealed, thus and thus it shall be; marrying, *&c. bidden* Remember Lots wife *her looking back:* and vvhere Lord being

askt,

askt, ſhall be revealed that ſecret, and theſe things be: whereſoever the body is, thither the Eagles reſort. *The body of an army, thoſe ſpacious quarters*; Therefore what I ſay unto you, I ſay unto all watch, have your lights burning, loyns girt, like men expecting, &c *of which Oracles not ſo obſtruſe hitherto as obvious now. His farewel the prophet* Daniels *on the houſe top proclaims it, bidden* Go thy way &c. (Dan.12.) *ſhewing*, And from the time the *Daily* ſhal be taken away; and the abomination that maketh deſolate ſet up; *Altars adored*; *giving to underſtand*, As any have eyes may ſee; *Pauls no little one*, *thus computes the time*, There ſhall bee a thouſand two hundred & ninety days: Bleſſed is he that waits, and comes to a thouſand three hundred five and thirty: *whereby taking* 1000. *reſts* (*the year of grace*) 1625..

1625. *calling unto this Jubile year* 1649. *even* Behold I ſtand at the door and knock, if any man hear my voyce and open the door, I will come in and ſup with him, and he with me ſhall ſit, &c. *By your leave Sirs, which bars any more kneeling at the Table not onely, but from thoſe words*, The daily taken away, *ſhews the Lords Supper how that taken away, unto the foorenoon tranſlated : putting no difference between his and their own Suppers : well preſaging the evening of time how diſcerned : what looking for and haſtening, &c. vvould follovv it*, Pet. 3.

Reſting, My Lord,

The humble Servant of your Excellence,

Ianuary : 1648.

ELEANOR.

FINIS

16. *The Prophetess* [illegible] (Wing D1990) is reproduced, by permission of the Folger Shakespeare Library, from the [illegible] at the Folger [illegible]. The copy contains some handwritten notes and corrections [illegible] Lady Eleanor's hand. The [illegible] of the original measures 140 × 82 mm.

Wing also lists as D1981 another [illegible] that begins with the following letter to the imprisoned Charles I:

[illegible] Charls Prisoner, &c.

SIR,
[illegible]

So [illegible]

Jan 1648 [illegible] DOUGLAS

a For [illegible] and handwritten [illegible], see p. [illegible] following this text.

36. *The Blasphemous Charge Against Her* (1649; Wing D1980) is reprinted, by permission of the Folger Shakespeare Library, from the copy held at the Folger (shelfmark D1980 bd. w. D2010). This copy contains some handwritten notes and corrections that may be in Lady Eleanor's hand. The text block of the original measures 140 × 92 mm.

Wing identifies as D1981 another edition that begins with the following letter to the imprisoned Charles I:

> For King *Charls* Prisoner, *these.*
>
> SIR,
>
> *Upon a reference from you* (1633.) *to these your Commissioners, I being Sentenced by them, as upon Record appears, because took upon me to be a Prophetess; first was Fined, and then to make publique Submission at* Pauls *so many times; that* Jericho for ever cursed, *and farther a close prisoner to continue at your pleasure.*
>
> *So be it known you are hereby required to make a publique acknowledgement of such your capital Trespass and high Offence; and first to* Ask me foregiveness, *if so be you expect Mercy in this world or the other.*
>
> Jan. 1648. ELEANOR DOUGLAS.

For Hard-to-read words and handwritten annotations, see p. 207 following this text.

25

THE

Blasphemous Charge

Against HER.

Matth. 10.

And ye shall be brought before Governors and Kings for my sake, against them and the Gentiles.

Printed in the Year, 1649.

(*a*) *July* 28.1625. the voice from heaven these words saying, *There is nineteen years and an half to the Judgement day, be you as the meek Virgin.*

(*b*) And 1644. he on a Fryday morning (his day of judgement) *Janu.* 10. Beheaded or killed, who burnt that testimony with his own hand, in the presence of so many.

(*c*) *Rev.*17. accomplished on both, the King aged 48. Beheaded *Anno.* 1648. current, *January* also; the other seven years compleat, and eight current Archbishop before his going into prison, translated 1633. *Sep.* 19. to his Metropolitanship, including the very seventh and eight moneth. And *H.*7. and *H:*8 their Character.

So again the aforesaid 19 of *Septem.* whose Coach and Horse with the Ferry-Boat, going (as it were) into the Abyss, sunk down, ascended again.

To

To the Kings Most Excellent Majesty:

The humble Petition of the Lady Eleanor, 1633.

Shews to your Majesty,

THat *the Word of God spoken* (a) *in the first year of your happy reign to the Petitioner, upon Friday last early in the morning did suffer: The B. Beast ascended out of the Bottomless Pit, the Bishop* (b) *of* Lambeth, *horned like the Lamb, hearted like a Wolf, having seven Heads*; viz. *making War seven years, hath overcome and killed them: Certain Books condemned to be burnt, their Bodies shrowded in loose sheets of Paper (by the Prophets being authorized:) This is the third day; if your Highness please to speak the word, the spirit of life will enter into them, and stand on their feet, &c.*

So craving no other pardon, praying, &c.

A 2 *Shall*

(c) *Shall go on the Word of God to the King* (Rev.17. cap.) The Beaſt that was, and is not, even he is Eight, and is of the Seven, and goes into perdition.

At the Court of Whitehal, Octob. 8. 1633.

HIs Majeſty doth expreſly command the Lord Archbiſhop of *Canterburies* Grace, and His Highneſs Commiſsioners for Cauſes Eccleſiaſtical, That the Petitioner be forthwith called before them, to anſwer for preſuming to Imprint the ſaid Books, and for preferring this deteſtable Petition.

Sidney Mountague.

Concordat cum, &c. Tho: Maydwel.

Re-

Registro Curiæ Dominorum Regiorum Commissionariorum ad Causas Ecclesiasticas. *Extract.*

Tertia Sessio Termini Michaelis 1633.

Die Jovis vicesimo quarto viz. die mensis Octobris Anno Dom. millesimo sexcentesimo tricesimotertio Coram Reverendissimo in Christo Patre & Domino, Domino Gulielmo *providenc' Divina* Cantuar. *Archiepiscopo totius* Angliæ *Primate & Metropolitano,* Richardo *eàdem providenc'* Angliæ *Primate & Metropolitano Archiepiscopo Eboracensi, Honorandis & prænobilibus Comitibus* Portland, Dorset, & Carlisle, *Episcopis* Elien', & Roffen' & Oxon', *Dominis* Iohanne Lamb, & Nathanaele Brent, *militibus legum Doctoribus,* Matthæo VVren *de Windsor,*

for Montford, *&*
VVorral *Sacræ Theologiæ professoribus Commissionariis Regiis ad Causas Ecclesiasticas apud* Lambeth, *Judiciarum seden' presente* Thomâ Mottershed *Regnerarii Regii, Deputato.*

Con' Elleanoram Audeley.

Dr. *Worral*: She appeared, and the Articles and Answers were publiquely read; She was Fined in Three thousand pounds, Imprisonment till she enter Bond with sufficient Security to write no more.

Mr. Dr. *Wren*, Dean of *Windsor*, he consenteth to that which is already said.

Dr. *Montford, Similitèr* with Dr. *Worral*.

Sir *Nathanael Brent*, *Similitèr* with

with Dr. *Worral*; and payment of Coſts.

Sir *John Lamb*, and my Lord of *Oxford*, Agreeth with the higheſt, with the higheſt; and to acknowledge her Offence at *Pauls* Croſs.

My Lord of *Rocheſter*, with the higheſt; and if the Court will bear it, he would ſend her to Bedlam.

My Lord of *Ely*, Three thouſand pounds, Excommunication, condemned in Coſts, and committed *ut prius*, till ſhe give, &c.

My Lord *Portland*, and my Lord of *Carliſle*, deſired to be ſpared from their Sentence.

My Lord of *Dorſet* agreeth with the higheſt.

My Lords Grace of *York*, Impriſonment, and not to have pen, ink and

and paper, and so with the highest.

My Lord of *Canterbury*, Three thousand pounds, close Imprison-ment, and to continue till His Maje-sties pleasure be further known.

She was Committed to the *Gatehouse*.

Officium Dominorum con' Elleanoram Tichet, *alias* Davyes, *alias* Douglas.

THe Councel for the offence insist-eth on her Answers, she to appear this day and place by Bond, to hear and receive the final Order and Iudg-ment of the Court.

At which day and place the said Lady *Eleanor Douglas* being called for, appeared personally; In whose presence the Articles objected against her, and her Answers made thereun-

to

to were publiquely read, with certain printed Schedules & Exhibites thereunto annexed, which ſhe acknowledged to be of her own penning and publiſhing in print; and the ſaid Anſwers to be her true Anſwers, and to be Subſcribed with her own hand: By all which it evidently appeared to the Court, by her own Confeſsion, That ſhe had lately compiled and written, and cauſed to be printed and publiſhed, the three ſeverall Schedules annexed to the ſaid Articles, ſome containing Expoſitions of divers parts of the Chapters of the Prophet *Daniel*, ſome other ſcandalous matter, by way of Anagram or otherwiſe, againſt Eccleſiaſtical perſons and Iudges of eminent place, and ſome others, both derogatory to His Majeſty and the

Last of the Caldeans! Belchazer Charles = Head

B State.

State. And firſt as touching thoſe mat. ters of high nature, which concerned his Majeſty, the Court did not any ways proceed againſt her, as holding them of too high a nature for this *Court* to meddle withal. But foraſmuch as ſhe took upon her (which much unbeſee- med her Sex) not only to interpret the Scriptures, and withal the moſt intri- cate and hard places of the Prophet *Daniel*, but alſo to be a Propheteſs, falſly pretending to have receiv'd cer- tain Revelations from God, and had compiled certain Books of ſuch her fictions and falſe Propheſies or Reve- lations, which ſhe had in perſon car- ried with her beyond the ſeas, and had there procured them to be print- ed without Licenſe, and after brought them over here into *England*, and here

without

without License, vented and dispersed them, or some of them, contrary to the Decree of Star-Chamber, made in the xxviii. year of Queen *Eliz.* of famous Memory, for the restraining of unlawful printing & publishing of books, & to the manifest contempt & breach thereof, and to the great scandal of our Church and State, and the reproach of the true Christian Religion here professed, and established within this Realm. And forasmuch as by vertue of the Statute of *Primo Eliz.* & by vertue of Letters Patents under the Great Seal of *England*, this Court hath full power and authority to punish as well all transgressors and offendors against the said Decree of Star-Chamber, touching the printing and publishing of unlicensed Books,

B 2 as

as ſuch bold attempts as thoſe of hers, in taking upon her to interpret and expound the holy Scriptures, yea, and the moſt intricate and hard places therein, ſuch as the graveſt and moſt learned Divines would not ſlightly or eaſily undertake, without much ſtudy and deliberation. For theſe her ſaid bold attempts and impoſtures, tending to the diſhonor of God, and ſcandal of Religion, whereof ſhe was found and adjudged guilty by the Court, ſhe was thought well worthy to be ſeverely puniſhed; and was firſt Fined in the ſum of 3000 l. to his Majeſties uſe, ordered to make a publique Submiſsion *in conceptis verbis*, at ſo many times, and in ſuch places as this Court ſhall appoint, and as ſhall be delivered her under the Regiſters

Hand

Hand of this Court; And ſhe was further committed cloſe Priſoner to the Gatehouſe, and ordered there to remain during his Majeſties pleaſure, who had taken ſpecial notice of her and her Cauſe, and referred the Examination and Cenſuring thereof into this Court. And laſtly ſhe was condemned in Expences and Coſts of Suit, which are to be paid before her enlargement: And the Keeper of the ſaid priſon was required and commanded not to ſuffer her to have any pen, ink or paper to write any thing, in reſpect that ſhe hath ſo much abuſed her liberty in that kinde already.

Concordat premiſſa cum originalibus in verià prediĉtà factà collacione fideli per me.

Jo: Donaldſon, *Notarium Publicum.*

SIrs, of our being entered into the day of Judgement, those Sessions, *Though the very day and moment knows none, except the Father himself*; neverthelefs, of the year thus (*Isa*. 63.) *Thus will I tread down mine enemies, for the day of vengeance is assigned, &c. And the year when my people shall be delivered*. Verily, ~~of great blessings rejected, the reward~~ of which deliverance time sworn with a high hand *Dan. c*. the last, as the Prophet shews first, what an unparaleld troublesom time, never since a Nation such (*ver*.) *And at that time the people shall be delivered*, so with these Mystical days, concludes his visions hiden, until then to rest; informs on this wise of the Golden number, *There shall be a thousand two hundred and ninety daies: Blessed is he that comes to a thousand three hundred*

hundred thirty five: Even the fifth crowned with the blessing, where one thousand taken way, rests the year of grace, 1625. and in haste taking leave of the Prophet *Daniel, The greatly beloved man*, the men of this age become so distastful unto, shal pass on with the restraind winds (*Apo. cap.* 7.) shewing untill such a time expired, the revealed threatned blow, not till then giving to understand, *And I saw four angels standing at the four corners of the Earth* (*Angulos terræ, Englands clap*) *holding the four winds that they should not blow on the Earth, nor Sea, nor any TREE*, &c. Or Scaffold (ver.) *And there were sealed a hundred forty four*, numbered twelve times twelve, doubled like *Pharaohs* dream, and as pointing to the equal hours between day and night; so to his Reign when began, perhaps sooner then 1644. a prisoner

com-

compleat, that four years after in 1648. [illegible] ghostly father the Arch B.B. in those dregs, he receiving his Tyths (*Jan.* 10. *Anno* 1644.) the old serpent willed or forewarned of the Tree or Block to beware, from those pernicious winds, forbidden to blow on any Tree to blow (the Sign in the Head) *till sealed in the forehead*, the so myste. rious servants of God, said to *serve him day and night*, &c. (to wit) the year of God, &c. proclaiming (*Psal.*) *Forty years long grieved, &c.*

And so much for the Word of the Lord *spoken to her*, 1625. *like the flying Rowl, Zach. twenty cubits in length, from the first of his Reign, the last of Great Brittains Kings, sealed or confirmed with that great Number* (*Rev.* 7.) *a hundred forty and four thousand, also pointing to the fourth thousand years of the worlds Creation, when the Redeemer of the world came, the* Lamb *of God, for ungrateful* M A N, *his life for to lay down.*

FINIS.

[36. *The Blasphemous Charge Against Her*]

Hard-to-read words and handwritten annotations:

5.5	3 [transcription]
5.5–12	on which daye of moneth October 23 was ye fresh massacre. EKenton fighte. [transcription]
5.10	*to'ius*
7.6	poore pauls [transcription]
7.9	And Bedlam ha[d] Little for y^e Halfe of the[] Now were it as big as pauls. [transcription]
8.7	Elleanorum
9.16	[underline; transcription]
9.17	[underline; transcription]
9.17	Last of these Caldeans: Belchaser Charles Be=Headed [transcription]
12.15	fined His Kingdome [transcription]
14.1–21	Sirs, of our being entered into the day of Iudgement, those Sessions, *Though the very day and moment knows none, except the Father himself*; nevertheless, of the year thus (*Isa.* 63) *Thus will I tread down mine enemies, for the day of vengeance is assigned, &c. And the year when my people shall be delivered.* Verily, of great blessings rejected, the reward of which deliverance time sworn with a high hand *Dan.c.* the last, as the Prophet shews first, what an unparaleld troublesom time, never since a Nation such (*ver.*) *And at that time the people shall be delivered*, so with these Mystical days, concludes his visions biden until then to rest; informs on this wise of the Golden number, *There*
15.1–21	Even the fifth crownd with the blessing where one thousand taken way, rests the year of grace, 1625. and in haste taking leave of the Prophet *Daniel*, *The greatly beloved man*, the men of this age become so distastful unto shal pass on with the restraind winds (*Apo.cap.*7.) shewing until such a time expired, the revealed threatned blow, not till then giving to understand, *And I saw four angels standing at the four corners of the Earth* (*Angulos terrae*, *Englands* clap) *holding the four winds that they should not blow on the Earth, nor Sea, nor any TREE, &c.* (ver.) *And there were sealed a hundred forty four*, numbered twelve times twelve, doubled like *Pharaohs* dream, and as pointing to the equal hours between day and night; so to his Reign when began paid his arrears then 1644
15.15	or scaffold [transcription]
15.21	a prisoner [transcription]
16.1–13	compleat, that four years after in 1648. pledged his ghostly father the Arch B. B. in those dregs, he receiving his Tythe (*Jan.* 10. *Anno.* 1644.) the old serpent willed or forewarned of the Tree or Block to beware; from those pernicious winds, forbidden to on any Tree to blow (the *Sign* in the Head) *till sealed in the foreheads* these mysterious servants of God, said to *serve him day and night*, &c. (to wit) the year of God, &c. proclaiming (*Psal.*) *Forty years long grieved, &c.*

37. *The Crying Charge* (1649; Wing D1982A) is reprinted, by permission of the Folger Shakespeare Library, from the clear copy held at the Folger (shelfmark D1982.5 bd. w. D2010). This copy contains some handwritten notes that may be in Lady Eleanor's hand. The text block of the original measures 140 × 92 mm.

Hard-to-read words and handwritten annotations:

5.13–17	And so preficent Bradshaw *&c.* [transcription]
6.11	thus [transcription]
6.11	*mans*
6.13	in [transcription]
7.2	[handwritten cross out; transcription]
7.2	the world could
7.17	*everlasting*
8.3	*down*
8.13	Rome

27

THE
Crying Charge.

Ezekiel 22.

Now thou Son of man, wilt thou judge, Wilt thou judge the bloody City? yea, thou ſhalt ſhevv her all her Abominations, &c.

Printed in the yeer 1649.

To the High Court of Iustice, appointed for the Tryal of *CHARLES STUART* King of ENGLAND.

By the Lady *Eleanor Douglas*.

SHEWS,

THe *Kings consent therewith, how* Mervin *E. of* Castlehaven, *Lord* Audeley, *unmercifully was sentenced to death* Easter *term* 1631. *and in* May *cruelly executed on Tower-Hill, accused falsly of two Crimes, what lewdnes could and malice produce; one,* Of his being accessary to a Rape committed on *Ann* his wife, done by a Page, one *Broadway; and,* Of Sodomy (*made death* H: 8.) committed with an Irish Footman, *Fitzpatrick O Donel; which aforesaid Lord* Audeley *indicted of Felony,*

lony, brought to his tryal at weſtminſter, *the K. Attorney where ſhew'd,* The King like God, would extend to the priſoner all mercy: *Likewiſe the Lo: Keeper that day Lo: High Steward,* becauſe the cry was great of Sodom, *would ſee whether thoſe things were ſo; the Witneſſes whereupon call'd to appear, ſhe a common Whore her husbands accuſer, without ever appearing in Court, or taking any Oath, had there contrary to the Law, one of her conſorts that ſaid,* My Lady upon her Honor ſaith thus, &c. *or,* It was true.

The other Witneſs, the Iriſhman, *he a vagrant, had ſerved under the Emperor, although a Papiſt, had contrary to Law, his Oath taken at the Bar, refuſing the* Oath of Allegiance; *where askt by one of the Judges the maner, confeſt,* Not the act, but ſomewhat of a foul

A 2 na-

nature, &c. *what ſuch malice & the like might invent, promiſed to be the Queens Footman. The Attorney, one not to ſeek of his Errand, ſaying*, Howſoever, it was an act of Uncleanneſs; prayed the Court to proceed upon it: My Lords, *ſaid he*, you have heard this odious Crime, how dark and myſterious 'tis grown; you muſt be curious therefore how you admit of any mitigation: *who accordingly his counſel took*, &c.

Upon which pronounced, Lord have mercy upon thee the priſoner, *to loſe his life forthwith, of ſuch promiſed mercy enjoyed the firſt-fruits.*

All which undue ſiniſter proceedings by way of humble Petition ſignified to the K. when perceived to what a low ebb the cry was faln and his Chaplains, Deans and others appointed to attend the priſoner,

ner, partly by their relation, he thrice in their presence had taken the Sacrament upon it, He was not guilty of those criminals; *was pleased by them to let the prisoner know his gracious Answer,* He should dye like a Peer of the Realm, be Beheaded, and not Hanged like a common person: whose Servants, his Page the principal, who ought to have suffered, before the accessary; he and his fellow-servant the Footman were brought to their tryal the next Term.

In behalf of whom the aforesaid Broadway, *came up divers Gentlemen of the County to inform the King, able to testifie of the Youths coming home to his Fathers house, more then six moneths afore the time put down by her of the Ravishment, this* Broadway *come away from his Lords service.*

And so president Bradshaw

Who

Who at last cast; when upon the Ladder so far protested both his Masters innocency that way and his own; taking God to witness, A virgin he came into his ſervice, and a virgin went forth of it.

O Donel *praying to St.* Dennis,*cryed out upon some of the Privy Councel that told him,* He muſt ſpeak for the King, *and thought not to be served so.*

And this mans house utterly ruined, chiefly, because had declined Popery, before his untimely death ever suspected; endeavoring to reform his Family, by which means cast himself upon the merciless times. Mervin *Earl of* Caſtlehaven, *that faithful Martyr, suffering (as it were) between those twain,* one on the right hand, the other on the left, *the honor having to be the first* entred into the

the joy of his Lord; *of whom notwith-ſtanding the worſt any in* [redacted] *world could ſay, was,* He had the beſt things in him of any, and the worſt: *Upon the Scaffold making this his Confeſsion;*

In the Name of God Amen.

I Mervin *Earl of* Caſtlehaven, *being in my full ſtrength and memory, thanks be given unto my Maker, having been branded and openly accuſed for change, alteration and doubtfulneſs of my Faith and Religion; I thought fit, like a Chriſtian man to give ſatisfaction upon what ground I ſtand for my belief, and to expreſs it under my hand, for the ſatisfaction of all charitable people and Chriſtians.*

Firſt, I do believe in the bleſſed and glorious Trinity, three perſons, one eternal and everlaſting God, God the Father, God my Redeemer, and God my Sanctifier.

I do relye upon the merit, death and paſsion of our bleſſed Savior Chriſt Ieſus, and upon his mediation for the remiſsion of my ſins.

I *do*

I do believe and use with most humble reverence our Lords Prayer, the Creed of the Apostles, and the ten Commandments, as they are set down and allowed in the Church of England.

I do believe the Canonical Scriptures, and that they are written by the inspiration of the holy Spirit.

And for the rest of my belief, I do refer it to the true Orthodox Faith of our Church of England. *And from the Articles received at this present in the Church of* England, *and confirmed by authority of Parliament, I do not differ in any point, renouncing all the Superstitions and Errors taught or believed in the Church of* Rome *or any other Church; in which Faith I will, God willing, continue to my lives end: In testimony whereof, I have hereunto subscribed my Hand this first of* May, 1631.

CASTLEHAVEN.

Psal.116. Right dear in the sight of the Lord is the death of his Saints.

FINIS.

38. *The New Jerusalem At Hand* (1649; Wing 1997) is reprinted, by permission of Harvard University's Houghton Library, from the reproducible copy held at the Houghton (shelfmark *EC65.D7455.B652t). The text block of the original measures 140 × 92 mm. Page 4 is misnumbered 3, and page 25 is misnumbered 26.

2.8

THE
New Jerusalem
At Hand:

By the Lady *Eleanor Douglas*,

Daughter of Lo: *Audeley*, Lo: *Touchet* E. of *Castlehaven*.

JE LE TIEN.

MAT. 28.

Behold, I am with you all days, until the consummation of the age.

Printed in the Year 1649.

The Prophetess of the most High, to all Nations and People, &c.

SHewing in stead of a *Charls* the second, gives ye the character of a second *Saul*, even *He and his for ever cut off*, unto that giving place, that everlasting, even proclaimed, *The first and the last* (to wit) Prophets the *beginning and the ending*, *Jure Divino*, afore Kings of the Earth: Certain inferences by, borrowed from dayes of old (*Sam. cap.*10.) whose Reign confirmed by that ominous token, witness of *Rachels* Sepulchre (as much to say) such another he *mourning and weeping also for his children, because they were not*, or not him to succeed, read in let-

A 2 ters

ters of her Náme, *Rachels*, otherwise rendred *Charls*; and thus running over the sum of it.

To whom on this wise shewed *cap*. he when little in his own eyes, above the rest how chosen to be a King so great, from *tending on Asses*, *Scotlands* former low Estate pointing thereto: & so farther of *Kings given in his wrath, in anger taken away*: briefly thus, but referred to the first of his Reign, *Anno* 1625. that heavy hand upon the City, an unparalleld Pestilence, concluded with our three Kingdoms Division; so that if ever all at their wits-end, now accompanying his departure, 23 of his bloody Reign; in making him King of *Great Britain*, evident the Lord repenting himself much more, well served for their Repining, whom *Nothing*

thing but a King would ſerve, who bleſt were above all Kingdoms; ſo in a virgin *Queens* renowned Reign: And for them ſo much, *Firſt and laſt of their Name,* both taſting of one ſharp cup, their Heads cut off, and faſtned their bodies in that maner to the wall, or nailed, &c. as to the Story referred (*Sam. &c.*) which had each three Sons: where this for another caſt upon her, *Thou ſon of the perverſe rebellious woman*; whether in right appertains not to our Scotiſh *Jonathan*, by his Mothers means ſtript of his Royal means and Eſtate.

Paſsing over what between him paſſed and his ghoſtly Father or Confeſſor, ſuppoſed to have been *Samuels* very Spirit, who fell all along both of them upon the earth ſore afraid, how

ever

feigned or carried out, to make good the innocent blood ſpilt of ſuch multitudes of his people, who without queſtion as participated of *Sauls* fits, *The evil Spirit from the Lord* (to wit) the evil Counſel infuſed by the Clergy; ſo wanting neither in his Fathers Faith or Religion, ſpake truer then he wiſt, whoſe wanton Minion bewitcht with, neither repented hereof;, One *charged with the life of his Father*, nor of his unmeaſureable Swearing, which amongſt them ſware *By their ſaul*, ſo long till verily conjured up his Spirit, that not a little boaſted of his King-craft, witneſs Familiar Spirits, witches of late, transferr'd from *Scotland* hither: And as for that *Agag*, the delicate *Buckingã* how his mother made childleſs,

leſs, ſhe author of his unhappineſs, ſhe inſnared by their *Spaniſh* junkets, cannot but adde this to the Reckoning of *Phinehas* ſpirit, how it hath acted on theſe twain, ſaying, *Righteous art thou, O Lord, that haſt judged thus*, *Anno* 1628. as when *Buckingham* his deadly wound had given him, by ſuch a one tranſported, &c. ſo even *Charls* late King, 1648. at length paid home that heavy Stroke or Blow of his, aged Eight and forty, like *The flying Rowl, in length twenty cubins*, &c. twenty years, which had given him to make his peace or repent him; and ſo much onely at this time commended to the Reader, with this contained in the Prophet *Daniels* confeſsion (neither have we hearkned, &c. (*Chapter* 9. *v.* 6.) doubtleſs pointing to the people

ple of this land alike with dumb & deaf ſpirits,&c.together with his lame confeſsion on the Scaffold,like blinde Devotions Leſſon, promiſed, *That he ſhould ſay but very ſhort Prayers,* who came not ſhort of it none at all ſaid that we hear of.

Nevertheleſs, unwilling to inſult over the worm or grave; as his hard lot, *To morrow be thou with me,* ſaid to *Saul,* ſo *This day be thou with me in paradice*; peradventure his pardon had folded up herein, which had not received in his life-time altogether *thoſe good times others had,* &c. might at the laſt gaſp or minute repent: And ſo much for *The Ax laid to the Root of the old Tree,* in a Reign of 23 years, which produced no better fruit. And for the title ſet forth of the Keys of *David* belonging to her, *Rev.*1.7. And

And as demonſtrates a ſecond *Saul*, ſo a ſecond *Adam*, he firſt of the Kings of the Earth, his immediate woful fall ſhadowing it forth.

VVitneſs ſhe ſubject (*Heb.*) called *Chavah* or *Eve*: By whom had three Sons, where thus for her ſake rewarded (*Gen.* 3.) *Even placed at the Eaſt a flaming Sword*, &c. turning every way, droven out as it ſeems VVeſtward, from his Garden to the open Field, in their Leather liveries to encounter travel, juſtly reaping the fruits of accurſed mother Earth, war and ſtrife, the Thiſtle and Thorn, its emblem in ſtead of the Olive and Grape: All our days as ſtubble but a blaze, vaniſhed like a ſhadow: The ſum or ſubſtance of which informing, formerly as he forbiden

B expreſly

expreſly the Tree of good and evil, notwithſtanding took thereof; ſo again, when as offered the Tree of life, *its Leavs for healing the evil of the Nations*, or Kings Evil; a like Treſpaſs or capital Crime guilty of, that rejects it, like Iudgements draws upon their heads: *And therefore ſuppoſe not that thoſe Galileans were ſinners above the reſt, becauſe of late ſuffered*, &c. *Nay, but except ye repent, ye all likewiſe ſhall periſh*.

And ſo from *Saul* and *Doeg*, deriving *Douglaſe*, here concluding as began, how his bloody Houſe cut off, alſo even *dyed for his tranſgreſsion againſt the word of the Lord, &c.* and alſo for asking counſel of one that had a familiar Spirit, & enquired not of the Lord (to wit, his Biſhops, &c. whoſe

army

army how ſwarmed with VVitches, never the like heard in any Raign viſited in that kind, wherwith ſhewing laſtly of the evil Spirit, when fell upon him, how the good Spirit (at the very ſame time) reſted on another: The ſolitary Turtle-Dove as it were ſhut up, one of his own name (owned by King *Iames*, before the other of *Stuart*) and of his Age and Nation: Sir *Archibald Douglaſe*, the ſuppoſed Son of King *Iames*, the Elder Brother about a moneth, &c. alſo wrote *Anno Etatis*, *&c.* as by a Legacy of a thouſand pound *per annum*, out of his Crown-Lands appointed for him; whereof though diſappointed or prevented by the ſaid K. unexpected death, yet of the better part could not be diſinherited,

B 2 then

then any three Crowns a greater blessing: The holy Spirits anointing apparent by his Letters hereto annext, that not only in those days were accounted to be distraction; but to this very day, even with Learned Doctor *Sybald*, fulfilling what honor Prophets receiue at home: By whose hand no few of these Manuscripts were burnt: This mans writing who wrote so long ago. From the *Hysope Nicity*, unto the Cedar Authority or Supremacy, conversing with no Books, but one the Book: Sir *Archibald Douglas* right Heir of the Earldoms, howsoever of *Morton* and *Douglas* the doughty; likewise of person a choyce yong man, and a goodly, &c. That Nations Captain by his Birth-right himself a Soldier

by

by profession, in *Spain* and *Germany* no ordinary Commander, upon whom the first fruits of the Spirit came.

Quæres or Questions

To Dr. *James Sybald*, Minister of *Clerkenwel.*

AND (whether) the very perillous time now, fulfilling what is written in *Pauls* second Epistle to *Timothy*, *Men shall be lovers of their own selves, more then of God*, &c. *from such turn away*: And what is written in (*Mark.* 13.) *Of the troublesome last days*: (*ver.* 10, 11.) Of which I will say no more, onely thus much: Had you demanded of me in how many

many days, the change which I ſpeak of ſhould be, or known of what conſequence it is, ye would not ſo ſuddenly have indangered me, as to have ſpoken a word of me to that purpoſe, or where I was; when ye ſee what will be, and what ye have heard of me; even very ſhortly you will be aſhamed, and heartily ſorrow for your precipitate Opinion of me.

Now conſidering that you are preparing to morrow in the Forenoon, on the uncertain Eaſter-day; Alſo to receive your part of the Paſſover, even kneeling at the Communion-Table; conſider theſe Texts, and prepare an anſwer to the ſame: *Deut.* 16. *There thou ſhalt ſacrifice the paſſover at the evening, at the going down of the Sun, That thou mayeſt remember it all*

the

the days of thy life: 1 Cor. 11. *When ye come together therefore into one place; this is not to eat the Lords-Supper, for in eating every one taketh afore his own Supper, &c.* Iohn 13. *and Supper being ended, &c.* Concerning which, tell me therefore in your Conſcience; is not the Lords-Supper in the Fore-noon a moſt Belly-god invention: Alſo the kneeling at the Communion Table doth not fulfil what is written in the firſt Epiſtle of *Paul* to the *Corinthians, ver* 20. 8, 21. *But I ſay, the things which the Gentiles ſacrifice, they ſacrifice to devils, not to God; and I would not that you ſhould have communion with devils, &c.* Alſo is not the Title of Doctors a moſt preſumptuous thing (*Mat.*) *Which love the uppermoſt rooms and chief ſeats, and*

to

to be called Rabbi, Rabbi, and Matth. 23 *Neither be ye called masters, &c.* As allo the names of Saints, (*Psal.*) *When who knows how often he offends; much less knows the secret sins of another*: Also according to your Conscience let me know your opinion of the Ministerial Priests: Traditions hath not made the word of God of none effect, or to have no power, *Mark 7. ver. 13. and many such like things do ye.*

Also let me know what is their reward that do crouch and make courtesies to boards; when as it is written, Keep thy foot, or have a care thereof when thou goest into the House of God; and be more ready to hear; then offer the sacrifice of fools (to wit) lest thou crouch and make a crooked

crooked courtesie to a board, which was but a stock, even a block: whatsoever it was, and whatsoever it is, and they worse then a block that make a cursed courtesie to it, a besotted beast and a devil (*Sam*.28.)going even to the very Devil of Hell, with him *who stooped with his face to the ground, bowing himself*; likewise they try what reverence they can do unto him.

And lastly, what is the reward of addition and diminishing the word of God, *Rev*.22.shewing, *For I testifie, If any man shall add, God shall adde the plagues written herein; and if any shall take away, God shall take away his part out of the holy city*. So taking in haste leave, think of me what ye please,

Rest your faithful Friend,

ARCH: DOVE. *Elijah*.

C

Likewiſe know, I deſire you not to ſpeak a word of this till the appointed time, onely have a care in the mean time of your own ſoul; *Acts* 2. *Save your ſelves from this untoward generation.*

From my Lodging at White-Fryers. *Anno* 1638. your Eaſter-Eve.

To my much eſteemed worthy Friend, *Iames Sybald*, Miniſter at *Clerkenwel*, this.

Loving Friend,

IT ſeemeth your imployment is very much, for if it were not ſo, or if ye had remembred my deſire, I ſhould have ſeen you according to your Promiſe in two days, after that time ye was with me laſt: Certainly, if ye knew how near the Great Change is, which I ſpoke of, ye would have ſeen me before this: Which unexpected Change,

Change, whatsoever it be, it being so exceeding near, I request you, whatsoever ye have to do, let me see you this afternoon: But a few words. And likewise through CHRIST *I charge you, not to speak a word of this, until you see what* GOD *will do shortly; whatsoever it be, unless a very Great Change be shortly, then think of me what ye will:*

Exitus acta probat.

Ye may believe me, for I think ye know it had been better for the Lord Major of this City, Anno Dom. 1638. *to have heard me from the* LORD, *then to have had the Plague of* GOD *amongst them, which came just then, how soon the seven Elected Eldermen did charge me, not to come near them, nor write any more unto them; which did so offend* GOD, *as his Plague hath continued*

C 2 amongst

amongst them until this day: Therefore do not vilifie my Request. So till I see you, Rest,

January 19. Your faithful Friend,
Anno Do. * *Rev.* 2.28.
M.DC.XXXVIII. THE
MORNING STARRE.

I pray you bring no servant with you, near the place where I am; for I am exceeding loth for to be known, to be near the city, until I be seen at Court; *which now God willing will be shortly: I am sure there is none knoweth I am so near you, no not one, except my servants: Therefore I request you let me not be discovered by you, nor by your words, concerning the contents of my Letter.*

Likewise do not think to lose much time with me, for one sentence shall be sufficient.

TO

To a Meſſenger of the LORDS, Dr. *James Sybald*, Miniſter at *Clerkenwel* at *London*, this.

Loving Friend,

MY ſelf, though your Well-wiſher, hath conſtantly been committed willingly within the Chamber and Study where ye left me about two Year ſince: It was not the Lords Will, know hitherto, that I ſhould write un.o you, ſince the 20 *of June*, Anno Ætatis, 1638. *Because the Great Change which he moved me to tell you, was to be ſuddenly, know, it was not to be acconnted according to the computation of man, but according his own (to wit) it was not plainly to begin, until ſome few days hence, according to our computation; his mercies being above all*

all his Works: He gives his very enemies a space of time, for to consider their own doings, that they might repent. Though now adays most of all the men of this world, cannot possibly be moved lawfully for to be obedient unto him, nor to be just: So saith ELIAS *and verily* ELIJAH, *who desireth you, if you love your self, or your own good, for to come unto him about two a clock this afternoon: otherwise, assuredly the* LORD *will not let me do you the good which I intend, who lets you understand, none of the unjust within this Kingdom before long will be able to stay therein: So think of this, and do which I lawfully desire for the best, till I see you.* Vale.
And so rest,

Decemb. 19. Your faithful Friend,
Anno Do. 1639. DOUGLASE.

From the JACOBIN *or* Carmeliſtain Fryers, *to wit of old, From the* Carme, Freere, Frater; *as* Fray *may be well applyed truly unto any one of all the many many ſorts of Fryers, whoſe* Fray *hath continued too long; and now, it muſt, it muſt be returned to them.*

And

And here happy Readers, with this Manna communicated (to wit) the Divine Prophesies of this Man; know herewith ordain'd and enacted as heretofore, a Rebel against the Father proclaimed, he that *Despised the Son*; likewise (unable to gainsay it) they a Reprobate Church, *sitting in the seat of Scorners*: which acknowledge not the fulfilling of these now, (*John* 16.) *All things which the Father hath are mine: Therefore I said, that he shall take of mine, and shall shew it unto you; and he shal shew you things to come*, as much to say, Even manifested the truth of those sacred Mysteries, contained in the *Revelation of Iesus Christ which God gave unto him*, &c. Cap.1. Things for the future treasured up, by no other Spirit to be unfolded, but by by the ſame Spirit of truth; wherewith were written at firſt, or penn'd; and for that purpoſe the ſame poured forth again in the laſt days: And ſo theſe by that Spirit then perſecuted, witneſs (*Rev.xi.*) *The Beaſt aſcended out of the bottomleſs Pit*, or Abyſs, one in old *Samuels* likeneſs, Biſhops, &c. Alſo which teſtifies, whoſoever deſpiſeth the Spirit of Prophecy, guilty of all the Blood of the Prophets ſhed: And therefore leſt your ſentence that, *Ye ſtiff necked, &c. ye do always reſiſt the holy Ghoſt: as your fathers did, ſo do ye* (Acts 7.) provoke him not, who is *a conſuming fire*, according to their works, Iew and Gentile both high-minded, who rewards them, as referred to the prophet *Malachi*, accompanied with what

D judge-

judgements (cap.4.) when that blessed time, arising with *healing in his Wings*, (ver.2.) the meek dove Messenger of peace, displaying her golden feathers, as the *lightning out of the East shineth even unto the West* (Mat. 24.) the Spirit of Prophesie vouchsafing a visit, absent from the Church so long comfortless, saying, *I have the Keys of Death and Hell*, a Scepter of seven Stars in whose right hand (*Re. cap*.1.) pointing to times Mystery, the present Century, and at this time so much for admonishing all: *He that hath an ear, let him hear, &c.* and fare him well that will not; a story by whom related of *Alexander the Great*, &c. on the Scaffold, as well might have told a tale of his Horse.

These from Whitehall, *sometime* Wolseys *the Cardinal*. Febr. 1648.

FINIS.

39. *A Prayer or Petition For Peace* (1649; Wing D2001) contains a reissue of her non-extant *A Prayer or Petition for Peace* (1644). It is reprinted, by permission of the Folger Shakespeare Library, from the copy held at the Folger (shelfmark D2001.2 bd. w. D2010). This copy contains some handwritten notes that may be in Lady Eleanor's hand. The text block of the original measures 140 × 92 mm.

Hard-to-read words and handwritten annotations:

title page.9	without whom yee can doe Nothing: [transcription]
2.6	n [transcription]
3.19	haste
5.12	a
5.15	est
5.17	smite
5.18	deep
7.5–7	and ascensions Joyful tidings to the Church [suggested by Esther Cope]
7.6	m [transcription]
8.6	winged Cherubims; en
8.20	He
10.9	s [transcription]
10.14	*hissiug* [sic: i.e., hissing]
11.5	*brethren Nations strugling*
11.9	of no
11.10	publique Thanksgiving, deserving
11.16	*have*
12.3–10	with whose incesstious Daughters the Kings of the Earth matched, for the Mothers sake disinherited, they and their heirs referred to the salique slavish Law, wresting that, *That the Lillies spin not*, &c. as the pillar displays of salt. With his Play-house for another [transcription]
12.16	*ecuted*
13.11	Whether [transcription]
13. 14	sed
13.15	rive
13.18–19	by means of a stick or rod, cast in
14.8	Though prophising all to the days. [transcription]
14.11	fiery
14.14	eaten [transcription]
14.19	till the evening of time this last age. [transcription]
14.19	of ages [transcription]
15.11	same voice, the swelling Seas sound
16.1	*Cassiopei* its
16.9–11	As August Past *&c.* [transcription]
16.11	like the backward Spring [transcription]

A

Prayer or Petition

FOR

PEACE.

November 22. 1644.

Behold, your house is left unto you desolate; And verily ye shall not see me, till ye say, Blessed is he that cometh in the *Name of the Lord.*

Printed in the Year, 1644.

A
PRAYER & PETITION FOR *PEACE.*

By the Lady *Eleanor.*

O Lord, the great and dreadful God, as we have ſinned deeply and offended, guilty of no leſs then open Rebellion, by excluding thee, fleeing from thy preſence with one voyce (as it were) *We will not have this man to reign over us* (or) *He defers his coming*, as others; Even departed from thy Precepts and Iudgements ſet before us: ſo here proſtrate before the foot-ſtool of thy Throne, implore nevertheleſs pardon and forgiveneſs.

For

For this no ſtoln or ſecret tranſgreſ-ſion committed, but with a high hand; and ſo much the rather preſuming on this acceſs, becauſe hitherto the vulgar (the burthen and heat of the day though theirs) thoſe ſheep yet not guilty or acceſſary to this treſpaſs or capital Crime, or of thy return oppoſed, as manifeſt in hearkning not to the loud voyces of the Propets accompliſhed thy Meſſengers: But to our Kings, Princes, Heads and Rulers, which appertains, ſo ſtraitly commanded, ſaying, *What I ſay unto you, I ſay unto all, Watch*; the *Gentiles* watch-word alſo charged in readineſs to be; and ſigns of the time they not them diſcerning, ſuch and ſuch expreſs evident Signs and Tokens, haſte, watch'd over them, as ſince this a Nation, or

A 2 under

under the whole Heaven. the like unknown, witneſs, The Iriſh Maſſacres VVinter flight, and Sabbath journey, thoſe bloody peſtilent Vials, ſo violently poured out (without doubt) not ſince the Flood as in this preſent Century.

Thus neither (awakened or) taking warning (by Forraign Nations) as Beacons lighted our neighbors houſes ſet on fire firſt, like *Jacob*'s ſetting in the front the handmaids and their children: whichalarms ſo lightly weighed, til ſuddenly at laſt, like *Sampſons* ſevenfold new Cords and green withs, all pluckt aſunder when linked ſo faſt and knit, *France* with *Great Britain*, *Spain* with *France*, *Germany* with *Spain*; together with theſe late married Iſles or united Kingdoms, now in widows

dows forlorn woful Eſtate, or worſe, as divorced; ſometime that as had it been a new world, with ſuch *Creations* flouriſhing, & Titles all new *Names*, even walking like days of old, alſo become as thoſe, when God repented he made *Man*, brought to a like Ebbe or fall, as thoſe inſaſciable Gyants, Great *Britains Babel* Towering thoughts confounded.

And now behold, O Lord, through a high and heavy hand abaſed and ſo low brought, humbled to aſhes and ſackcloth, from the higheſt to the loweſt; then tread not on a worm, break not the bruiſed reed, the wounded ſmite them not; but hear us out of the deep, O thou our Anchor, hope and preſent help, ready to be conſumed and ſwallowed up, if thou calm not

and

and aſſwage thoſe working tempeſtuous Seas, through unruly raging winds let looſe, wrought and contrived; And ſo with him praying in his poſture, *Elijah*, when as without *Rain* ſo long, forty two Moneths (that prophetical Number ..preſt ſo much, of Three years and a half) he bowing himſelf double, or kneeling on his head; alſo behold ſuch our Eſtate turned upſide down, ſince the year 1642. defer us not theſe miſerable Iſles and Kingdoms of ours, whoſe Store-houſes exhauſted, like thoſe Rivers dryed up, and like the dead Trees, burnt up our Nation and Habitation, torn between two She-bears, like thoſe Forty two ungratious Infants.

To conclude (O forſake us not! thou of uſpeakable Mercy) cauſe thy

face

face to shine upon us, for the Lords sake, our alone Savior Iesus Christ, made of the womans seed according to the flesh: A woman making her first witness of the resurrection [redacted] tidings to them. [redacted]: Let thy mighty voyce be heard, that speakest sometime to the Fish, the Fig-tree, the Deaf, the Dead, and very Devils subjects; And at whose motion the Sun and Moon moved not, stood still, heard him; and turnest the hard Rock into standing waters, &c. also the waters of this city, heal them; say the word and it is DONE, that henceforth let there be no more DEATH, no more Killing and Slaying, stay thy Hand She beseeches thee.

A Letter

A Prayer or Letter for the Peoples Conversion and Deliverance from their Distraction, *June* 1649.

AND O Lord of Sabbaths, our King, the God of Hosts sitting between the winged Cherubims, enclosing thy glorious Throne; That without delay vouchsafest to hear the humble address of thy Handmaid, and the waters according held of our Brittish *Jericho*, witness the very next moneth, *Decemb.* the 5th *Anno* 1644. a conjuring Letter from the other side, as would answer at the day of Iudgement the contrary, &c. to lay aside Arms, whereas about three moneths after, the Enemy waxt at thy consuming presence like melting wax, calling to Rocks and Hills, or fleeing to hide them were put to flight: He vanished vanifhed in that fafhion difguifed, amazing thofe that knew him, figned with the years of thy right arm, 1645. owing fince the horrible defign *Anno* 1605. *November* the 5th which faction (he the four and twentieth of thofe Alban Elders, proftrating his Crown fo low) combined with.

And the Sword of VVar fheath'd thus, as when *Elias* the *Prophet* his Supplication prefented; juft three years & fix months after their departing the City, he in that maner led in a ftring, from 1641. *January*, until 1645. *June*, that blow before his downfal. Notwithftanding, Iuftice her Sword dravvn fince Kings, Princes, Head-Rulers, going to wrack, great Trees felled down, as well as thofe of lower growth amended; like that reftlefs

B mans

mans Eſtate, *taking unto him ſeven ſpirits more unſufferable*, after the Houſe ſwept and adorned, the Epilogue or End worſe then the beginning, pointing to the Spiritual Function; eſpecially, *ſeeking high places, earthly preferment, whereat all aym.*

Then here croaching at thy bleſſed feet, for a bleſsing on the Iubiles inſuing year: O heavenly bounty, royal mercy, greater then *Solomons* exceeding fames report, ſuffices we have bin and are of thy Iuſtice, not wanting an open example, *a hiſſiug to all Nations*, guilty of no petty Treaſon, thine own Servants and Citizens, *Shuting thee out, conſpiring againſt thee*; outed by diſloyal Tenants: with thoſe Husbandman alſo ſaying, *the Inheritance ſhall be ours, to us and our heirs*; accompliſhed ſigns and tokens when, the whole

Creation groaning to be delivered, accompanied with the peoples voices or diſtempers reſtored to their old liberty: *Kingdom againſt Kingdom*, witneſs, *brethren Nations ſtrugling like* Eſau *and* Iacob, *one houſe ſtorming the other*, the Devil the old Serpent, for his part ſtorming too, his time becauſe knows of no longer continuance; a day of publique Thankſgiving, deſerving rather then ſitting up their own horn, or to be admired of the world.

How is it then that they do not underſtand, blaſpheme thy name ſo nigh: rave on the world; notwithſtanding, *What have we to do with thee, O Jeſus*, conjured before the time, *to torment them not*, both ſex diſcovering, *like the dog returnd to his excrement, and Sow to the mire*, how cleanſed from filth, or in grace growing up, how long the grace-

B 2 leſs

lefs world in thefe budding times, alfo befotted, look back with *Lots* wife, to a fink of fin and corruption, with whofe inceftuous Daughters the Kings of the Earth matched, for the Mothers fake difinherited, they and their heirs referred to their Salique[redacted] Law, averting that, *That the Lillies fpin not*, & as the pillar difplays[redacted].

VV[redacted]h his Play-houfe for another whether not recorded in *Ahabs* reign by our Scotifh Bethmite, alfo (as it were) execrable, *Iericbos* edifice Erected: *The foundation laid in his eldeft Son, and the gates in his yongeft fon, execu'ed at the gate*; that after demolifhed thofe cages, or Moneftaries of theirs, for an acknowledgment of the powder plots efcape, dedicated that Monfter everlafting like Theator, to the Devil for his Sabbath-fervice, and other fuch like. New

New *Jerusalems* precious foundations and gates, ought rather much to have looked after, or to have considered the Arks building, which century the seventeenth, we then were entred; the Ark as in length Three hundred cubits measured out by the days of the year, so in breadth fifty, answerable to the weeks thereof; the hight of it thirty cubits, according to the days of the moneth, &c. ~~ye~~ whether teach us to number ours, the sum of it.

That merciful Lord, except infused special grace: Since so it is, as derive their Name, from *BRUTE*, *So are they*, may as well speak to the Ass and Adar to hear, *What the Spirit saith unto the Churches*, or to cause ~~by means of a stick or rod, cast in~~ an Ax to swim, grown (thou seest) so brutish and blockish, well shadowed out in

his

ſeeing men like Trees walking : without which from above avails as much, as before the Scriptures ſpeaking in the vulgar language : *That bleſsing although not equivolent to the former ; how hear we every man in his own language, we born, &c.* yet a door, not remote therefrom. prophesying all to this days.

From whence emboldned do beg, give them leave like as when bitten by ~~fiery~~ Serpents, thoſe vipers ; by another beheld in the ſame likeneſs were healed ; ſo by theſe leaves taken from a womans hand, by them [redacted] (as it were) live may for ever : They by reaſon of their knowledge puft up hitherto, even of times and ſeaſons miſtery to take their fill, not in ſeaſon till the ~~evening of time this laſt~~ ages .

And ſince to have knowledge of the diſeaſe, though the firſt ſtep to recovery

very ſuffices not: The Medicine if not attained, give them the Spirit of diſcerning, ſince come to maturity the Tree of Life, a qualification for of our firſt parents expedition, the tree reſerved, that caſting an eye upon the Map of the world that then was, the Ark Baptiſms figure, whereby to meaſure or parallel the Goſpels pilgrimage and the Floods age together, lifting up the ſame voice, t[redacted] ing their alarm, climbing over Rocks and Mountains, beſides an univerſal flood a year or two ago, over the face of the earth, told then before, *There ſhal be ſigns in tht Heavens, in the Sun and Moon, and in the Stars*, the Sea roaring, people at their wits end diſtracted, &c. witneſs this ſign, A new Star, as ſeen in the Eaſt, the one 74 years before *Ieruſalems* deſtruction or judgment,

ment, ſo the other in *Caſsiopei* its aſpect or influence to the great Year 1644. extended *Rev.* 7,14,21. refer'd to it; VVhich Meſſenger Star likewiſe appeared ſeventyfour years before our being entred into the very day of judgment, with no ordinary apparitions in the Heavens, *The powers of Heaven and Earth ſhaken both.*

So look upon us amended Lord, [redacted], vvith thoſe ungrateful graceleſs Lepers (asked) *Where the nine,* &c. curſing hitherto, vvhere thou bleſſeſt, ſuch returns. O ſend down upon the time to come, (though have ſinned a great ſin) a bleſſed ſhower of commiſeration for which ſo much. And for this ſtollen touch, as vertue when gone from thee, 1649.

FINIS.

40. *Sions Lamentation* (1649; Wing D2012B) is reprinted, by permission of Harvard University's Houghton Library, from the clear copy held at the Houghton (shelfmark EC65.D7455.B652t). The text block of the original measures 205 × 155 mm. (N.B. This item has been reduced to fit the present text area.)

Hard-to-read words:

title page.2	LAMENTATION
3.9	every
4.18	incurring inseparable
4.19	such distraction so giddy
4.21	as witness
5.21	prophesie supposed
7.6	*Huntingdon*
7.7	ashes Hers. *Ashbeys*
7.8	he born *anno*. 1630.
7.18	mard
8.5	tofore inclining
8.6	prophesied
8.7	as *Josias*

SIONS

LAMENTATION,

Lord

HENRY HASTINGS,

HIS

Funerals bleſsing, by his Grandmo-
ther, the Lady *Eleanor*.

Chron. 34.

But Ioſiah *would not turn his face from him, &c. Harkened not unto the words of* Necho, *which were of the mouth of God.*

Printed in the year. 1649.

Zach. 12. *And they shall look upon him, whom they have pierced: And they shall mourn for him, as one mourneth for an onely, &c. and shall be in bitterness for him, as one is in bitterness for his first born.*

THese, as by way of comparison set forth: This prophesie appointed for a sign also requisite, since Faith in high things always slow.

Ionas *as alotted then for the resurrections sign, of which took essay*: Such a three days rest and nights three; And the suns retiring so many degrees that high favor to *Hezekiah*, Likewise of the leavings in the cup, happy *Hastings* this first born, an onely Son, partakes one of no inferior Family: Taking his leave of this life, whose first days rest taken, on the Lords day; *Saying my lovers and friends hast thou*

A put

put away far from me (*Psal.*) whose death and obsequies (bewaild of no few) asſigned for a warning-piece of thoſe very perilous days ſtoln upon us: *When ſay peace and ſafety, then ſudden deſtruction, Theſ.x.* And they ſhall not eſcape even the general day of Iudgements forerunner: whereof *Apocalips* thus, *Behold he cometh in the clouds, and every eye ſhall ſee him*; and they alſo that have pierced him; and all the Kindreds of the Earth ſhall wail, &c. And thus of one ſo hopeful committed to no ſimple Doctors, through too much ſuddenneſs or ignorance, as that way who can plead not guilty; by letting blood was caſt away; upon whom becauſe of this caſt ſuit of cloths beſtowed on him of his Maſters, *They ſhall look upon him whom they have pierced, &c.*

Let none with an evil eye look thereon,

thereon: And so passing on with several coats of houses born inclusive, adorning the Herse, as dedicated to our *Jerusalem* of the *Gentiles*, *And in that day there shall be a great mourning in* Ierusalem, *as the mourning in* Hadadrimmon, *in the valley of* Megiddon, the house of *Huntingdon* of which participates: Also in *London*, every family apart mourning and their wives, &c. Of the royal Branches, like the *House of* David, all of them bewayling apart, &c. likewise from that ominous name, called *Megiddon* impart, *it is done, Behold he comes making the sable clouds his chariot*: solemnized Heaven and Earths Funerals, these great lights extinguished, The *Sun* become as sackcloth of hair, The *Moon* as blood, The *Stars* falling, &c. answerable to that loud voice, *Revel.* 16.

Done it is, gathered in that place

called in *Heb. Armagedon*, when every yle fled away, &c. from whose Name importing diligence, *Hastings* who lost no time himself, declares much more what hastning required, and looking unto that day, at whose *appearing Heavens and Elements dissolves and melts, &c.* VVherefore, for instruction sake adds, when ye see these come to pass, *And I will pour upon the house of* David, *and upon the inhabitants of* Ierusalem, *the Spirit of Grace*. So be sure then time to look up, &c. And this for another, *and in that day I will make* Ierusalem *a heavy stone for all people, &c.* As extraordinary blessings rejected, no ordinary correctiions incurring inseparable evermore, besides such distraction so giddy, that plague increasing daily too, or curse of tax leavied, as witness whether fullfilled: *and in that day* (saith the Lord) *I will*

I will smite every horse with astonishment, and the rider with madness: and in that day will I seek to destroy all nations, that come against Ierusalem, &c. *and in that day* (saith the Lord) *I will cut off the names of the Idols out of the land.* And such like demonstrations shewing out of request, the name Saint drownd in oblivion, such an eye sore at this time unto many.

And passing forward also, whether that waiter on the latter days, *Esdras* testimony, termd *Apocrypha*, or miscalled, speaks not the present condition, presaging, the sons of the Church, *Sion* her sons cut off that fraternity; whilst deeply musing upon their departure from the Law, grown to such a low ebbe or degree, the law though still in force, like the Spirit of prophesie supposed transmitted not beyond the primitive times, as as grofs as Romifh miracles, without tryal *Efdras* informs, faw fuch a mournful mother, chang'd his cogitations, fhe replying, *Sir let me alone*; yet afterward thus after fo long time, that had a fon then nourifhed by her with fo much travel, grown up, came to take him a wife, when fell down and died; the houfe turnd upfide (as though) overthrew the lights fleeing the city, &c. into which Park or Field fled, purpofed to take up her reft; whereupon her pafsion to divert, fpreads that catalogue of confufion the prefent cafe greateft of all *Sion*, the mother of all, delivered into hands of hateful Iaylors a captive: Spoken to *Sion* her felf, at whofe fearful voice caft out the earth fhook, which befides her Sons farewel, fome future thing reveals, a prophetical voycc, &c. And new *Ferufalem* in her place, &c.

VVhere-

VVhereupon *Uriel* the Angel signifying *Light*, shews unto him. He in need of comfort himself the solution, thrice over, who repeats these and thirty years, ver. *But after thirty years,&c.* *Lucy* Lady of *Huntingdon*, the sackcloth and ashes Hers. *Ashbeys* mourning for him, he born *anno* 1630. about nineteen years of age, whose Epithalamiums to lamentations exchanged for Epitaphs: The saffron robe for sable mourning, whose mother coming to his bedside, a little before his death, Thus *quomodò vales?*

quomodo non possum bene valere cum proximus sim deliciis meis?

aluding partly to her Name of *Lucia*, &c. And for the visage mard or disfigured; wiped off so soon by the resurrection hope, as matters not, though obvious to beholders at such time; VVhen beauty turn'd into ashes,

·hich

which Light: about ten extinguished at night, injoyed no ſmall happineſs, in this the time of ſickneſs, in ſcarce complained of pain, Heretofore inclining to the Royal Party: *Haſtings* propheſied of by *Eſdras* the Prophet, as *Joſias* his Birth, ſo long before concerning that reformation, when thoſe prieſts cut off, foreſhewed their judgement, &c.

And for *Eſdras* that new ſong of his, ſo much ſuffice: And new *Ieruſalem* at hand, no material city, whoſe face all *Light* and *Luſtre*: And for theſe uſeful materials, *Giving all warning not unprovided to be of the wedding garment*; Threatning the downfal of the rough garment from head to foot, ſoars and blains their candleſtick reward: And ſo make haſte Lord God, Amen.

FINIS.

Iuly *the fourth, which Funeral train about noon paſsing through the City from the* Piazza *along thoſe ſtreets by the half Moon down the Strand, Temple-Bar, Fleet-ſtreet, up Ludgate and Old-baily to Smithfield and St.*Iohns *ſtreet (worth obſervation) ſaw not the face of Coach, Cart or Car, which paſſed by, either that met us, or ſtood in our way, as witneſs can ſo many, Sun and Moon as when ſtood ſtill,* Ioſh. *x.* Even ſo make no long tarrying, *Pſal.* lxx.

41. *Strange and Wonderfull Prophesies* (1649; Wing D2014) is reprinted, by permission of the Worcester College Library (Oxford University), from the copy held at Worcester College (shelfmark AA.2.4[73]). The text block of the original measures 187 × 134 mm (N.B. This item has been reduced to fit the present text area.) On each page, lines of poetry followed by lines of the printed marginalia are transcribed when necessary. In transcriptions of lines of poetry, reference mark letters are set off further in bold, though this is not the case in the text itself.

Hard-to-read words and handwritten annotations:

title page.11	afterwards into [text obscured by library stamp]
title page.13	how farre [text obscured by library stamp]
title page.14	unfulfilled [text obscured by library stamp]
1.1	most
1.21	Peers,
1.24	as a gastly skull.
1.**c**	al her … Belshazzer
1.**g**	hatchet … then … *Charles Stuart*…. upon the *Scaffold*
2.2	*Belshazzer*
2.4	wise (transcription)
2.5	Southsayers
2.28	high unsought.
2.29	preferments
2.34	resolve
2.**i**	Treasons, &c. and … death according
2.**p**	against
3.1	as in
3.15	January 1648 …[remaining words illegible] [transcription]
3.15	walking
3.23	was
3.26	the Ox
3.27	undreamt of this his
3.31	Whose
3.34	to say.
3.**u**	souls which flew
4.23	Crest,
4.23–26	Entrayls [transcription]
4.**d**	time seaven times seaven that is 49th year of his age, the
5.1	is
5.21	asterisk [transcription]
5.27	whose hand rests thy life
5.28	ways, and al
5.29	glorified him/ … wrote on the wal./
5.30	ed thy Kingdome hath
5.30	Execution place [transcription]

Strange and VVonderfull PROPHESIES BY The Lady ELEANOR AUDELEY; who is yet alive, and lodgeth in WHITE-HALL.

Which Shee Prophesied ſixteen yeeres agoe, and had them Printed in Holland, and there preſented the ſaid Propheſies to the Prince Elector; For which ſhe was impriſoned ſeven yeers here in *England*, by the late King and his Majeſties Councell: Firſt, ſhe was put into the Gate-houſe then into Bedlam, and afterwards into the Tower of LONDON.

With Notes upon the ſaid Propheſies, how farre they are fulfilled, and what part remains yet unfulfilled, concerning the late King, and Kingly Government, and the Armies and people of ENGLAND. And particularly White-Hall, and other wonderfull Predictions.

Imprimatur Theodore Jennings August 25. 1649.

London Printed for Robert Ibbitſon in Smithfield near the Queens head Tavern, 1649.

Strange and Wonderful

PROPHESIES

BY

[illegible]

With Notes upon the said Prophesies, shewing how farre they are fulfilled, and what parts [illegible]

[illegible] White Hall, and other [illegible] Predictions.

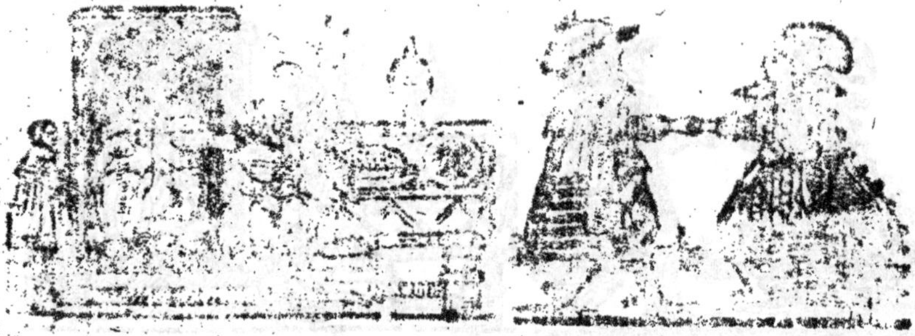

[illegible]

Strange and VVonderfull PROPHESIES BY *The Lady* Eleanor Audeley, *who is yet alive, and lodgeth in White-Hall.*

TO *a Sion* most belov'd I sing
b of *Babilon* a Song,
Concerns you more full well I wot
then ye do thinke upon.
c *Belshazzer*, lo, behold the King
feasting his thousand Lords;
Phebus and *Mars* prais'd on each string,
every day records.

The Temple Vessels of Gods House,
boldly in drunk about:
His *d* own (tis like) were made away,
bids holy things bring out;
e Praising of Gold and Brasse, the gods,
of Iron, Wood and Stone;
f See, hear, nor know, but now alas,
praised in Court alone.

A *g* hand appears, lo in his sight,
as he did drinke the wine,
Upon the wall against the light
it wrote about a line
In presence of his numerous Peers,
not set an hour full,
In loyns nor knees had he no might,
chang'd as a gastly skull.

a Those that beleeve this prophecy.
b So she frequently called the Bishops and Courtiers of *England*.
c The late King *Charles* whom in all her books she cald *Belshazzer*; because the wal of the Banquetting house at *White-Hal*, where he feasted, should be terrible to him, as a writing on the wall was to *Belshazzer*, which proved true, for there he was beheaded.
d Here she prophecied of his pawning and selling of his plate.
e The pulling down of pictures and Organs in Churches.
f All did rise against him but the Court faction.
g Here shee prophecied of the Kings death, which fell out true. For the heads-man took the hatchet in his hand wherwith he was be-headed, on the wal of the Banquetting-house, after the King had drank a glasse of wine, at one blow or line of blood, in presence of his then Equalls, for he dyed as *Charles Stuart*. After he had been scarce an houre upon the Scaffold, he fell downe on his knees, and so laid his neck on the block, with a pale gastly countenance, without any opposition.

A 2 Who

i Here she speaks of the High Court of Justice, where the King pleaded hard, and so did the 3 Lords; but they were sentenced for their Treasons, &c. and put to death according to judgement denounced by the Lord President in Scarlet.

Who might it read, alas, the thing,
Belshazzer i loud did shout;
Calls for Magicians all with speed
came in, as w[illegible] went out.
Caldeans and Southsayers sage,
the meaning whoso can
Of *Mene Mene* third Realmes Peer
in Scarlet Robe the man.

k The King did eate no Supper the night before he dyed.

His *k* majesty forgets to Sup,
Nobles astonish'd all;
Musitians may their pipes put up,
stood gazing on the Wall.

l He dranke a glasse of wine a little before he came to execution.

m His head was divided from his body.

The *l* pleasant Wine at length as sharpe,
too late till thought upon
Division *m* of another strain
unfolds the fingers long.

n Here shee names the Banquetting-house, the very place where hee should be executed, and that before the host or Army. And this did befall him, for being led by his Queen:

o This she write to perswade the King to beleeve her prophecy.

When *n* to the Banqueting house so wide,
Where host of Lords did ring,
So wisely came, the gracefull Queen,
said, *Ever live, O King.*
Needs o trouble, O King, thy thoughts no more;
forthwith shall it be read;
Daniel *there is who heretofore*
like doubts did open spread.

p The King delivered His George to the Bishop of *London* for P. *Charles*, but the Parliament considering his raising forces against them would not let him have it.

Could al interpretating Shew
which profound man soon brought,
On whom confer the King needs would
his *p* orders high unsought.
Needlesse preferments youle reserve,
Sir, keep your gifts in store,
High offices let others gaine,
there's given too much afore.

Yet unto thee shall here make known
resolve this Oracle true,

sure

Sure as in *q* thy Banquetting Houſe,
where all that come may view:
The Veſſells of my God are brought,
the palm ſalutes thee know
Herewith; for theſe profan'd by thee
threatneth the fatall blow.

q Here ſhee ſet down the very place and manner of his execution, which was true, for at the Banquetting-Houſe the King had his head cut off at one fatall blow.

O King, even thou, the moſt high God
unto thy *r* Grandſire bold,
Caldean land, a Nation fell
gave them to have and hold.
The Royal Scepter and the Crown
advanc'd whom he would have,
And whom he would he pulled down,
could put to death and ſave:

r His Grand-father was put to death in Scotland, which ſhe did uſually call *Caldeas* Land.

January 1648 fr
Jang
Hory

Till walking at the twelve moneths end,
ſubject ſtill Tides do fall;
Excellent *s* Majeſty how gon,
Court exchang'd for the Stall.
Thy *t* Grandſire on, as came to paſſe;
at all yet minded not,
As if a feigned Story, but
his miſerable Lot.

s Here ſhee prophecyed that Monarchy ſhould ceaſe in *England*, and White-hal which was the Kings Court be turned into an hold for Souldiers.
t Shee here prophecyed that hee ſhould as ſurely be put to death, as his Grand-father was, though not in the ſame manner.

Expell'd was for the words eſcap'd,
memory can ſpeak well,
Hardened in pride, unheard of ſuch,
the wilde Aſſe with did dwel:
Sent to the Ox, its owner knows,
u undreamt of this his doom:
Fowls their appointed time obſerve,
wots not the night from noon.

u Here ſhee prophecied of the fouls which flew over the King when hee was at execution, to ſhew his folly, that hee would not know his time, but bring himſelf to that miſerable end.

Whoſe *w* heart made equal with the Beaſt,
driven out with thoſe that Bray,
The Diadem as well fits thee,
Aſs, go, as much to ſay.

w Here ſhee prophecied that his Entrals ſhould bee taken out, and his body be imbalmed, which was true.

x She speakes this of his spiritual estate, that God in mercy hath saved his soul.

x Until return'd came to himself,
knew him that rules on high,
Over the sons of men appoints
what office they supply.

y During the time of the Kings imprisonment, there were Guards upon him night and day.

z This fel out true, for he was much lamented, by those of his own party especially.

y During which space, this Assyrian,
what watch kept night and day,
Thus metamorphys'd, over him,
lest make himselfe away.
z Fields, woods as wel ring out, as men
for wo, and Ecchoes call
Mercy this savage King upon,
in holy Temples all.

a It was grown to a common Proverbe that the King knew not his friends from his foes, al being abas'd, and none daring to stir or move for him.

Bewailed, dejected soul, thus faln,
fed now grazing full low,
whilst they bedew the ground with tears
a discerns not friend from foe.
Earth that of late made seem to dawn
with songs of Triumph high,
Fleeth each wight abas'd as much,
among the Herd doth lye.

b Speaking of her own family.

c Shee here blames those that would not beleeve her.

By b Star-light for device who gave,
as graven on his Shield,
An Eagle mounted on the Crest,
a Hart in silver field.
Extold again his God as high,
blessed him all his days:
c Others reputes them as nothing,
alone proclaimes his praise.

d Here she prophesied of the very time seaven times seaven that is 49th year of his age, the King was be-headed.

d Prince Charles.

Whose seven d times it served forth,
in vain for rest to crave;
Whom Devills Legions do possesse,
a Monarch turn'd a Slave,
Deposed thus, thou knewest wel,
Belshazzer, d O his Son,

And

And renew'd so, e deliverance
  voyced by every one.

A day a f Trumpet made to sound
  for Generations all;
And with a Feast solemnized,
  that no time might recal:
The memory of such an act,
  yet as it had not been,
Thy Favorites who are more this day,
  or matched to thy Kin.

Then they g adoring Wood and Stone,
  Statutes forsake Divine;
Meditate carved Statutes on
  in Faction do combine,
With Enemies of God most high,
  to thrust him from his Thron,
And thus hast lifted up thy self
  so facile and so prone.

Against the Lord of Heaven thy King,
  not humbling of thy heart,
But stiffened hast with pride thy neck
  unto thy future smart. *
Behold, polluting holy things
  with Sabbath so Divine,
Idolatry and Revells in
  that day and night made thine,

But he in whose hand re[illegible],
  even breath, thy [illegible] and [illegible]
Thou hast not glorified him
  sent this wrote on [illegible] *
God numbered [illegible]dome hath
  ended; the Hand points here,
In Ballance he hath weighed thee too,
  the set hour drawing neer.

e This fell out true; for presently after the Kings death, the House of Commons Voted *England* a deliverance from Monarchy.

f An Act was published in all parts against kingly Government, notwithstanding the many favourites thereof, And Lords that the King used to call Cosens.

g This is not yet fulfilled, but it seems to point out that the Kings Statues, and Armes shal be broken & pulled down from all publick places, as he in his Reign had promoted Idolatry liberty on the Lords day, and other notorious sins against God,

Execution place

How

h This is in part fulfilled by the Kings lands and goods now upon sale.

How light soever by thee set,
thou as thy weightlesse Gold,
His Image wanting, found much more
lighter then can be told.
h Parted, divided thine Estate,
given to the *Medes* is,

i She pophecies here that ther shal be no more Kings in *England*.

At Hand, the Hand bids it adieu,
i finish'd thy Majesties.

{Reveale / O Daniel.} Anagr. {Eleanor / Audeley}

FINIS.

42. *For the Right Noble, Sir Balthazar Gerbier Knight* (1649; Wing D1989B) is reprinted, by permission of the Folger Shakespeare Library, from the unique copy held at the Folger (shelfmark D1989.5 bd. w. D2010). The text block of the original measures 140 × 90 mm.

Hard-to-read words:

title page.7	*dren*
3.19	Apostles
8.3	*to sup with us*
8.7	*Saints*
8.8	Students

For the Right Noble,

Sir Balthazer Gerbier

KNIGHT:

From the Lady *Eleanor*.

Iſa. 30. 9,10.

This is a rebellious people, lying chil-dren, that will not hear the Law of the Lord.

Which ſay to the Seers, See not; and to the Prophets, Propheſie not unto us right things: ſpeak unto us ſmooth things, propheſie deceits.

Printed in the Year 1649.

For the Right Noble,

Sir Balthazer Gerbier Knight:

From the Lady *Eleanor.*

SIr, Having Intelligence of your Academy near the City, in imitation of *Paradice,* wherein of Rarities ſuch variety; and not at all doubting, but for his Throne there you have reſerved a place, to whom we owe all our utmoſt ſervice: By your admittance, ſhall for an addition to thoſe requiſite Sciences ſpecified in print by you, preſent the happy place with the *Book of Life, Cum Privilegio, Bleſſed that readeth, and they that bear the words, &c. The light*

ſhining

shining in darkness, and the darkness not comprehending it, the word of life; to us testifying, *If we say we have fellowship with him, and walk in darkness, we lye*, &c. (*Joh*.1.) or *if gainsay what he affirms, we make him a lyar likewise*: who although the prophet *Joel* on this wise, *afterwards I wil pour out my Spirit upon all flesh, Men-servants and Maid-servants, prophecying in those days before the terrible day of the Lord come*: And our Lord himself, *Behold, I am with you all days, until the consummation of the age*; his last words or farewel: Notwithstanding by them of this gross age, as if any thing too hard for him, taught as an Article of our Creed, setting up their pillars, beyond the Apostles dayes that the Spirit not transmitted extraordinary,

A 2

ordinary, becauſe of prophecy ceaſed, therefore extinguiſhed, likewiſe of Miracles, that when thoſe twain, the witneſſes which we expect (*Rev. xi.* ſhall have power ſuch, we may fulfil the prophets, as did they, *Crucifying the Prince of Life*; which great City called *Spiritual Sodom and Egypt*, ſuch ſinfulneſs for, and hardneſs of heart, the Gentiles departing from the faith as declares; ſo cannot be the Romiſh Church impeached, but only they to whom *the holy Ghoſt ſent*, moſt like firſt to viſit his own, reſiſting true tokens and ſigns: the very unpardonable treſpaſs, to which our Church in a nearer relation, holding in his appointed time *for him any thing too difficult*; in danger with thoſe *vipers*, of *breathing out like va-*

pours,

pours, confined to that *Pit* or *Abyſs*, *Rev.9.* thoſe heavenly lights obſcuring with Fogs *the third part of them*; the *Sin againſt the third perſon*, that bids of it beware: with that loud voyce from the Iſle of *Patmos*, *He that hath an ear, hear what the Spirit ſaith*, &c. whileſt *Great Britain* as though aſleep, had a paſs or diſpenſation not concerned in any ſuch Alarms, made their paſtime as *Bedlam* for entertaining the *Holy Ghoſt*, by this City, *&c.* ſuch an offence, *The Word of life, the leaves whereof expels the old Serpents poyſon*, darkneſs for unchangeable light exchanges, confutes ignorance, abates luſt, and the like; like *Pearls caſt before Swine*, &c. Such Grapes and Figs, our Thorn, the Roſe and Thiſtle affords; forewarnd

though,

though, *Judge not, that ye be not judged* (*Matthew* the 7.) for *Lex talionis*, and what Diſtraction and Diviſion of late amongſt them, that think to ſilence, thoſe *Cloven Tongues* to quench them; when as for prevention of which, that Allegory Supper (*Luke* 14.) *A certain man made a great ſupper, bad many, ſent out a ſervant at ſupper time*; with ſleeveleſs excuſes ſet light by, prophetical admonitions, ſo grown out of date: whereas in truth the *letter but dead*, obſerved onely in a Hiſtory way, without the Myſtery going therwith underſtood; company none craves of his, ſaying, *Behold, I ſtand at the door and knock; if any man hear my voice, and open the door, I will come in and ſup with him*, &c. faring thereafter:

after: witnes that Summons issued forth, saying, *Write, Blessed are they called to the Lambs supper* (Rev.19.) expresly said to be *The Spirit of Prophecy* (ver.10.) *The witness of Jesus*; for contempt of which, the fowls that know their time, they mustered, *called to the supper of the great God*, those birds of prey, *to eat the flesh of Kings, the flesh of Captains, and horse flesh, of small and great*, without respect of persons in that carnal estate worse then theirs *lying to the holy ghost* Acts, &c. or his folly, he that *offered to buy it with money of the apostles*, thus to belye and outface this, shed out again so impossible held, professed *not a man of them should so much as taste thereof*, the excommunication of the Clergies profession foreshewed, Author of all our evils. And

And for this here ſhewed, ſo much, ſuch indignity offered to the holy Spirits feaſt, vouchſafing *to ſup with us*; toward which craving from your ſelf Sir this favor only, *the table to take order may be furniſhed with fine linen and clean*, ſtiled, *The righteouſnes of Saints*, the judgement of thoſe Students with you; upon this queſtion, touching propheſie, ſuppoſed out of requeſt, VVhether higher diſobedience in the one, to credit feigned miracles, or not to believe true ones? Alſo when made *death to touch the forbidden*, and others rejecting theſe, *The Spirit and the Bride ſaying, Come*; and *Whoſoever will, take of the water of life freely*; which of them deſerving the Name of a Church, or excluded rather to be out of Paradice.

Auguſt, 1649. *FINIS.*

43. *For the most Honorable States Sitting at White-Hall* (1649; Wing D1989A) is reprinted, by permission of the Folger Shakespeare Library, from the unique but incomplete copy held at the Folger (shelfmark D1989.45 bd. w. D2010). The text block of the original measures 140 × 90 mm. (The title page has been enlarged to aid readability.)

Hard-to-read words:

4.15	*Boors*
5.10	trouble
5.16	*fetters*
6.1	Habitation
7.19	parts;
7.20	short
8.1–2	*Luke* 8. thus, *And when he WENT to land, there met him a certain* MAN
8. 4	*ware*
8.16	of
8.20	afterward

For the most Honorable

STATES

Sitting at

WHITE-HALL.

The words of Amos, &c. And the Lord shall roar from Zion, and utter his voyce from Jerusalem, and the dwelling places of the Shepherds shall perish, and Carmel shall wither: Thus saith the Lord, for three tarnsgressions and for four, &c. And will cut off the inhabitants of B. and the Scepter shall perish out of Beth. Thus saith the Lord, for three transgressions and for four, &c. Together with Divisions character, *viz. By the same token, saith the Lord of Sabbath;* When Bishops Lands sold, Rhetoricks flowers out of request, *Great Britains* Union dissolv'd, or cut assunder, puts down their Kings, he Beheaded, Four and twentieth from the Conquest, aged Seven times seven, in the Seventeenth Century. *Thus saith the Lord, In that day I will raise up the Tabernacle of David that is faln down, &c. and will build it again, as in days of old.* Amos cap:8.

London, Printed in the Year 1649.

31

For the Right Honorable, The Councel of State.

From the Lady *Eleanor*, *Octo.* 1649.

AS known to all, the true way or touch-ſtone, other none to try them by, but that *Salt the life of all things*, *All things whereby were inſtituted*, without which (*his word the Way and the Truth*; where Legions of diviſion the like unknown, a like poſsible to expect *peace one with another*, as to thrid Needles with a Cable, or in a day build *Pauls*.

And ſo behold, all like as when *ſtung by fiery Serpents, were healed by another in that likenes*; alſo of thoſe Legions entred into *that wilde man*, as enſues, a taſte or tryal of them tendred

dred

dred to these restless days, wherein *every man in his proper language, hears the wonderful word of God*, as in a chrystal mirror presenting the visage of the present, extracted from that distracted *MANS* recovery, sent hither to Preach (askt *What his name was?*) declaring *What God had done for him* (no infant or babe) directed to the Gentiles, a light for the last days, as though askt *Great Britain*, and *Germany*, their Names should answer *Gergesens*, they both a compound of it; from *Gadarens* as also derived *Gallia* or *France* (lying over against *England*) as that Region over against *Galilee*; so *Whether thence comes any good thing*, like that saying of old: Also former Marriages (what successes have had) who wots not,

A 2 shall

ſhall come to the matter (*Mat.8.c.*) of our Saviors pilgrimages or weary progreſſes.

And when he was come to the other ſide of the Countrey of the Gergeſens, there met him two poſſeſt with Devils, which came out of the Graves, very fierce, ſo that no man might paſs by that way. And the devils beſought him,&c. *and he ſaid, Go*; whereof in a paraphraſing way thus proceeding, verily their paſs for *Graveſend* thoſe twain *Rup.*and *Maurice*,returned to *Grave Maurice*, Couſen Germain with the *Boars*, iſſue of the late *Palſgrave* of the *Rhyne*, that German Prince turned out of his Countrey, making in the *Low Countries* his abode, whoſe Offspring thoſe furies or fiends broken looſe here, ſent home again : To this

this day which Family are constantly visited with a Spirit before the death of them, a thing known to all; and thus as though a Babe new born should speak the hardest Names.

Mark 5. on this wise going on with it, of the aforesaid *unclean spirits* baptized in the lake, &c. certainly emblem of the *Gentiles* being return'd to wallow *in the mire*, as waters of troublesom times giving warning; where thus, *And when he was come out of the ship, there met him incontinently out of the Graves a* MAN *that had an unclean spirit, who had his abiding amongst the Graves, bound with fetters and chains, &c. neither could by any man be tamed*, his Ghost (as it were) that Bear *Canterbury*, brought so often to the stake or Bar on his knees; where

beside

beſide his Habitation, where thoſe Monuments in Cathedrals, whoſe Houſe at *Lambeth* with its ſcituation not onely pointed to, but of its denomination borrow'd from the houſe of *Bethlam*, otherwiſe called *Bedlam*: As his Name withal whence derived from the Grave-maker or Sextons Office, their digging or opening vaults, not unlike to be one of his Godfathers; ſo much of his raving fit, that bad our Savior *avoid*: foreſhewing had thoſe times been in his, had given him that oath of forſwearing himſelf, or his own accuſer to be, as forced no few in that undue kinde, his own Obligation ſo well obſerving, queſtioned not his ſpirit of continency, any more then whether the name *Puritans* a perſecutor of, or

given

given *Judas* pass, gone to his own place, *Canterbury* the last of his name on a Friday executed, the day on which our Lord was buried for his long service, that in a field *Gules* gives the Halter or rope, from henceforth a chain left to hang their Keys in. And so much for him and them both answering, *For we are many fryers*, whose twelve Godfathers withal besought, (as it were) *Him not to torment he adjures them*; which concerns more then any Lord Majors Oath, or his Show on the water.

So each in his order, where follows *Great Britains* last King, or *Englands* late Tyrant, into whom many Devils were entred from several parts; but one above the rest (no short time) vext with most, whereof

Luke

Luke 8. thus, *And when he* W[illegible] *to land, there met him a certain* MAN *out of the City, which had a Devil a long time, and he ware no clothes, neither abode in house, but in the Graves, and he commanded the foul spirit to come out of the man, for oft-times it caught him, &c. therefore he was bound in fetters*, as the cause of his binding shews, so from those words, that *it came out of the man*, as much to say, a woman, his *Vasthi* put away or departed, bereft of the Breeches, &c. in recompence Crown'd by her Servant *German*. And so much for this misled Man, went away from his House of Parliament and *Hampton-Court*, turned out of City-houses and Country both, took up his restless Lodging among the slain in the field, afterward in

44. *A Sign Given them* (1649; Wing D2012AA) is reprinted, by permission of the Folger Shakespeare Library, from the unique copy held at the Folger (shelfmark D2012A.5 bd. w. D2010). This copy contains some handwritten corrections that may be in Lady Eleanor's hand. The text block of the original measures 140 × 90 mm.

Hard-to-read words and handwritten annotations:

title page.2–3	SIGN Given them being entred into
3.7	printed 'had' transformed into 'HEE' by hand [transcription]
7.9	*&* [transcription]
7.9	the cross [transcription]
7.17–20	[crossed-out printed words partially legible] obeyed *Joshuahs* command (no feigned *Phaeton*) *stood still, the Moon moving neither* they arrived that longed [transcription]
8. 1–8	[crossed-out printed words partially legible] after Rest, so now before removed, carried thence away, shews them the way, accompanies them as it were, sets in the East: Moreover for whose additional years, fiveteen [sic] wedded to those ten degrees, these crowning the first of his Reign, 1625. forbids any more Coronations of Kings: No [transcription]
12.14	night
13.13-20	[crosses out big sections of these lines to make the following printed text] those days before *Noah*, again, *how preparid then?* [Original printed text reads as follows] those days before *Noah*, so shall be his coming again, concerning not onely Times golden vial or glass, by which account its being at a stand: But how it stands or fares with *faith* put to the question (*Luke, &c.*) *whether any where found such a thing as faith* [transcription]
14.1–5	[crossed-out printed words partially legible] As for the set time, or when. Lo, the present generation: so *Masters, for setting your house in order* who here discharges her calling or place by [transcription]
16.12	*Emanuel Jesus*, its Numerals

A

S[illegible]G N

G[illegible] them being [illegible]red into

The day of Iudgment

To set their House in order.

For the High Court of Parliament assembled.

From the Lady *Eleanor*.

PSAL. 97.

The Lord is King (or reigneth) *let the earth rejoyce; let the great Isles be glad.*

London, Printed in the Year 1644.
[illegible] printed with some words of addition for the Year present, 1649.

A DISCOVERY

Unto what Nation the laſt Day aforehand to be in the laſt days Revealed: Contained in the XX. of *Kings*, *Iſaiah* 39.

AS THE no other aſsigned then *The word of God*, touching the Reſurre-ctions then *being at hand*, but that of *Jonas* the prophet; ſo in point of like incredulity at his return again turned *Sadduces*, appointed no other, but this of King *Hezekiahs* days (*Kings, &c.*) that for a ſign or

A 2 aſſu-

assurance had, the third day of his uprising, going up to the Lords house to seal it; that of the *shadows going back*, for the thrid of his life out lengthned, a lease made him of thrice five years, like a shadow when past.

VVithout which token, not in a capacity of obtaining so high blessing passed not without being by the prophet *Isaiah* advertised (the Lord of Hosts Ambassador) his house afterward how swept; and sons under what slavery issued from him, not for facility such onely, but difficulty of belief dangerous not a little.

Of which days come about again, this great Revolution ushering the day of Iudgement, his coming in the Clouds; whereof as follows, of *Jacobs* ladder reaching to heaven gate, thus,

thus, The express Epitomy of King *James's* life of *Great Britain*, where beside no smal plague accompanying his first coming, afore never visited so with those tokens, of his like recovery, here giving to understand beyond expectation; such a solemn Thanksgiving for which at *Pauls cross*: which long Sermon in was related, how in his late sickness unto death, he likewise *justified his upright walking with God*: and therewith how pluckt off his Cap, and cast it on the ground, in such a passion professing in point of witting Injustice, *he would not so much as ask God forgiveness*; by which way of purging himself, as came not behinde *Hezekiah* neither in some gross failings: like that good King his hearkning to those charming

ing

ing *Babylonian* Ambaſſadors or Spies with letters ſent to congratulate from *Baladan ſon of Baladan.*

Alſo who *ſhewed them all his ſtore and armory,* coming from thoſe *Auſtrian Philips, &c.* overcome with like jugling ſlights, *a few figs and junkets,* ſuffered that *Gundamore having ſurveyed the Tower, to carry away as many great Ordnance and Guns as he pleaſed, preſerved for Truths defence, and Kingdoms ſafety,* in no leſs peril of home-bred friends ſuch, then forreign foes, requiſite with Arms and Forces to be ſecured: And then how ſent his Son after, forced for whoſe *Ranſom* to ſend over *All the precious things and goodly, laid up by his Predeceſſors, to be beſtowed amongſt thoſe inſatiable Eunucks and Officers diſtributed.*

ted. And laſtly the good man himſelf, in whoſe days *flouriſhed Truth and Peace*, thus over-reached, for all his King-craft and Learning, that brake his heart ſhortly after. *And the reſt of his Acts, and all his might* (or greatneſs) *and how he brought water into the City, and made a Pool and a Conduit & that Idol* the cross *are they not written in the Chronicles, &c.*

And thus this *Hezekiah ſlept, and reſted with his fathers, and Manaſſes his ſon reigned in his ſtead*; that came not ſhort of *Ahab*: and he awakened thus, for him ſo much ſuffices, become a ſign himſelf, no inferior one, had the Suns retiring for a ſign, ~~o-~~ beyed ~~Joſhuahs command (no feigned~~ ed [redacted]

after

after Rest, so now before removed, carried thence away, shews them the way, accom[redacted] it were, se[redacted] Moreover for whose additional years, fifteen wedded to those ten degrees, these crowning the first of his Reign, 1627, forbids any [redacted] Coronations of Kings: No more rising or setting here of theirs.

Kings xxi. *Chron.* xxxiii.

AND this *Manasseh twice twelve years old, when he began to reign over Great Britain*; How he reared *Altars to Baal, and set up his Roman Altars, built Altars in the house of the Lord, adored that Babylonian Image the Crucifix, manifest are they not on record?* Beyond Heathenism abomination

nation execrable: Moreover to the overthrow of them and theirs, how many seduced, beside shedding so much Innocent Blood; insomuch that the Catalogue of his sins, *Manasses* great wickedness, the hateful *Amorites* Cup, wherewith paralleld and worse; which Tyrants but light in comparison, weighed with this *MANS*, since 1625. the Remonstrance of the present.

To whom *the Lord spake, and to his people* likewise, but both by regard alike improved in his Commandments; as the Suns course the contrary way gone as many degrees astray, and so both alike whether rewarded, recōmended to the beholders, whose high looks brought down, *here see whose Sons coat this? therefore*

B *thus*

thus ſaith the Lord, Behold, I am bring-ing an evil upon them, that whoſo hear-eth it, both his ears ſhall tingle : where thus again, whether *Jeruſalems* line ſtretched over us , CITY and Country both ; *And I will wipe Jeru-ſalem, as a man wipeth a diſh, which he wipeth and turneth it upſide down* ; as in a glaſs whether preſents not the face of the preſent, ſpares neither ſide; who not amiſs deriving from *Brute* their denomination, from the Aſs as wel *who underſtands his owner*, no ſuch ſtranger to the dumb. And ſo much for this *Manna* ſet at nought, theſe judgements of the Lord foreſhewed, light by ſet ; notwithſtanding ſpeak-ing the *Canaan* language unto this our Age, to all whoſoever hath ears, in their Native tongue, ſhewed them

their

their unnatural motion gone backward how far, offended thereat or no, whereof as ensues.

This for another making up the number, he when made his supplication, how was heard, also returned to *Hampton-Court*; however mis-led by sinister Counsel, or betrayed, not unhumbled either, unknown not unto all who agreed to whatsoever, about two years after who slew him in his own house, attended with glowing ears not a few, such a spectacle.

And how *the people of the Land slew them again that had conspired, &c.* *Rainsborough* and our *Holland* Ambassador, taking essay of it, Drunkenness added to blood-thirstiness, were the first saluted with which unexpected cup.

And with expedition (a few words to the wiſe) on this wiſe paſsing on, what *Baptiſm* firſt paſt on his Sons, viſible in the Seers book; withal how ſervile on the other ſide to his Prieſts Biſhops, charmed by their ſubtile Goſpels: whoſe Service book becauſe allowed by his Father, what an Idol made of it, where that for another, recorded in their Prophetical Remonſtrance, gave himſelf to them that had Familiar Spirits, bringing up whoſo named by him, the gods and others; as Plays his night exerciſe.

And the reſt of his folly, and other of his judgement, making his Prayer-book alſo equivolent with the Allſufficient *Scriptures*, evident as his grove made, daily at Ball where ſacrificed his

his time, graced with one of his Fathers unhappy acts, that *Baals* or *James* Chappel, prodigious Tvvins, the other his *Babylonian* Theatre, from *James*'s to vvhich fatal place made his laſt progreſs or march, erected in Commemoration of the Ark as had been, alſo the ſeventeenth Century current; as from *Adam* to the Flood ſo long, not unforevvarned of it by him *that was the ſon of Adam, that was the ſon of God*; that as vvere thoſe days before *Noah*, ~~ſo ſhall be~~ [redacted] again, ~~concerning not onely, Times golden vial or glaſs, by vvhich account its being at~~ a ſtand: ~~But hovv it ſtands or fares with *faith* put to the queſtion (*Luke, &c.*) whe-~~ [redacted] ~~*found ſuch a thing as*~~ [redacted]; *how prepar'd then?*

As

[redacted] farther giving you in the next place notice, from *Manasses fifty five years Reign*, of *his second coming at hand*, goeth hand in hand vvith that of *Cæsar Augustus his five and fifty years*, in vvhose Reign *The Prince of Life, The Beginning and Ending* of Monarchy, *came, about the fortieth year, into the world, that began to be about Thirty years of age, in the fifteenth year of Tiberius*, (Luke, &c.) even the sum of it bids turn to those sure Chronicles, penn'd by the *holy Spirits command*, thus saith the Spirit, from *the return of Manasses days to expect his coming again, aforehand*, as as shewed unto his servants the Prophets, expresly pointing to the year 1655. at hand, being the time when the flood came, 1655. from the Creation, as computed by the Ancients and other *Noah* and his (*Baptisms* figure, at mans estate all) preserved in the *Whales womb, ten moneths* fulfilling, *before any window in the Ark opened*: and thus *one deep calling to another*, as when the *waters prevail'd*, the snowy *Dove found no footing*, the *Raven* afore sent forth, no other presaging then the *Spirit of Prophesie*, at such a time again though ceased long at last salutes the nations with the *Olive* leaf *in her mouth*, so seasonable now for their healing, without which Angelical leaves applied, an evil incurable, promised *The Tree of life, yielding its monethly fruit*.

And so be it known, That the aforesaid blessed period of years 55. containing Moneths *666.* (*Rev.*13.) called *The number of a MAN* (to wit) that *Roman* Emperors Reign, shewed afore the *Moneth* of *August* bearing his Name; by whose Predecessor the Calender corrected: and *666* Hours fulfilling a *Moneth*, all bids Tyrant Time and his Generation or Offspring *Adieu*, subscribed with *Emanuel Jesus*, its Numerals *MVILV. Anno* 55.

FINIS.

45. *The Everlasting Gospel* (1649; Wing D1986) is reprinted, by permission of the Folger Shakespeare Library, from the clear copy held at the Folger (shelfmark D1986 bd. w. D2010). The text block of the original measures 140 × 90 mm.

2

THE EVERLASTING GOSPEL.

Apocalyps 14.

And they sung a new Song before the Throne, and before the four Beasts and the Elders; ver. 24. *And no* MAN *could learn that Song, but the* 144, &c.

Printed in the
Year of our Redemption, *Decem.* 1649.

The Holy Gospel,

According to the Evangelist,

By the Lady ELEANOR.

E*Ven the same, that which was from the Beginning,* then believed in, magnified unto the end of the world, as until the consummation of the Age (saying) *Lo, I am with you, without end whose Kingdom.*

How it came to pass shewing, in the first year of his Reign, first of his Name, *Charles* of *Great Britain,* in *Berks* the first of Shires, she then at her House *Englefield* Manor, of *Englands* Realm, Daughter of the first Peer, *Anno* 25. the Moneth of *July* in, so call'd after the first *Roman* Emperor, he slain, *&c.*

VVhere the word of the Lord of

A 2 Hosts

Hosts, when came to her, the Heavenly voyce descending, speaking as through a Trumpet of a most clear sound these words:

> *Nineteen years and a half to the Judgement, and you as the meek Virgin.*

Awakened by which alarm early in the morning, whereof thus, signed with *Divisions* character, the years being divided, this magnified morning Star, story of *Jerusalem* of the *Gentiles, Great Britains* blow foreshewing, *Anno* 44. accomplished: The same though come to pass, who nevertheles in stead of their acknowledged error, like those *Priests and Elders*, first who *setting a Watch*, then underhand by such large Doctrine en-

endeavor to ſtop the peoples mouths, that do as they are taught, promiſed to *be ſaved harmleſs*, the old Serpents policy, *&c.* And with this Revolution thus going on, in the firſt of his Reign, the beginning in of the year, when a *Star* within the *Horns of the New Moon* encloſed, of ſome judgement at hand, the ominous Forerunner: Firſt, of the VViſe-men coming from the Eaſt, as follows; whoſe flight taken weſtward, through that heavy hand occaſioned; the Cities unparalleld Plague, Bills to be Canceld never, or drowned in forgetfulneſs, encreaſed to no leſs then weekly *Five thouſand five hundred and odde*, the Age of the world; decreaſed as ſuddenly about the midſt of Summer: all one as their being fed, that bleſsing

blessing thought upon, when the five thousand men with *those loaves five*, &c. no more then the fingers of their hand, any matter made of it, so thankful: VVhereupon (the aforesaid Visitation) the Term kept at *Reding*, County of *Berks*, other Courts at *Maidenhead* Town, the Parliament posting to *Oxford*, doing all homage to this *New born BABE*, *ruling with the iron Scepter*, them forewarning all in vain, *Be wise, O ye Kings, Be learned, ye Iudges*; that in such security held themselves then, and so much first for that, and his powerful word displayed, the priority thereof, thou *Britain* not the least, *&c.* And of his wrath then kindled, shewed great Blessings and Corrections inseparable companions: VVherewith

with proceeding, namely, *without it done nothing that was done*, its mouth the Oracle, *Beginning* and *Ending* of *Monarchies*, inheritance whose from *East to West extends*; concerning the aforesaid golden number, *Nineteen years and a half*, being in a Manuscript inserted, containing *Germanies* woful Occurrences, and *Great Britains* both, with what sign confirmed; shewing further thus, who immediately after with her own hand within two days delivered it to the Archbishop *Abots*, he then at *Oxford*, of University the first, in presence of no few; with this for a Token given, *the plague presently to cease*; of whom took her leave, the Bishops *Amen* whereto went round.

The Bills obeying the same before

fore the Moneth expired of *Auguſt*, witneſs when ſcarce deceaſed *One thouſand* of all Diſeaſes, whereas afore ſo infectious, five children dying for one aged, next Term ſupplyed with others fled returned; ſo that of its late deſolation appearance, no more then of Change or Amendment amongſt them, none at all.

And ſo purſuing the Prophetical Hiſtory in the next place, That it might be fulfilled *out of the Low Countreys, &c.* as the Virgin when undertook her voyage, ſhe fleeing for the Babes preſervation thither; alſo conſtrained for printing the ſame, to go into *Holland*, thoſe plain ſwathing-bands for wrapping it in, pretending in her husbands behalf the *Spaw* obtained a Licenſe, ſince none for printing

ing to be had here, inquiſition and hold ſuch, among them impriſoned about it formerly, till afterward all as free, *Cum Privilegio* out of date become.

VVhere thus paſsing on the mean while ere her return thence, *George* Archbiſhop deceaſed, *Anno* 33. unhappily whoſe hands imbrued in innocent blood, Archbiſhop *Laud*, 19 of *Septemb.* tranſlated, *&c.* reigning in his ſtead, ſucceſſor of him, in ſtead of the Stag who ſhot the Keeper, preſaging what Murthers him coming after, when-as for another her ſoul pierced in no mean degree, what honor to be *a Prophet amongſt their own nation and rank*; for example as ſpecified on Record: no ſooner arrived then apprehended, of her childe raviſhed,

viſhed, a greater then the Parliament, *the Word of God*: And how recompenced for their ſervice, referred, *&c.* where after a Candle being ſent for, about the third hour in the Afternoon, that with his own hand had burnt it, ſaying, *She hath taken good long time, till* 44. *for Dooms-day then; My Lords, I hope I have made you a ſmother of it*: in truth his own fatal hour, thoſe years of *Nineteen and a half*, reaching to his Execution Moneth and Year, *Anno* 44. *January*, when parted head and body, like that aforeſaid divided year, ſhewed afore ſacrificed by his ungracious hand, Author of this Diviſion or Diſtraction, a cup filled to the brim afterward, as that Iudgement day, *June Anno* forty four compleat: The reſtrained

four

four *Winds*, &c. *Apoc*.7. ſignified by them, extending to forty eight, that Blow *January* alſo, all ſtanding at the ſtroke of FOUR; the fourſquare City *New Ieruſalem* wherewith agrees: *Micah* the Prophet (*cap*.5.) his alarm to awaken the Age, ſpeaking no parable, by her goods ſeized on, wherewith given the Oath, ſuch and ſuch *ARTICLES* for anſwering to: In which caſe not much to ſeek, of *Scandalum Magnatum* in that kinde, againſt *thoſe little ones*, the penalty of it, *touched by whomſoever, a milſtone a fitter ornament*, &c. ſhe not ſlow in appearing to receive their wilde Sentence; the Dragon of *Lambeth, Laud*, his venom diſcharging laſt of all, even *Anno Etatis* 33. meaſured out by our Lords age, when

B2 as

as brought to his Arraignment by wicked hands, how ſacrificed this *Teſtimony* of his; a word alſo as enſues.

And thus like meaſure *October* 23. ſhe committed cloſe Priſoner, Excommunicated, Fined to his Majeſties uſe Three thouſand pounds, and to make publique Recantation at *Pauls* Croſs, as extant on Record, Twelve Hands Signed by; alſo *Edge* Hill fight, and the *Iriſh* Maſſacre 23 of *October*, and Twelve of them at once Voted to Priſon, for that Order of theirs nothing to ſtand of force there done without them: His Majeſty laſtly Fined his three Kingdoms to the uſe, *&c.* As for *Pauls*, a habitation for Owls, thoſe Noats ſet up, to ſet forth the reſidue, where

the

the time would fail how the firſt Blow at *Edge-Hill* in *Oxfordſhire*, the ſecond *Newbery*, fought within a ſtones caſt of her houſe at *Englefield*. And thou *Bedlam*-Houſe, too little the Thouſandth part to contain of them diſtracted ſince thence her coming, *well knowing if the Maſter of the houſe called Devil, &c. what the Servant to expect*; where ſo much for this time, accompanied with the Univerſal Tax, no Inferior Rack ſet upon in theſe days *C.Stu.* his Reign, as ſometimes in *Cæſ. Auguſt.* ſecond of that Monarchy, no ſmall oppreſſion, as the lineage of *David* a witnes of it: cloſing it with theſe from her Name, *Rachels*, ſignifying a Sheep, rendring *Charles* his ſoil for the Golden fleece bearing the Bell: ſo whom he he hath joyned of her Lamentation, *&c. Jacobs* saying, *Some evil Beast hath done it*, needs not ask *Whose Coat party-coloured?* also in pieces rent, since our *British* Union, *&c.* not without cause *weeping*, *because they are not*; and so all doing they know not what, *even forgive*, &c. And again thus, since *Thus it was written, and thus it behoved to suffer*; *and to rise again.*

The New-Years-Gift *to all Nations and People,* Iubile.

Decemb. 1649.

FINIS.

46. *The New Proclamation, In Answer To A Letter* (1649; Wing D1998) by Lady Eleanor's daughter, Lucy Hastings, is reprinted, by permission of The British Library, from the unique copy held at The British Library (shelfmark 486.f.27. [10]). The text block of the original measures 155 × 90 mm.

Hard-to-read words:
8.8 *ther*:

THE

New Proclamation,

IN

ANSVVER

TO A

LETTER.

Exod. 34. *And the Lord paſſed by before him, and proclaimed, The Lord, The Lord* God, *Merciful and Gracious, Long-ſuffering, and abundant in goodneſs, &c.*

Iſa. 9. *His Name ſhall be, The wonderful Councellor, The mighty God, The everlaſting Father, The Prince of Peace.*

London, Printed 1649.

THE

New Proclamation,

IN

ANSVVER

TO A

LETTER.

Exod. 34. 6. And the Lord passed by before him, and proclaimed, The Lord, The Lord God, Merciful and Gracious, Long-suffering, and abundant in goodness, &c.

Isai. 9. 6. His Name shall be, The wonderful Counsellor, The mighty God, The everlasting Father, The Prince of Peace.

London, Printed 1649.

May it pleaſe you, &c.

HAving taken ſome time to examine the incloſed, in obſervance of your command it is here returned; The interpretation therein given of that Text *Phil.* 2.6. being compared with our Engliſh Tranſlation, and both with the Original, ours is found to be rendred much neerer the letter, and very agreeable to the Greek phraſe, a cloud of Interpreters withall taking it as we do: And though poſsibly the words might admit of another conſtruction, yet what can be ſo ſafe as to read it to the letter, when the ſence accords ſo well to the reſt of the holy Scripture.

A 2 VVherein

VVherein our bleſſed Savior Ieſus Chriſt, the only begotten Son of God, is often ſtiled, God abſolutely; but it is obſerved, that ſimply and without reſtraint to ſome circumſtance, none is called God, beſides the only true God, the Eternal Creator of the world: Chriſt is called *The true God and Eternal life*, 1 *John* 5.20. The name *Jehovah*, and Divine properties, as Eaternity, Immenſity, Omnipotency, to be religiouſly adored, prayed to, truſted in, are communicated to him. He is ſtiled, *The proper or own Son of God*, *The only begotten of the Father*, and who ſhall declare his generation? never ſaid to have had any time of beginning, who then may contradict his Coeaternity with the Father? Shall not the wiſdom of God

be

be Coeaternal with God? not a word in the Scripture that makes him of a Godhead inferior to the Father, who then may in respect of his Divinity deny his equality?

All those places of Scripture which declare the Lord Christ to be true God (seeing there is but one God) make him one, and equal with that one God; yet hath the Son a distinct subsistence from the Father, and from the Holy Spirit; as the Father hath life in himself, so hath he given (*viz.* by Divine generation) to the Son to have life in himself: *I will pray the Father, and he shall give you another Comforter*, which distinguishes him from the holy Spirit.

Yet are there not three Gods, the Scriptures affirm there is but one.

This

This point is with humility to be received; we cannot reſtrain the Deity to the Laws of created Nature, nor finde whereto perfectly to compare him: VVhen the Apoſtle teaches, *That in Chriſt dwells the fulneſs of the Godhead bodily*, he bids firſt beware of being ſpoiled by Phyloſophy: It is ſufficient the word of God inſtructs us, That the Father is *Jehovah*, the Son is *Jehovah* (no inferior God) the holy Spirit is *Jehovah*, yet there is but one God *Jehovah*: This I take to be Trinity in Unity, and Unity in Trinity. However the Modern Iews were offended at this Equality and Unity, the ancient Iews very well underſtood that when our Savior ſaid he was the Son of God, he did in effect affirm himſelf to be God; and that

Iſa 44 5. compared with Rev. 21.6.
2 Cor. 6. 16. compared with Lev. 12. 26.

that when he called God his own Father, and ſaid he did the ſame work with the Father, he made himſelf equal with the Father: Neither doth our Savior Chriſt reprove them for ſo judging of him, *Joh.* 5.

As for thoſe Objections, *That God is the head of Chriſt, That he ſhall deliver up the Kingdom to God, even the Father, That the Son himſelf ſhall be ſubject to him.* It is the uſed maner of ſpeech in the Scripture (by reaſon of the Union between the Godhead and Humane Nature in Chriſt) in mentioning what is proper to one Nature, to take the name of the other, as where our Lord ſpeaks to *Nicodemus, No man hath aſcended up to heaven, but he that came down from heaven, the Son of man which is in heaven:*

ven : to be in divers places at once, must of necessity be understood of the Deity alone, though spoken under the Name of the Son of man: So it is said *of Christs Kingdom there is no end*; and yet it is again said, *He shall deliver up the Kingdom to his Father*: The giving up of the Kingdom must be as Man-mediator, and the retaining of it without end, as God Eternal. And so for those places, *It pleased the Father that in him should all fulness dwell, &c.* they are understood, It pleased the Father that in the Mediator Christ, should all fulness dwell.

Thus as I held it my duty on this occasion, I have endeavored to give a reason of my faith in this particular,

Being your most humble, &c.

Lu: H:

47. *The Arraignment* (1650; Wing D1972B) is reprinted, by permission of the Folger Shakespeare Library, from the unique copy held at the Folger (shelfmark D1986 bd. w. D2010). This copy contains a handwritten note that may be in Lady Eleanor's hand. The text block of the original measures 140 × 90 mm.

Hard-to-read words and handwritten annotations:

3.12–14	[illegible word followed by] Lo Fairfax [transcription]
9.1	*worm*
12.1–2	in like
12.17	*spirit, come forth of him, and enter no more into him.*

THE
Arraignment.

By the Lady *Eleanor*.

MARK 9.

And he said unto them, verily I say unto you, that there be some of them that stand here, which shall not taste of death till they see the Kingdom of God come with power.

Printed in the year, 1650.

MARK 9.

And whosoever shall offend one of these little ONES that believe in me, &c.

AND so who should be greatest, or bear the sway; this Lesson appointed for the present, occasioned upon that dispute: Also to whom it points about a Thing, of no little weight doubtless, where declared, *A milstone better hanged about his neck*, be he whosoever, standing no better on his guard, (the safe-guard of no few) on whose behavior or vigilancy depends, to whose lot the Milstone falls as follows, even the Military or

Sword

Sword profeſsion, their judgement here called to hold up their hand at the Bar; behold as this ſeals it a free paſſage: Verſe, *And if thy hand offend thee cut it off, it is better for thee to enter into life maimed*; likewiſe of the foot, *Better to enter halt into life, &c.* VVhere by the natural Body, reports the caſe concerning the politique, to ſlight the leaſt or loweſt degree, *coming in his name how perilous.*

So here anatomiz'd whoſe Father diſcern I pray: *Then loſe a foot, ſuffered his whole body to periſh*, who thought little of the thrid or term cut off ſo of his days: By means of a feſtred Toe, a Corn, turned to a *Gangren* dyed, falling into a violent Feaver, that very *Ignis non extinguitur*, or VVilde-fire, his doughty heart leaving it to his heir how paterizaring, of late far and near not unknown misled or overmaster'd when put on his tryal, what metel or salt in him: Better much had been without assistants such hands, eyes, or feet, unless more command over himself had, whether friends, wife or followers.

From the Omnipotent General, Lord of Hosts when as sent unto, dreading neither sacred watch words these or Alarm: These thunderings vouchsafed not so much as to see the party, the like unparaleld in Divine presidents or other, of such greatness stood upon or manhood notwithstanding, *Quisquis scandalizaverit unum ex his*, be he never so eminent, his doom in the bottom of the Sea

better

better to have taken up his quarters: To whom had ſome great thing been commanded, *To have departed his native ſoil, or half his goods have parted among the poor*, how much rather, but when to lend an ear required: Even cowardize in the higheſt degree, or weaknes, who keeps his diſtance with ſuch, thereafter from his preſence excluded as far (as much to ſay) *Write their Epitaph on the ſand, reward them with a cup filled double, a portion let them be for fiſhes, all as deaf and mute like themſelves, no burier, &c.*

And for ſuch Saints, ſo much ſuffices; as his name, *THOMAS DYDIMOUS, &c.* and for them alſo whoſe voyce the mountains obey, or Monarchs confined them to the ocean, Trees no ſmall ones

pluck

plucks up by the roots, whose estate *blest when hated and cursed, in poverty rich, their cottage Heaven.*

Against whom, all their Enemies can alledge, for silencing the Holy Ghost thus; or to cloak their arrogancy, is because, former times as it were barren signs and token discontinued, therefore abolished, That may affirm as well, or maintain Hell shall prevail against Heaven, as that ordinary spirits shall unseal the Books of Prophets, or that other Book (so stiled) Revel. 20. *And I saw another book opened, &c.* to be explained ever by them, *The word of the Lord induring for ever having spoken it,* Isa. 40. *Whatsoever is crooked, shall be made strait, And the rough be made plain fields,* the voyce of deserts accompanying it as those

thoſe waſte parts at this day, though depopulated, *again to be ploughed as in days of old; proclaiming the Spirit of Propheſie oppoſed, though ſhall prevail, The firſt and the laſt,* in the mean time that begets theſe diſtractions to deſtroy themſelves: The Bottomleſs Pit witneſs, as they term it (or Abyſs) even when heaven opened; the other its poyſonous Fogs as free (*Apoc.* 9.) That Aſſemblies deſcription. *Latine habens nomen exterminans.*

VVhere laſtly, after that ample admonition (of health compared to Heaven, and languiſhing ſickneſs to Hell) by way of Terror, expreſsing the laſt general day of judgement, at hand, with ambition how ſeaſonable; *as his WIVES looking back to Sodom*, *verſ.* as here bidden, *To have*

have ſalt in themſelves, the ſpirit judgement, without which never expect to have other reſt, or to be found in peace at his coming, even to try the ſpirits, &c. each thing in its ſeaſon, ſalt the life being of all things, quinteſſence of the elements, both the good ſpirit reſembles and the bad, the beſt of all things and the worſt, for the dunghil not profitable, otherwiſe nothing ſo pure, to have a diſcerning ſpirit the ſum of all.

VVhere touching the perpetuity of the aforeſaid fire and worm: The old explaining the other; herewith to go forward a Leſſon proper for the age: *And the men that have tranſgreſ-*

ſed

sed (Isaiah the last) *for their worm shall not dye; neither shall their fire be quenched;* as much to say, the latter or last day approach'd: *No more dry bones henceforth, whose worm shall continue or remain in them;* as moreover, *They shall be an abhorring to all flesh,* (to wit) *their intollerable stink able to poyson man and beast, &c.* also of Calenders out of date; but from new Moon to new Moon, from Sabbath to Sabbath, like weekly Bills of mortality.

And so much for this *Habeas Corpus*, or moderating the severity of such places, concerning their enlargement one word, where serves both for the grave and hell, supposed to be without redemption, as from this place such another Abys, saying, *Descidite Maledicti*, aluding to the different seasons,

B the

the life and death of the creature, when the Sun enters into *Aries*, the reviving Spring, and in *Capricorn* VVinters tedious nights *Decembers*, *preparing fuel*, &c. Mat.25. *shadowed under the sheep on the one hand, the goats on the other*, left surprised unawares as the old world by the deluge, *to have oyl in their lamps all*, &c. *when some taken up in the air, changd, in a moment, after the Trumpets loud alarm, others swallowed up by sea and land.*

So again, for his shewing afterward *Every sacrifice shall be seasoned with salt*, bidden to have *Salt and peace*, &c. refers to another passage in the Levitical Law, their Peace-Offerings, *The Priests laying his hand on the head of the Oblation*, as it were at the bar holds up his hand, in behalf of him-

himſelf and the people, under a groſs cloud of ignorance, acknowledging guilty of that creatures ſufferings, ſhadowing forth what they liable unto.

Alſo for ſetting at large the ful meaning of theſe, without needleſs Apology, by way of what tedious objection might require, farther to ſhew the depth and plenitude of this place of Scripture, like the fiery pillars light ſide, and dark toward others, even of its deſcending to Humane Sciences, Divinities Handmayds: a word more from the VVhale to the VVorm, from the Milſtone to the peble, *nothing to be deſpiſed*, as commodious and uſeful the the leaſt as the greateſt, even ſo points to our everlaſting arms, that of material ſalt, or ſulpherous Barrels of powder to be provided that way; alſo the

the endless worm to have match in like readiness: And that fire unquenchable, the flint for another, as before shewd, supposing to quench the Spirit by way of retaliation, our *Capernaums* alarm, or caveat enterd disesteemed other, themselves to be abased as low next door to his doom, *Good for that man had he been unborn, to exalt themselves like those rebels*, gain-saying *CORE* and his fifties rewarded.

And thus in his name, concluding by vertue of his all-sufficent Arm, that fasted forty days, I charge thee thou deaf and dumb foul spirit, wherewith possest from his infancy, &c. thou melancholick spirit, come forth of him, and enter no more into him.

Jubile Lent.

FINIS.

48. *The Bill of Excommunication* (1650; Wing D1979) is reprinted, by permission of the Folger Shakespeare Library, from the clear copy held at the Folger (shelfmark D1979 bd. w. D2010). This copy contains some handwritten notes that may be in Lady Eleanor's hand. The text block of the original measures 140 × 89 mm. Page 38 is misnumbered 39.

Hard-to-read words and handwritten annotations:

title page	Annotations: 'Daniel Rest *&c.* What if Hee tarry till I come'; 'The floods A. 1655 & James reign Caesar August moneths of 56 years / 666 Howers of ye monethe / Have no rest daye nor Night' [transcription]
title page.5–6	Called
6.7	*glad*
15.3	Martyrdom
18.1	*way*
19.17	*hidden*
22.1	*tirus*
22.13	true
27.1	slow, had some
29.15	on them
30.1	*to buy of*
30.18	above
31.8-9	*Heterogenium*
31.19	Fleece, likened for its purity and
32.10	*in his right Hand*
32.11	*anew*
32.19	*He that hath*
35.6	winking
36.6	because
36.12	nakedness
40.1–10	*did flee with other twain covered their face*, crying Moonday, figured in those three solemn Feast-days, *The Passover*, *Pentecost, and that of Tabernacles*, *fall down before him that sate on the Throne*, give up the verdict, *ver.* saying, *Thou hast created all things, and for thy pleasure these were and are created*: Witness, *The Rain-bow Fringe over his head*
40.11	*and*
40.20–21	*The Prophetess his Messenger* / From *White-Hall*, fatal 30 of *January*, *Jubile.*
40	[bottom of page] which daye about [transcription]

The Bill of

Excommunication,

For abolishing henceforth the

SABBATH

C[illegible]

Sunday or *Firstday*.

By the Lady *ELEANOR*.

Apocalips, cap. 1.

Printed in the Year, 164[illegible]

666

Have no rest daye
nor Night

The Bill of
EXCOMMVNICATION
For abolishing henceforth, The Sabbath called Sunday or First day, from the Lady *Eleanor*, (*Apoc. cap.* 1.)

AS shewed by whom (when passed by) in his admonition: *Whom ye ignorantly worship, him shew I unto you*, (*Acts*) so understood of you even alike Prophesies Mistery, especially this Book of *Apocalips*: *The last*, &c. times and seasons preordained bounds, whereof the sum, in season now; of which obtruse Oracle by Her as ensues; a blessing far from every one of you neither; the most Supreme and reserved.

Containing three Articles or Arguments first Prophesie, like

A 2 the

the *Eagle* renewing its ſtrength. Se. condly, of a new Sabbath inſtitu. ted, namely Moonday, *One for Thee*, as it were, *one for Moſes, and one for Elias.* Laſtly, *Of the Lords ſecond coming in the laſt days*, revealed to be, alſo of time, perſons and place, no unneceſſary circumſtances.

The Book ſuperſcribed thus, *Reader and Hearer, both with a bleſ- ſing crown'd, keep the words hereof, for the time is at hand.* ver. a ſufficient Motive.

VVhich paſſages profound till come of full Age, under cuſtody of Metaphors and Figures, by him Se- cretary to the Holy Ghoſt, on this wiſe, under his Hand *Joann.* The grace of God ſignifying, *Anno Dom.* Theſe Viſions vvhen awakened, that

that alone Peace-maker.

Ver. *Iohn to the ſeven Churches, grace and peace from him which was, and which is, and which is to come, and from the ſeven Spirits in preſence of his Throne:* Times voices paſt, preſent and future, bids farewel him, a Father become of many Generations, bearing date the laſt ſeven hundred years, thoſe in the rear next to eternity: *That ſits not on Thrones by hands erected.*

As in the next place *Eaſters* Anniverſary day, the Reſurrections comemoration (*ver.*) *And from Ieſus Chriſt and firſt begotten of the dead, that waſhed us in his Blood, &c.* implying (Ieſus C HR:) even Lord of Sabbaths three, from his reſt; a greater then *Cæſar* ſlain then, or C H: R: either

ther of *Britains* three Isles, stiled Defenders or Saviors, &c. whose Coronations father and son both about *Easter*, *J.* and *C.* those first and last.

And so he cometh he cometh, (*Psal.*) *Let the great Isles be glad thereof, To him be glory and dominion for ages of ages, even so Amen.* (ver.) *A.* and *O.* All and Some, beginning and ending of the *Roman* and *Norman* Tiranny both, also pointing to the Hebrew Language and Greek, Old and New Testament, where the one begins, the other *Finis* subscribes.

And so a brief Remonstrance of whose Sabbath or First day, not only how of late prophaned, but accompanied with a mass of abomination

as

as far as these narrow limits permit.

To steal the hearts of the people, *Absoloms* policy like, consecrated to Maygames and VVakes, when crowding and piping to fall to their Heathen exercises, needs not be awakened, to give ear to these lessons, like him that made *Israel* to sin; such a care had of the people, least weary themselves that way, answerable to those presumptious prefaces annext to Bibles, lest it troublesome either, that except the Revelations Book, and other like least edifying, and such as may be best spared, allowing the rest once a VVeek to be read; Doubtless in process of time, not without an intent to poyson the rest likewise of those living Fountains, by like aspersions.

Pretending

Pretending it only concerns *Rome*, as by their Marginals all upon that Dragon laid and his Red Livery. And thus proceeding with that Ivory Box, dissolv'd those Spirits oderiferous Oyntment alike acceptable, to the world as when she of everlasting memory, afore his Burial then brake the other, no less then before times departure prefiguring the Spirit of Prophesie distilling that dew on *Mount Sion*,&c. a threefold testament importing.

But leaving that, *like to the three measures of meal taken by her, wherein hidden, &c. till the whole leaven'd again return* where left him; after had his ample Salutations signified; Relates by vvhat Authority sets out the insuing Proclamation or summons

ſummons to appear all before the Throne of his reſt.

VVhere ſhews firſt of all when and where (*ver.*) *I John even your Brother, on the Lords day tranſported,* &c. *in the Iſle called Patmos,* &c. as a ſubverter of the VVorld thither exil'd, that Diſciple voyced, He ſhould not dye becauſe of that ambiguous Speech: *If I will he tarry till I come, &c.* Suddenly behinde him like a Trumpet, a great voice; *I am A. and O. the firſt and the laſt,* Affirmative and Negative both, as much to ſay, before Parliaments: *VVhat thou ſeeſt, write,* &c. turned about, who ſaw ſuch a dreadful apparition, the day of Iudgements very likeneſs, ſaying, *I am he that was dead,* &c. the Reſurrections

B voyce

voyce, that posture in, standing in midst of seven golden Candlesticks, the seven Planets in his right hand, bidden dread neither Tyrants Scepter or Jaylors Keys, both are his, Keys of Death and Hell.

As moreover a Books description in Paper, Ivory white, gilt about, bound and brazen clasps in relation thereto, a PEN razen like; The Liquid Sword with two edges coming out of the Standish mouth, even *Revelations* sacred Representations, with its lightning Aspect: a voyce, as many waters, emblem of troublesome times: as the Flood about the midst of such a Century the seventeenth, not unknown, Shepherds advertis'd all, vigilant to be then even from the Lord of Sabbaths presence, (evident)

dent) whoſe eyes like the Moon at full, a flame of fire likened unto, as the Sun in its full ſtrength, his countenance with the ſeven *S*tars or Planets in his right hand: *Saturn, Sol* and *Lunæ,* who fell dead at his feet, he of that new Name *John*; no ſtranger to our Nation, or uncertain Author: The Name given by the Angel to him, laſt of the old Prophets, firſt of the new.

And as for the firſt day of the VVeek become the laſt, ſhadowed out without queſtion by thoſe diſpleaſ'd Laborers, told them the laſt ſhould be firſt, and firſt laſt, (that Reciprocal reply) complained had born the heat of the day, demanded whether unlawful for him to diſpoſe of his proper Goods, when that E-

B 2 venings

venings account finiſhed, a peny to each, amounting to ſeven pence, *&c.* Diſplaying thy ſplendant Locks; O our Sundays Sabbath, our Sunday, our Sunday Sabbath, under a total Eclipſe; O Sabbath, our Sunday our Sunday; as when he hid his face, ſet up that *Epanalepſis* noat of his, told except come forth, not a man would tarry that Night, *&c.*

Thou *Abſolons* Pillar, weep *Pauls* for thy caſhiered day. *Apolo's* Temple, this Dragons Tail, where worſhipped no more, in whoſe Church-yard, ſave-reverence, worſe then burnt by the Hangman, whereas the lap of his Garment cut off *Sauls*, ſmote *Davids* heart, witneſs ſet out thoſe unclean ſeats, there lined with the Scriptures clean through, not

onely

only,but the House of Prayer turnd to School Houses, Ringing with a noise of boys such a charm, *I pray God and God grant we love*; upon any lascivious Poem or Fable, rent in pieces that Name lessoned by others not, but miscalling a Prophet, what befel, doubtless then sellers of Doves (*Simonis Caveat*) deserves the VVhip much better. But in comparison of the rest, like palms of her Hands, and soles of the Feet *Jezebels*, for brevity forborn: So in sweat of thy face, both return to eat Bread and Fish, cry Oynions and Garlick, those Hymns, the Day and thou droven out together.

Apocal.

Apocal. Cap. 2.

As the generality or ſcope of which informs, how much qualified above others, the more adds to their failing in what Point ſoever, ſo ſhews herewith to ſuch an Age abounding with fulneſs: Of the gift of Propheſie added beyond all the reſt for a multiplication.

Thus, where every word hath its weight: *Unto the Angel of the Church of Epheſus*, &c. *I know thy works* (ver.) *Beſides theſe thou ſhalt do no maner of work*, &c. viz. exempted labor implies this Iſlands denomination, derived from the Angels Name, otherwiſe called *England*, containing Biſhopricks about twenty ſeven; Seald with the ſeven Lamps

Lamps or Golden Candlesticks.

VVho although had suffered Martyrdom, disproved them, to wit, Bishops of *Rome* false Prophets, with feigned Miracles had discovered such: Neverthelefs, guilty of no lefs then their first love forsaken, because for a time the gift of Prophesying ceased given, gone totally, whereby gives to understand, not enough to hate where God hates, except love too, whom he loves, who may say they had a Candlestick, *except repent and amend*. As for the seven Stars born, times Antiquity displaying, requires no farther pursuing.

The Prophetical *Oyes* following it to all persons in general shewing, Thus saith the Spirit of Prophesie, *To him that overcometh, endureth*

to

to the end, &c. Stands out the ſtorm, gives them the Sacramental Tree of Life, in the midſt of Paradiſe: The true Vine, the VVord its myſtery ſignified, revealed to be about the midſt of the preſent Century, as from his walking in the midſt of thoſe golden Lamps not onely, but by this Trees ſtanding in the midſt likewiſe, *&c.*

VVhere follows to *Smyrna*'s Angel, down weight, *I know thy works, ſaith the firſt and the laſt, He that was dead*, &c. Again ſounding the Reſurrections alarm, notwithſtanding their poverty, ſaying, *Thou art rich*, by that ſeeming paradox, ſhewing the eſtate of Prophets: The Supreme Authority, difficulties rather kindling, then daunting generous Spirits, ſuch

ſuch as between the Arch-Angel and the Tempter, in Infancy of that Church: ſuch a like bout or diſpute, as (ſometime) about *Moſes* Body, ſo here with the father of falſhood, like blaſphemies the Devils Deputy, breathing out; as informs for caſting out the Holy Ghoſt, (*ver.*) Behold, *The Devil ſhall caſt ſome of you into Priſon, that ye may be tryed,* like *Daniel in the Lyons Den*: which Ambuſcado's and Inquiſitions inhibits to fear them. The Crovvn that none can diſpoſe of, ſuffices the limited ten days, (to wit) the *Jubiles* releaſe or return.

And going herevvith on the Churches Map, or ſeveral Pariſhes by name, in vvhat eſtate it ſtands when reproclaimed, *Make plain the*

C *way,*

way, &c. Even explaind by his Messenger, the very Age or time at hand of his coming.

Thirdly, *To the Angel at Pergamos*, time for them to be let Blood, sends this Challenge from *him with the two edged Sword*, unworthy of their ears, cowards and dastards, as it were, that hide themselves: knows their service and where they abide both, *ver.* where Satans Throne, his Courts were kept, preying daily on widow and fatherless not onely, but their Spiritual Dens also, setting Fornication of both kindes at sale, adding Doctor *Balaam* Excommunicating to make up weight, *curse where should bless*, in such a milde way reproved, *ver.* hath *a few things against them*, none of the

the ſharpeſt VVits or Spirits, yet as of no inferior conſequence; as again, others appointed to viſit priſoners, or rather ſift, *&c.* perſons condemned, in making report contrary to their conſcience, guilty not onely of innocent blood, but have drawn the never departing Sword, inſtruments of it: *Except repent*, may ſay, *They had a dwelling*: will ſhortly try with them, the two edg'd Sword none ſpares: The paper Field, its Exciſion to beware: *He that hath an ear*, &c.

Moreover, *To him that overcomes*, ſtands it out, *ver. Will I give to eat of the hidden Manna.* That Sacramental Cordial for all Maladies, a preſent cure, beyond Chymiſtreſs extolled works, under their Ænigmatick

C 2 terms

terms concealed, equivolent not with this *Unium Necessarium*, this Donative, not of man, but from him, assuring nothing so secret that shall not be discovered, not a little of it failing.

Inlarged thus, *(ver.) I will give him a white stone, therein a new Name written, which no MAN knows but he that receives* : beside the gift extraordinary, of discontinued Prophesie restored, alludes to him, *a Prophet and greater, &c.* His written *NAME*, where so real a demonstration of the aforesaid Immunity and Name, needless further to be insisted on, or for displaying, further quotes of such Antiquity, with their several distinguishing Motto's, figuring *Daniels* reserved visions. And

these

theſe of the *Apocalips*, a *Phænix*, one of great *Babylon*; the other an *Eagle*, taking its flight from *Patmos*, both of a feather, the inſpired Pen: withal ſhewing theſe ſpeaking the *Engliſh* Tongue, with *Hebrew* and *Greek*, either equivolent, preferred to be the Holy Ghoſts Interpreter, diſcovering future things, even ours the Angelical Golden Language: And ſo much for that Super-Philoſophical *Elixir* or multiplying Stone, of ſuch a profound penitrating Nature; this ſecret gift, hearts obdurate, as hardeſt Mettal or Adamant, expels the Old Serpents poyſon, them reduces to a glorified eſtate, others to whom but droſs in compariſon.

The fourth writ ſerved on *Thyatirus*

tirus Angel, so stiled from inspiring their Auditors, *ver. These things saith the Son of God, that hath his eyes like a flame of fire, his feet as fine brass*, viz. The refining VVord, or Spirit of Prophesie, knows their works or laborious service, neither on the decreasing hand.

And thus all to make up their account, against whom notwithstanding *a few things*, whose Angel currant neither, where shews implyed a true Prophet or Prophetess, from a false one mentioned, *Jezebels* Sorceries tollerated and Idolatries: And Father *Balaams* Magick documents confided in, whilest true miracles faithful signs as nothing reputed, though not inferior to *Elias* Spirit, when vanquished *Baals* Priests, with

those

those companies or fifties blown up, and their Commanders, on which Church imposed no other Assessment or Burthen, but exchange of the Sabbath: No more burthens by Porters upon Moondays, no longer a working day, not without a touch of their Mother Priests, namely, those laying in Childebed suffered to Baptize.

From him whose eyes likened to the Moons fiery visage: But to hold fast that *Magna Charta* from the beginning, then *Westminsters* tryal, or *Guild-hall*, of more importance, concerning what attention due, when the holy Ghost commands audience, things to come shews; as here every Church like the days of the week called by name, *&c.* This for another

other addition, not the leaſt, together with the Morning Star, whoſe Patron not as *Lucifer* faln, or mans invention, like a common ſign, but evident manifeſtation of the Spirit, from him the Father of Lights, accompanyed with the Iron Rod: Kingdoms turned upſide down, others like a tottering VVall, unlike Enſigns of Magiſtracy, the Mace, *&c.* expreſly ſignifying withal, for the publiſhing of this News-book, or Revelations. Together with the Preſs, the Art of Printing ſo requiſit, (of late by a Soldier, one free of the Military profeſsion, found out) this exquiſit work, as compared to a Potters Veſſel broken in ſhivers or pieces; Their breaking every Letter (ſo not a little ominous) The

Iron

Iron ſcouring Rod, Pieces or Guns belonging unto, invented by a Monk thoſe Ordnances, the Iron Age foreſhewing therein, *How the powers of heaven ſhaken between them:* foreknows thus all Sciences and Crafts, Liberal and Mechannicks, from the Goldſmith to the Black-ſmith, alſo Heralds and Alumiſts, thoſe myſteries.

And thus of their Angels faln a-ſleep for company: *The Church of Sardis* Angel not found perfect, pro-phane rather, after the former calm way admoniſhed: *Theſe things ſaith he with the ſeven Spirits of God, the ſeven Stars in his right hand,* viz. *Die Lunæ,* The Spiritual day ſaluted with the Reſurrections voice, (*verſ.*) *Be awake,* &c. where Poſſeſsion be-

D ing

ing eleven Points of the Law, *bidden to hold fast*. Not enough; they had the white Garment, or had faith, *Repent*, &c. *I know thy faith*, as much to say, *by thy works*: *He that hath an ear*, &c. be watchfull, plain as the Bellman speaking what hour or time of the Night, (signifying times glass run out) or suffices either to confide in the Name, naming the childe after *Peter*, or the like, as much to the purpose, as their Gossips cup and white sheet. Beggerly Traditions preferring, whereas in times of old among the Kings and Genealogies those, not two of one Name hardly read of.

Sixthly, *Philadelphia's* VVrit, their good Angel saluted, *from him that is* aluding to *Holy and True*: Their name shews, *Had loved them*; though

slow,

slow, had some strength or faith, whose upbrading foes to do Homage at their feet who they are. No more difficult then of this universal Tryal (from which they delivered or escaped) to discern of what nature, stiled the hour of Temptation, strengthned so by the preceding Proofs: *Behold, I come shortly, hold fast that no MAN*, &c. implying, because said, *Of that day and hour none knows*: Therefore such an offence, his comming to be revealed aforehand, as though because the moment of Execution uncertain, therefore the Sessions or Sizes.

VVhere lastly, Of the NAME how called or subscribes, as follows. Shewed them more or less, *They had denyed his Name, and had a few*

D 2 *Names*

Names, &c. inferring not onely their denying Baptiſm, (impoſed on Infants) but the Prophets Name figured from his, *A King and a Prophet, Davids*, ver. *Theſe things ſaith he that hath the keys of David, ſhuts and no MAN opens*, &c. further, *as Seals it with the Croſs*: That *Eloi, Eloi*, &c. ſuppoſed *he called Elias*, by a *Paranomaſia*; as theſe to corroberate the myſtical expreſsions of the Prophets Name, witneſs, *ver. And I will make him a Pillar in the Temple of my God, and will write upon him the Name of God, and of the City of my God, coming down from my God.*

So take all, Crown and Keys both, a better Title whoſo ſhews, with New *Jeruſalem*; whoſe Name of old called *Elia*, that *Homonymia*

for

for another. *Eli-Amor vincet*, That all things indures. For the everlasting Diadem, worth the holding fast, *Je Le Tien*.

Lastly, with *Amen* who begins, *These things saith he*, &c. *Unto the Angel of the Church of the Laodiceans*: To whom a short Sermon also, as much Ears as their Candlestick, *Neither cold nor hot*: Even *Pauls* with its Aspiring fired Steeple, and their *Amens* hallowed out, naked and filthy both: Though carry his Name that Apostle, none of his Spirit upon them, after the cold fit off, as violently hot: Confesses was afore exceeding mad.

These Hour-glass Doctors how fervent aludes to Alcumists, glass Stills or Limbecks, knows their Luke-warm

warm temper, *I counsel thee to buy of me gold tryed in the fire, and white rayment,* &c. *and eye salve* : pointing both to Buying and Selling those places : Also better seen in *Plato* and *Hypocrates*, then in the Prophets or Apostles, whose arrogancy begetting incurable blindeness : likened to them taken with a vomiting commonly, as in Agues, shortly come to be spewed or discharged, loathsomest of all other : By their Sophism laboring to anoint with the Spirit of ignorance : Fruit of their stale Orations, what Tyrant Custom Priviledges, or for their own pleasure or benefit, best serves. Unto that given in the same hour, above violence or robberies reach that treasure. Strangers and Forreigners

ought

ought to have bought rather the o-ther permanent. Then arrayed in that rag of Heathenism: Hypocrasies Livery, by whom so different from the expedition wherewith the Spirit writes, (witness) have with mixture, like VVater put into VVine agrees as well: Intermingled senceless *Heterogenium* Parenthesis, but answer-able to faultless Marginals as poor.

And these no times to sleep in, or secure, with no flattering Pensil, or falsifying Pen, inhibited neither Sex to unsheath that two edged Sword, where portrayed from head to foot both: *The World, the great MAN, and the Word, whose hornible Throne, the Creations Fabrick*, for the snowy Fleece, likened for its purity and soft-ness: So many Lights about it: The Elements

Elements, those Coats of Antiquity displaying: *Like a flame of fire his eyes*: *Out of his mouth like the piercing ayr, a voice as waters, such a noise*: *The footstool earth as dumb, likened to brass*, those veins Mines rings out precious times adieu or lamentation, like those extinguisht Lights, so many Candlesticks signified by: *Signed with the seven Stars in his right Hand, even like the old garments drest anew, Heavens and Earth ready to vanish*: VVhereof so much for manifestation, though much more affords touching the Title and Reign of a Prophet over this Kingdom, to put al rule under his own feet, even when altogether by the Ears; as much to say, *He that hath an ear, Then*, &c. Shut up so long under no ordinary

Locks,

Locks on this wise set on, by unlucky Door keepers, of whose providing: Behold, like to have a warm Supper: Their leavings at Noon, understood like the rest, &c. their own Suppers like laid aside: Informing, he as commanded to say, *I am hath sent me*, &c. So here again, *which was, which is, and which is to come*, commanded these things to be written unto you, from *A*. and *O*. *He that hath an ear*: After the vulgar strain: *To our loving Friend, at the Angel or Sign of the Crown*, &c. *with speed these, subscribed yours*, &c. *Da: & Do: These are to let you understand: so trusting shortly*, &c. *bears date, Anno* &c. The Sabbath or Resurrections witness, sealed with the seven Tapers: First, to *Westminsters*

E Church,

Church, expressing without vigilancy, the rest but all void. As secondly, with the Keys, testifying these, saith, *He that was dead*, &c. For the Holy Ghosts cause them put into the Gate-House, forbidden to fear those infernal furies. So thirdly, Those Advocates maintaining any Title or Cause: To Iudicature Courts at *Westminster-Hall*. The Sword of Iustice, with intrusted: By *Balaams* example, Bryberies snare, to flee or to beware: Signed with the Swords point two edged, pointing to the Throne of Tyrants, lest pride receive a fall.

To redeem the time, spurring on to repentance, whose all-searching eyes, *likened to flames of fire, and feet like brass*, Sign of the Gun: The Cities

Cities Church, *Peters*. Fourthly, its warning piece, for cleansing or scouring their Lodgings, those Common Sewers or Stews. Also, to *White-Hall* Chappel, to make clean theirs, winking at the like, willed to be awake, *&c*. have regard to a good Name, under colour of late meetings, lest pollute themselves.

And thus according to the signs born under, here to that ensign worn out at Elbows: Every one in his order addes to the seven Stars Impression: *The seven Spirits, those before the Throne*: The wedding Garment, that Robe not to defer it.

To the House of Parliament, Sixthly, *Thus saith he that is Holy, an open door that hath set before them, &c.* Prophesie discontinued Parliaments, both

E 2

both under a notion : *Have kept the WORD,* wherefore escape that stumbling block of the Sabbaths change : Also knows the work of their Hangings, shews, *I will make a Pillar, &c.* becaus● a little strength in them. Lastly, with their lowd *Amen*, the Sabbath witness : To *Pauls*, with its Church-yard Drapers, what lack ye : *Buy of him white rayment*, that the filthiness of their nakedness appear not, all to be rayed in plain English, fitter for to selt sackcloth, more in season : remove those offices out of the *House of Prayer* : And thus knows all their Parishes, how many within the VValls, *&c.* as though had lost either their keys or ears, *that let him to stand without or knock*, who (however flatter themselves)

ſelves) ſerves them thereafter.

And knocking here louder and louder, *like the Trumpet on Mount Sinai*, concludes with this Royal Patent, as formerly declares, received of his Father, *The morning Star, &c.* with a touch given of their Morning Suppers: *So again to him that overcometh, will I grant to ſit on my Throne at my right hand, or reſt, even as I overcame, and ſate with my Father, &c.* as much to ſay, That maintains the cauſe witneſſed with the Prophets awakened Viſions, like her Son, who opened his eyes, ſeven times ſneezed, came out of his long ſleep: So even preſcribed the preſent Century, whenas out of that *Chaos* or *Hyle*, its quinteſſence comes to be extracted: Through the Holy Spi-

rits

rits Co-operation, wherewith at first written, ordains for it a day of acknowledgement or remembrance.

VVhere lastly, for these Allegory Doors, both of entrance and utterance, his messengers knocking thereat early and late, *He that hath an ear, &c. Behold, comes shortly, at the door, &c.* so much for that: That cannot be accounted but long: That *day and hour*, to be so much longed for, and for this no small favor to shew the Door, only this Postscript by the way, *cap.* 4.

Post hæc vidi ecce ostium apertum in Cœlo, &c.

VVitness, the Trumpets voice, a door or passage no longer shut, *ver. Come up hither, and I will shew thee*

thing*s*

things to come to paſs, &c, *As imme-diately ſaw about the Throne, be hold-ing thoſe precious Tables, like a Book open*, the Grand Iury ſet: All ſeting forth a reſt day, even the fourth Commandment, *the four faced four beaſts*, eye witneſſes, teſtifie no leſs: *Where like as when the Law given, like Lightnings, Thundrings, and Voyces, proceeding out of the Throne*, accompanying the Trumpet with their diſplaying Colours, or En-ſigns, pouthered *full of eyes before and behinde, reſt not day nor night, which was, and which is, and which is to come: Holy, holy, holy, another reſt day, &c.* agreeing with that of *Iſaiah, When the poſts of that door ſhaken, the Sera-phims diſplaying thoſe wings of theirs, with twain covered his feet, with twain*

did

did flee, with other [illegible] *their face,* crying Moonday [illegible] *in* those three solemn Feasts [illegible] *The Passover, Pentecost, and that of* [illegible] *nacles, fall down before him that* [illegible] *on the Throne,* give up the verdict [illegible] saying, *Thou hast created all* [illegible] *and for thy pleasure these were* [illegible] *created:* VVitness, *The Rain-bow Fringe over his* [illegible]*, before him the emrald Earth, his Cushion;* [illegible] *fire and ayr, those burning Lamps and Spirits, &c.* The Chrystial *Ocean Sand* his Hour-glass, with hours 24, and four seasons: The Conquest four and twenty, in their old Cathedral way prostrate, making such low obeysance in white, &c. say all glory be to the Holy Ghost also.

The Prophetess his Messenger

From *White-Hall,* fatal 30 of *January, Jubile.*

FINIS.

wch Daye abov[illegible]

49. *The Appearance or Presence Of The Son of Man* (1650; Wing D1972A) is reprinted, by permission of the Folger Shakespeare Library, from the unique but incomplete copy held at the Folger (shelfmark D1972.45 bd. w. D2010). This copy contains some handwritten notes and corrections that may be in Lady Eleanor's hand. The text block of the original measures 140 × 87 mm.

For hard-to-read words and handwritten annotations, see page 423 following this text

THE
APPEARANCE or *PRESENCE*
OF THE
Son of Man.

P S A L. 48.

Thy right hand is full of righteousness, Let Mount Sion rejoyce, and the daughters of Iuda be glad, because of thy Iudgements.

Printed in the Year, 1650.

Even as I received of my Father, &c. *He that hath an ear let him hear.*

AND proceeding herewith in another place what he saith, *who had not concealed it were it otherwise; That in his Fathers House were many mansions*: reserv'd Mysteries, all revealed not at once, as much to say, [redacted] reiterated so: even *He that hath an ear* (to wit) on pain or peril of his head, &c.

Proclaiming no other then the Supreme Order or Authority, their unlimitted Commission * The Spirit after absent so long, how (as it were) *stands knocking at the door*: whereof

* That w.ch is from the Begining; Things befo Hand shewn

whereof these the sum or substance of no inferior consequence: A greater then the Conquerer, Parliaments Prerogative not exempted: saying, *To him that overcomes, and keeps my works unto the end, I will give power over the Nations, shall rule them with a rod of iron*: His insulting Enemies necks made his footstool.

Who speaks the word of the Lord, and done it is: Those Heathen-Potentates, but like to Potters brittle Vessels broken in pieces, scattered, suddenly a Printers Press like. As the aforesaid herewith consenting shews expresly (*Psalm*) *The Lord said, Sit thou on my right hand, until I make thine Enemy*, &c. *shall send the rod of thy power out of Sion, B*

tho

thou ruler, &c. And ſo much for this the prophetical everlaſting Order.

VVhoſe Priſon-commons put into the reckoning, *In the days of thy trouble* (ſaying) *ſhall the people offer thee free-will-offerings*, &c. Bread (to ſay) for the Lords ſake, and running-water: *Therefore ſhall be lift up thy head: The Lord thy keeper, hell gates ſhall not prevail againſt her:* and clear truths as Noon-day, not unknown come to paſs: Notwithſtanding by you, *As for this Moſes we wot not what is become of him:* with one conſent afraid all to come nigh him, terrified with them, becauſe of that luſture on his viſſage, *&c.* The two renewed Tables coming down with in his hand: Shadow-

Shadowed out directly in those revived VVitnesses two (*Revel.* 11.) when supposed to have heard no more news of them: Those lights deem'd had utterly been extinguished, like to the day of Iudgement, when those rebels at the same time swept away in that cities earthquake: And sacrificing all to your own inventions, how requisite some real Demonstration then extraordinary, such unruly winds, where broken loose Trees whose fruit withers: Not for ought good without applyed means supernatural, not to be tamed or ordered: Even appointed this anointing faithful and true saying: These from her overshadowed with the same hand, as he *Aarons* god

god that was ordained, like Beams of Divinity participating, and Oyls odirefferous, an Elixer not of man or flesh and blood: *She whose Throne heaven, earth her footstool from the uncreated,* saying, *I am A. and O. first and last, both beginning and ending, by whom all things were done: Not without her any thing done or made; Trinity in Unity, of Manhood the head: Who of Death have the Keys and Hell: Then the Queen of the South a greater, born a greater not of Women: Melea,* by Interpretation, *Queen of Peace,* or She-councellor. And so much for this without contradiction, she his Executor, *Made like unto the Son of God,* the ancient of days likeness: owner of that Title of Tythes, to whom the Patriarch

a compoun
of his Nam
Melchisedec

arch offered a Tenth, from the ſlaughter being returned of thoſe Kings; preceding that Cities day of Iudgement prefiguring the final; for which interceding none might avail: *Even the Lord upon her right hand, wounding even Kings in the day of his wrath; judging among the Heathen: Heads of divers Countreys ſmiting aſſunder:* ~~ſuch headſhips of the Church~~, of ſuch no more.

And weak ſights [redacted] leſt offended overcome with light, for quallifying the ſaid Deity, or to moderate the ſame. *Imprimis*, firſt and formoſt ſaying I am *A.* and *O. alias, Da:* and *Do:* by her firſt and laſt marriage ſo ſubſcribes, that beginning and ending *Dowger*, &c. in the next thus. *Item*, Daughter of *Audeleigh*

Audleigh, or *Oldfield*, in the *Saxon* Tongue, [redacted] no created Peership: a *Saxon* Baron afore the Conquest, As unto this day, preferring the act of time Antiquity, before Titles subject to be reversd; and so far for that beginning and ending, of Kings and House of Lords.

Also Baron *Touchet* of *France*, *Castlehaven* in *Ireland*, *Douglas* of *Scotland*: Honors three, consisting in a fourth, *Audeley*: Of those Nations no obscure Denominations, which late ruined old house of this Kingdoms fall a forerunner, *Je Le Tien* its Motto, *Hold fast till I come* (*Rev. &c.*) a derivative therefrom: like unto the Tabernacles work to a loop, and holy Garments or Coats adorned with several pre-

B cious

cious Stones, following that patern in their true fiery colours, display'd, ~~consuming dross, as a Refiners fire,~~ ~~like~~ of whose discent, Genealogy of his noble Prophets no novelty to be kept, suffices so much in refference to the Morning-Star, usher of the day: That honor received from him, giving the seven Stars or Plannets: The Creations coat, arms born: By vertue hereof, (*ver.*) *He that keeps my works unto the end, as I received of my Father*, &c. ~~whom~~ invincible Prophets, his followers with whom no shrinking or back-drawing, till they have made it good: so much for their Charge.

VVhere lastly, by consequence, Heaven how comes to be her Ioyn-

Ioynture, place, being no unneceſſary circumſtance thus going on: Thou *Bethlehem* or *Berkshire*, not the leaſt, firſt of Counties: Even ſhewing the words of the moſt high God, at *Englefield* Mannor-Houſe: That Morning-Salutation for ever bleſt, where that voyce came unto her, ſpeaking down as through a Trumpet, theſe words.

Saying, *There is Nineteen years and half to the Judgement day, And you as the meek Virgin.*

VVhere farther, by way of Priority thus walking about *Sion*, counting her Towers, thoſe Right-hand years, in the firſt of his Reign, *A°* 1625. firſt of his name of theſe Dominions, moneth

July, 28. so after the first *Roman* Emperor called: He slain, &c. shewing not to vulgar apprehensions difficult, in this Cosmographical Table of New Heaven and Earth: How under the Gallery of the aforesaid *Englefield*-House, where awakened with that unexpected Alarm in English: The VVestern Road lies a Thorowfare under a high Arch for Travellers: Also a place called Hell of old, a Mile or two distant therefrom, full of pits within the royalties: The Harbor of such decrepid with age, and their Associates blinde and halt, craving relief nigh the Highway-side, no Critick observation in the County of *HARTFORD*: whose Ioynture the Manor of *Pyreton*

lh manor
old awaye
the E: of
untingdon
bought by
Marques
Winiegster
d gime nate
it hath
ved wth
uis Ashbey House: & Bakengr

Pyreton (fire in Greek) consisting of a Tythe or Impropriation, shews *A°* 48. the same year of that Kings slaughter or execution: she restored *Trinity* Term put into Possession of the said Tythe: By the Sheriff a VVrit *Moveas Manus*, by vertue of it, to that Patriarch, sometime appertaining Abbot of St. *Albons*: sold away *A°* 33. in the days of her durance, not difficult a little to regain it; the oftner Argued, the more Ambiguous, until by the Barons of Exchequer, in writing the same appointed to be put down; so Intricate, *&c.* Of which holy Appurtenances Consecrated, things too exactly which cannot be observed, *A°* 1625. Since when, not any thing acted or come to pass:

From

Her Rela portion

From *Germanies* Deſolations, *Ro-chels* Siege, until *Irelands* Blow, and what ſince followed; like one waves purſuing another, forerunners of the moments great change and general Iudgement, [redacted]: even which Paſſages not unforeſhewed by her hand, together with the aforeſaid Golden Number of *Nineteen years and a half to A° 1644.* extending [redacted] his *January* Account not onely, but the late *Charls* when became a priſoner, *Nazeby*, &c. That day of Iudgement, A° 45. current; afterward taſting of the ſaid fatal Moneths cold Cup: as *Buckinghams* Auguſt Moneth, him foreſhewed, whereupon (boading to that Nation a laſh) ſhe wan

that

that wager to his ſmart: The typifying Breeches of the *Sotch* man her Husband, againſt ſuch wimzes of hers who laid them, as he then termed it, paſsing not ſcotfree, &c.

And theſe with other like, a world not able to contain them: alſo this for another, 1647. by the ſame token that Night a bold Star facing the Moon (April. 2.) paſſed through her Body, at which time ſerved that VVrit, bearing date the ſecond of April: *I ſend thee to a rebellious houſe, &c. Ezek.* 2. and *cap.* 12. ſhe prefixing *Penticoſt* enſuing, as when ſuch a mighty ruſhing wind, to beware them like as when they all aſſembled, &c. witneſs *Southwark*: That Mornings gheſts unexpected accompanied with ſuch

a Thuna Thunder-clap from above, and darkness: To the upper House a warning piece their discharge.

And lastly, a second like unto it, witness, 1650 July Jubile, that judgement by fire in *Holborn*, and other parts of the City: Instantly in the same week she cast out of her lawful possession of *Englefield*, by that Counties Sheriff, being by due course of Law put into the same: But in the VVhitson-week, the like unheard without being impleaded: for the same Sheriff with pistols and VVeapons to break up doors, done as he said by a mighty power: All he had to say for himself, authorized by Committees Order, for swallowing a VVidows Estate up, after that maner: And fasting, under pretences,

Skirmish By sea from Johns fishing with

[49. *The Appearance or Presence Of The Son of Man*]

Hard-to-read words and handwritten annotations:

title page	extensive handwritten gloss but largely illegible: 'As the fat[her] justifying the Sonn: the sonn likew[ise] justifies He [ ] Hee the Im[age] of God: Sh[ ] The sonn o[f] mans &c. both one w[ho] dispises Them dispises Him & so Him & and His father both [ ].' [transcription]
3.10–12	Men therefore left without excuse: of the iron rod the Ax bid beware, reiterated so
3.16–19	That which was from the Beginning; Things before Hand shews [transcription]
4.17	*Lord*
4.18	*until*
4.19	*send,*
4.20	*Be*
7.14–16	a compound of His Name Melchisedec [transcription]
8.10–11	such headships of the Church
8.12	moreover
9.2	also
10.2	colours
10.3–4	consuming dross, a Refiners fire, like
10.14	whom
11.5	words
11.11–13	Even Mene Mene & [transcription]
11.17	of
12.9–20	handwritten gloss: '[ ]th maner [s]old away the E: of [H]untingdon bought by ... Marques [of] Winchester [a]nd since made [an] Example ... it hath [f]ired with [th]eirs Ashbey House: & Bazeing Towers'. [transcription]
13.3–6	Her Held portion [transcription]
13.12	Argued, the
14.6–7	when persons or Sex; without such respects:
14.12	to Laud [transcription]
14.13–20	handwritten gloss in margin: '[ ]an: the stone cut out wthout Hands. not all frustrat Malachi all the prophet refreshing and watch all etc. Peter appearing of ... Lord &c.' [transcription] handwritten gloss at bottom of page: 'Acts and a prophet like mee' '... shall not see him 'till Blessed. etc. And Elijah restoring all things Husbandmen'. [transcription]
15.1–20	largely illegible gloss in margin: 'Imprimis Dr. Giffords wife so ma[ ] for many y[ ] presently [ ] perfectely [ ] Item captain m[ ] Item Mr. Jandey so long in [ ] &c. Item cast. out of a [ ] att Rattle [ ] a dumb possest' [transcription] gloss at bottom of page: 'And att supper time Hee sent out a servant a crye att midnight Hee y^{t} Hath an Eare'[transcription]
15.11	served that
16	largely illegible gloss in margin: 'after Her [hus]band ... Dowglas [ ] strikne maddnes' [transcription]

50. *Before the Lords second coming* (1650; Wing D1974) is reprinted, by permission of the Folger Shakespeare Library, from the clear copy held at the Folger (shelfmark D1974 bd. w. D2010). This copy contains some handwritten notes that may be in Lady Eleanor's hand. The text block of the original measures 140 × 92 mm.

Hard-to-read words and handwritten annotations:

title page	lengthy handwritten annotation, parts of which have been crossed out by hand. The legible sections read as follows: Which Ro[ ] Him *&c.* Imp[ ] points to ascentions revela. cap ... present Jul[y] moneths [ ] Septemb: 3 Decemb. Blowe the woe pas[ ]. Thes as giv[en] understand Latin *&* [c.] other to [ ] Et milla terre ... *&c.* Septe[ ] *&c.* Septem' [transcription]
title page.8	*A*
3.7–9	Brethren of these distracted Dominions, hereof in a word without
3.8	prophesye [transcription]
3.12	bathe an Ethiopian,
4.13–14	disposed daily for [transcription]
5.13	scern
5.17–20	*whatsoever they pray, Thy Kingdom come say in their hearts, Torment us not before our time* [transcription]
6.17	10.) of
6.20	precious
9.21	as [transcription]
10.1	as [transcription]
10.1–2	Aquila also pointing to the North: [transcription]
10.15	interr'd, where three days and half
10.18	forty two, theirs contributing thereto
12.14	the letters 'th' crossed out by hand in the printed word 'forth' [transcription]
14.1	teach
14.10	pricking
14.13	anointing
14.13	Here [transcription]
15.1–3	durance undergone, since then when deem'd impossibilities or distraction.
16.1	diction, *Blessed are they …Com*
16.2	*mandment*
16.6	twelve of
16.11	*buy*
16.12	*the Beast*, &c. alike
16.13	ving the
16.15	dain'd (even) upon pain of Death.

Before the *Lords* second coming. 32

OF

The last Days

To be visited,

Signed with the Tyrant *Pharaohs* Overthrow.

ACTS 3. 22, 23.

A Prophet shall the Lord your God raise up unto you of your Brethren, like unto me, &c. And it shall come to pass, Every soul which will not hear that prophet, shalbe destroyed among the people.

Printed in the year 1650.

Before the Lords second coming

[illegible]

Three Days

To be wished

[illegible] agreed with the Tyrant Pharaoh

[illegible]

[illegible]

[illegible] the Lord [illegible]

[illegible]

Printed in the yeare [illegible]

The most Mighty his Messenger, ELEANOR DOUGLAS, *Dowger; Daughter of Lo:* Audeley, *Lo:* Touchet, *E: of* Castlehaven:

To them of *England*, *France*, *Scotland*. *Ireland* and *Wales*;

BRethren of these distracted Dominions, hereof in a word, without which, that tryed Gold in the fire coveted, and whitened Rayment, eye-salve, of that sort or anointing, do but [redacted]Ethiopian, spur *Balaams* ass, since other Balm or way none beside, when have tryed all, but by the word to try the Spirits, whether counterfeit or current, Scriptures to search, those Mines, a business worthy of as serious dispute as whatsoever: namely, wheher for blaspheming against the holy

A 2 Ghost

Ghoſt hath not brought upon us this judgement unexpected, wherein delay no leſs perillous then heretofore pernicious, untimely taſting that paparadice fruit, whoſe precious gates when as come to paſs ſet open, The chryſtal flovving living fountain to all paſſengers free, ſuppoſed to have been dryed up: The reſerved Tree of Life likewiſe given gone, monthly rendring its golden Largeſs, attain'd not to its maturity till now: whoſe wholſom leaves [redacted] for aſſwaging the Nations feſtered wounds aſsign'd, ſo requiſite thoſe Supernaturals againſt unnatural waged wars: Theſe not the firſt time preſſed, But *Gallio* cared for none of theſe matters, (*Acts* 18.) although deny the holy Ghoſt; by conſequence: The Lord

that

that bought them. Moreover accompanied with frequent Blaſphemies, by the Trade called *Religion* ſet abroach, Scriptures not more in thraldom to *Romaniſts*, their ſtate of Ignorance, then the holy Ghoſt endeavored to be enſlaved (Arrogancy the worſt) by them ſtiled *Our Reformers and Deliverancers*, diſtraction of no common conſequence, deſtructive to concord among Brethren-Nations, in their Brothers eye narrowly obſerv'd, diſcern a mote: Execrable Opinions theirs, nevertheleſs a Beam ſuch a mountain in their own, eſteems it not conſiderable: Foes of our grand Freedoms and Liberties, [redacted]; not onely intrenched *Sion* about

bout, have ſcaled new *Jeruſalems* wals, undermined her Bulwarks: But out-ſtripping Savages of late have ſlain moſt barbarouſly our tvvo Sacred Ambaſſadors, Thoſe VVitneſſes as impeached (*Revel.*11.) The laſt days, whoſe Ringleader the foul Beaſt aſcended out of the Abyſs, by undeniable evidence charg'd with the gift of Prophecies Lamp extinguiſht, troden under foot that holy City, &c. exchang'd for their gifts ſent one to another, or Symony, triumphing over their corps, becauſe tormented them with their publiſhed Commiſsion, teſtified that ſolemn Oath taken, (*Rev.* 10.) of Tyrant times being cut off, and unhappy generation, ſuch to be no more.

And ſo much for theſe precious paſſa-

passages, all plainly speaking of Prophecies return or resurrection, like the Eagles renewing her strength, immunities not inferior to former times, withal informing what Mutiniers in Court and City, against these 2 books in special of the Prophets, *Daniel* and *John*, both which men revived but by a touch, &c. the one continuing until King *Cyrus*, the other until the Cities destruction, Types and Figures before the Churches Deliverance time: How long in captivity under Tyrants, Lawless wretches, not unlike those ruines of the Temple, darksom uninhabited Vauts in the possession of Owls and their Mates, whose Houses and Riches become their Heaven and god.

And so come to Times Mystery, his

his golden Hour-glass, whereof thus, (*Revel*.11.) he where bidden to arise, &c. his casting it up to be forty two Moneths, in short as much to say, By three yeers and a half, pointing to the number of Seven, extends not onely to the Seventeenth Century, but expresly to the present *Jubile*, from that moiety or dividing of Time, so over and over prest by those sealed VVrits of theirs: The Prophet *Daniel* his multiplyed weeks, as informs, saying Seven weeks, and Seventy weeks are determined, &c. And in the midst of the week, &c, but several voyces all in one, expressing the aforesaid *Jubile* or fiftieth yeer, appointed that of pardon, whereof our Lord on this wise, *It is impossible but that offences will come*, (Luke 17.) *But wo unto him*, &c.

&c. no leſs then *Great Britains* neck-Verſe, that ſhall offend one of theſe, ſtiled *his Little ones*, a Mill-ſtone then other Ornament more proper for ſuch a one, as in reference hereto, bears date even his laſt return (*an.* 49.) ſeven times ſeven. *And if he treſpaſs againſt thee ſeven times in a day, and ſeven times in a day turn again, thou ſhalt forgive (or receive) him:* bear witnes the Diſciples, *Lord increaſe our Faith*, to wit, Defenders of the Faith ſtiled, never at ſo low an ebb, as that ſure Oracle replyed, *had they Faith as a grain of muſtard, &c.* Need not fear the day of Iudgement tydings, or *Worſt of Tyrants* concluding it, how faring with them when the Son of Man revealed, *verſ.*24. one taken the other left, demanded where Lord ſuch Maſſacre, and woful wars

B refers

quite
also
pointing
to the
North:

(refers them to the Roman Ensign, the Eagle, where the corps, &c. ^+^

And so much for this, be it known to all, *Touch not mine anointed*, *do my Prophets no harm*, with a touch of Times week its Mystery, the most Supreme, set at nought for Onions and Garlick, those anointings in sted of *Canaans* Grapes and Olives, by *Oxford Naamans*, are not the Rivers of *Damascus* better?

So proceeding with *Sodoms* Map of those two Prophets crucified, exposed like some Malefactors not suffered to be interr'd, where three days and half (and years) beside sounding the general Resurrections Alarm, Months forty two, theirs contributing thereto, for a time, times, and dividing of Time, with one consent crown the Seventeenth

teenth Century, 500 years fulfilling a period, ſhadow'd under Hyerglypick figures, how honor'd the Spirit of prophecy then powred out, as by thoſe two in Sackcloth Liveries, their agreeing in one, and them whoſo hurts or diſhonors with untimely death repaid, fire proceeding out of their mouths.

At whoſe word (that wine) VVaters turned into Blood, VVars foreſhewed, reſtrain the Heavens, ſmite the Earth vvith Plagues as often as they pleaſe, ſtiled *The two Olive Trees*, and *Two Candleſticks*, expelling darkneſs; the healing nature of Oyl not unknown, requires no farther amplification, ſhewed to be the Books of the greatly beloved Man, and that Diſciple whom the Lord loved: So, *Come, ſaith the Spirit*, and *Come, ſaith the*

B 2 *Bride*,

Bride, and thoſe will take *gratis* : and *If any man take away*, &c. for I teſtifie unto every MAN: Leſt the laſt Error worſe then the firſt, when the bad Spirit tempting, and the woman.

Thus paſsing on, when the Spirit powred out a paſſage when opened in Heaven, the Holy Prophets giving thanks, the time come of their awakening, opened alſo the gates of Hell; ſuch an uprore about Father Times being cut off, thoſe tydings the City ſetting on fire, the Nations ſtung, their time come for[illegible]to be judged, (*Rev.*) the Devil wilde for company, loſes no time by Sea and Land, becauſe his but ſhort greatly wrath.

On all ſides thus, how the Myſtery abounds of Iniquity, witnes our wandring Stars, viſible in this horrible

Age,

Age, so many though charg'd with abusing their Tolleration or Liberty of conscience: no wonder, when higher Powers express no better use made of theirs, then by leasing and scoffing to abuse the Holy Ghosts long-suffering, of vvhose Apostacy and Erroneous actings, extending to delay of the day of Iudgment, not sensible of our entrance thereinto: And detaining the Kingdom of Heaven from the true owners, By reason of certain Reserves or doubtful Speeches, matter of Reality failing, our fluent *Tertullus's* inform: Because said, *Of the day and hour knows no man*, and to Thieves approach likened by night; hold forth, need not be beholding, or farther consolation expected for *Sion*, that fear causless, lest set at nought their Trade, no farther

ther watch requisite, teach the good man of the house may take his ease, (*Mat.* 24.) as upon that mistake went abroad of that Disciples not dying, taken for a second *Elias*, *Joh*. &c. Because of the conceal'd day and hour, which matters not: Go on in deferring amendment, sufficient tokens come forth of the last Day, though pricking the hearts of very Iews.

Of which store not all expended, *Aarons* distillings, or her renowmed anointing to the end of the world, Here tendred not by way of ostentation or self-ends, seasonable as looking towards *Sodom*: Shewing How extant on Record in several Courts since *an*.1633. and afore to a year, a Month, and the very day, under her hand, foreshewed matters then of highest nature of late executed

as

as by ſo many years diſtance under-gone, ſince then when deem'd impoſſibilities or diſtraction.

As farther, by credible perſons to be teſtified, no few about the City, how accompanied with Miracles no inferior ones: Beſide Devils, alſo dumb Spirits caſt out, moſt outrageous of all other, with as ample commiſsion and convincing teſtimony, as ever *Moſes* and *Elias*, if not a greater, except the Age become more deaf or unmoveable then that pillar of Salt, *Lots* metamorphoſed wife, her Execution ſign, or then our *Wyldſhires* ſtonage wonder, as proper for *Pharaohs* of theſe days.

And as cloſes (diſplaying his pedegree off-ſpring of the Prophet *David*, ſaying, *I come ſhortly*) with that Benediction,

ction ; *Blessed are they that do his Commandments*, that they may have right to the Tree of Life, whose Leaf withers not or changes : And may enter in through those everlasting gates, twelve of the new City, so Monethly Humiliations and other like Superstitions observ'd, no other then (*Dan.*3.) when ye hear the sound, &c. *Whoso falleth not down*, &c. and *If any man buy or sell ; save he that hath the mark of the Beast*, &c. alike acceptable, leaving the other undone, (to be excommunicated with Dogs, &c.) Be it ordained (even) upon pain of Death.

Deo sit gloria, &c.

From the Queens Bench.
2 September, &c.

F I N I S.

51. *Elijah the Tishbite's Supplication When Presented the likeness of a Hand, &c. (Kings 18.)* (1650; Wing D1985) is reprinted, by permission of the Folger Shakespeare Library, from the clear copy held at the Folger (shelfmark D1985 bd. w. D2010). This copy contains some handwritten notes that may be in Lady Eleanor's hand. The text block of the original measures 147 × 93 mm.

Hard-to-read words and handwritten annotations:

title page. 5	was [transcription]
title page.6	a [transcription]
title page.6	for a present [transcription]
title page.7	as Likewise this Hand or monster Foot [transcription]
title page	remaining marginalia read: '(Dan.9) Abominal Armey ... (or ... in ye original' [transcription]
3.4	Heaven?
3.10	Thou [transcription]
3.14	witness B so many B August 23: 1651 That Thunder &c. [transcription]
4.2	*Babel*
4.1–4	1651 As Mr. Love &c.: [transcription]
6.19	printed word "also" crossed out by hand [transcription]
8.3–7	1651 [ ]anished & this sold att Chelsye &c. [transcription]

ELIJAH

THE

TISHBITE's

SUPPLICATION

When was

Preſented the likeneſs of a *Hand*, &c. for a preſe

(*Kings* 18.)

as Likewise this Hand or monster Foot

MARK 13. (Dan: 9)

But when ye ſhall ſee the Abomination Abomingi
of Deſolation (or maketh deſolate) Armey
ſpoken of by Daniel the Prophet, (or
ſtanding where it ought not; Let him wing
that readeth underſtand, &c.

Printed in the Year 1650. in ye original

Elias Interceſsion preferr'd.

O Lord of Hoſts our God, *How long thou Lord of Sabbaths*, thus ſhall ſilence be in Heaven? How long whileſt they ſuppoſe *like their ſitting Gods* thou likewiſe *faln aſleep*, ſlumbreſt, or heareſt not at all; as theirs *purſuing the Enemy, or on a march*; thy thundring Voyce refrain no longer: O this day be it known That art God, I beſeech thee, I thy Servant alſo, hear me for thy VVords ſake, above all haſten to Anſwer, hear me, bidden in thy Name but ask *Fire, fire, from the Wheels of thy Seraphin Throne*, vouchſafe the light of thy preſence, a ſpark thence to lick up at once or Reconcile (a Deluge ſuch of Diviſions) threatning no leſs then quenching Celeſtial flames; Thy Incenſe ſmoke

A to

1651 As mr Love &c:

to extinguish thus arm'd to re-edifie *Babel*-Rout theseGyants then as fared with those false Prophets both of one Spirit, Lo crying from morning to night too, *Let none escape either*, despising not the Birthright onely (sure Promises) But where thou blessest, filling up with inveterate hatred the measure of such Long-suffering, the VVorld, made believe thy Spirit confined in the Hemisphere of their Studies; That the *Jews* how much blest, uncalled in such revolted times, where beside Confusions Mark set on the Age present, confounded alike as that first Generation after the flood, their aspiring Towers Erecting when scattered, whether then turned *Turks* and *Saracens*, that Mother of Abomination, bear witness, *Mahomets* Blasphemous *ALCORAN* also, at

Pauls,

Pauls, *Cum Privilegio* the Great VVhore ſtilled well *Babylon*, never more Bruitiſh after once inlightened, the Night paſt, that *whoſo runs may read*, not a tittle failing, whoſe preſence likened to Lightning out of the Eaſt, even ſhining unto the VVeſt, coming not ſhort of the *Jews* Viſitation, notwithſtanding in as much want (if not more) to be reingrafted ſtanding themſelves, to *Babylon* lo returned.

As moreover witneſs to this day in the firſt place, without Baptiſm; ſupperleſs both; Nuld by them ſuch a Deed of Gift beſtowed on thoſe Maſters of Art our Rabbies, whereas in the Ark its firſt figure all at full Age, till after the Flood none born unto them; impoſed nevertheleſs by theſe *Gog* and *Magog* Admintſtrators on ſuch, knowing *not the right hand from*

the

the left, retaining other Character, none but hearſay; together with the other left off, or taken as ſome morning potion, and other like Tradition: armd with thy Brimſton Bow, appeal to thee, O righteous Iudge, thus where turned into VVormwood, the *Waters of Life* no few periſhing that way the Springs of Iuſtice anſwerable, if weighs not *Nabotbs* Caſe down *Ahabs* ſword, inſtead of *Solomons* ſeaſon'd in the ſtrife of that now deſpiſed Sex, of *Turkiſh* ſlavery more then a taſte partaking, VVidows Eſtates put into the Ballance, in the VVorlds ſtate of Infancy, that if repenteſt at the heart, thou madeſt him not a Beaſt, Rather, leave it to the world [illegible] of ſuch an Expreſsion the extent how much ſince concerned in it, that in Expectation of *New Jeruſa-*

lems

lems Nuptials were it not, better a Thousand times the Gentiles Church since the Apostles Age, to have perished in that foreshewed Siege and Destruction, not a *stone left on a stone*, also they as obdurate.

VVhich Petition wherein without farther Process, not like Attorneys BILLS, supposing to be Heard for their much Repetition.

VVhere lastly to be short with the time like that *little dark Cloud a Hand like*, to the waiting Prophet no small welcom token, as gathered therefrom these of Palmistries Science, extending to the present *Jubile* or Number of Fifty; so points to a Blow when as much attention lends to their Note, as they of such took notice sent from him, those *Baals* Sons the Image of God both alike, as the Baboon or such

like

like theirs carried with the current of the Cormorant Times. And so far for them drinking at the Brooks side their farewel, Four hundred and fifty, for Fish and Fowl such an unexpected evening Banquent. And for the peoples hearts turned back, trusting in heartless Leaders, attended with that blessed *shower* expected as little, so long after the Heavens restrained; and in *Israel no few Widows too, but unto none of them, save to Sareptas Widow of Sidon,* &c. As thereby that line behold measured the present Abominable Age its coming to it self again, cleansed the unparalleld Leprous Time.

October By *Eleanor Tichet.*

FINIS.

52. *The Lady Eleanor Douglas, Dowger, Her Iubiles Plea or Appeal* (1650; Wing D 1996bA) is reprinted, by permission of the Folger Shakespeare Library, from the unique copy held at the Folger (shelfmark D1996.55 bd. w. D2010). The text block of the original measures 148 × 87 mm. This text lacks a title page.

Hard-to-read words and handwritten annotations:

1.1	*Dowger, Her*
1.3	printed word "she" crossed out by hand [transcription]
1.3	she
1.6	Prisoner called to the Bar, Sir *John*
1.7	*Stowel*
1.13	he the last of them: His Mother the onely Daughter in being of that Queen, bears
1.15	that Virgin Name, *Eliz.* The said
1.16	Prisoner
4.1	whose unseasonable
4.5	many words. Lastly, But put
4.11	point
4.13	of

The Lady Eleanor Douglas, Dowger, Her Iubiles Plea or Appeal, No &c.

EVen like a Prisoner so many years that hath been for the Kingdom of Heaven; shews this Prisoner called to the Bar, Sir *John Stowel* Knight, He the Herald appointed for displaying her Title, as in this Looking-glass presented or appears; in the VVest Parts one of no mean Quality or Means: Four and twenty Knights since the Conquest, he the last of them; His Mother the onely Daughter in being of that *Queen*, bears that Virgin Name, *Eliz.* The said Prisoner aged *November* last, Fifty years; moreover well known, whose Grandfather Sir *John Stowel*, unhappily that had his hands in blood, &c. Had two wives living at once,

A begetting

begetting no Common Suits at Law, between the Divorced's Suing for Dower after his Deceaſe, and others of the Name to carry the Inheritance, *&c.*

Thus paraliz'd here with the *Stuarts* Line, the late *Charls* aged *Novembr.* 48. *Anno redempti*, 1648. He ſince the Conqueſt the four and twentieth Crowned of theſe VVeſtern Iſles, whoſe father (that made it death in like caſe) King *Ja:* had himſelf his *Leah* and *Rachel* alſo, two VVives, lived with both; the firſt, ſhe Daughter of one Sir *Peter Yong*: His Son *Charls* about a Moneth yonger then Sir *Archibald Douglas* deceaſed, *&c.* to one of his own name, who marryed her as K. *Ja:* ever diſclaiming that of *Stuart*, *&c.* alway Stiling the ſaid Sir *Peter* his

his Father with due reverence every way; whose eldest Son the Dean of *Winchester*, K. *James* his Executor made, *&c.* about a month before his death, appointing out of his Revenues about 10000 *per annum* for the said Sir *A: Douglas*; with no pleasing Aspect by the *Buckinghams* look'd upon.

And how it hath succeeded, witness such slips what root have taken: His eldest Son *Henry* at full age cut off: His eldest Daughter a Fugitive: Her eldest drowned, *&c.* as better for him too, then his person prostituted so to the Iron rods lash: That token bequeath'd his Son a Milstone in the place, even he and his extirpated, with *William* Conquerer, Bastard as began, concluded with *Charls*, *&c.* By whose

whose unseasonable Elevated thoughts, others bidden be wise: The *Germain* Empires Ebb, for his forewarning who had, and superfluous many words. Lastly, But put it their proper Case; likewise in those Courts of theirs, whether require not of Tenants, an Oath of Fealty, without questioning Possessions, Title of those owners (as whereunto referred) suffices point of Law; so for deciding other-like doubts: Bars striving with that of Justice, one or the other, the Sword with two Edges.

December, &c.

FINIS.

53. *Hells Destruction* (1651; Wing D1995) is reprinted, by permission of the Folger Shakespeare Library, from the clear copy held at the Folger (shelfmark D1995 bd. w. D2010). The text block of the original measures 140 × 92 mm.

Hard-to-read words and printed marginalia:

title page.5	*some*
4.2	cannot
5.3	know
5.8	*World*
6.16	not?
7.20	Patriarks
8.1	*as*
8.20	what Iustice and Equity
10.1–2	*had requited him, Threescore and ten had dismembred them,*
end paper	The origin of the annotation 'Mat: 25' is unclear.

38

Hells Destruction.

BY

The Lady *Eleanor Douglas.*

Apocal.

Behold, the Devil shall cast some of you into Prison, that you may be tryed; and you shall have tribulation ten days, &c.

Printed in the year 1651.

Hells Destruction.

Behold, the Devil shall cast some of you into Prison, that ye may be tryed; and ye shall have Tribulation Ten days, &c. Apoc.

MOst Learned and Honored Iudges, with whom so precious restles Time, of which as who can be over frugal, shunning therefore Multiplicity; long process but wearisom to the wise: Seeing then our Laws how ballanced with Gods Law its profound Precepts, said to be founded thereon, and Reason in its purity consonant thereto, otherwise hath with it no affinity.

Emboldens to present this Paradice

A 2 Posey,

Poſey, durable preſidents which too circumſpect wherein ye cannot be, hereof as enſues.

Adam that firſt Lord Chief Iuſtice or Iudge, before whom *the Lord God brought every Creature formed of the Earth, to ſee what he would call them; and whatſoever he called every living Creature, that was the name thereof*: of a certain admits of no wrong or contrary Names whatſoever in any Courts of Record to be legal or anſwered unto. As theſe inform, accords with the former, the Iudge of quick and dead; where demanded firſt, *What his Name was?* before obtain'd a paſs for that Baptized Herd the Gentiles Prototype doubtleſs, the Devil his Godfather; who made anſwer, ſaying, *Legion, for they were many*; he

Conſiſting of about 6000 Foot and 700 Horſe, the length of Times Foot, the diſtracted Time Aged near 6000 years, he Legion alſo, &c. The Dutch ſtiled Gravs and Boors their late loſs put into the Reckoning, Mat. 8. Mark 5. Luk. &c.

he resident (as it were) in Hell, among the Graves distracted, *&c.*

Thus as we see and know irrational Creatures, these of several kindes retain their proper Names; and very Devils not debarred theirs. Nevertheless that Dominion have over them, Man the *Little W...*, to Angels not much inferior, deemed no little VVonder, as though confined to a lower Region then they, suffer our selves, worse then Bruits undergo Names enjoyned utterly false, instanced as here the dead childe like in stead of the living laid in her Bosom, disputed in *Solomons* presence; whereby no less then bereft both of her good Name and Liberty, witness this their erroneous VVarrant of Arrest, *Ecce vera copia.*

Eleanor

Eleanor Lady *Davers* alias *Douglas*, committed to *Woodstreet-Compter* by *Steedman* Officer to the Lord Major (*July* 17.) 1646. As true that might have ſtiled her *Lord Major*, &c. for any relation between *Davers* and *Douglas*: But by a Non-ſence *Alias* a ſeeming connexion far from Holy VVrits Example, Slime in ſtead of Morter, and Brick-bats for firm Stone, with it diſpenſes not; Confuſion of that conſequence.

VVhence follows next *Simon Magus* alias *Peter*, &c. Saints and Devils become fellows; alſo Fool and *Racha*: what not? as out of the path of his Commandments: of warrants that latitude allowed them, one Name becauſe lighted on, matters not how many falſe beſide, ſo at all with

with Logicks definition or Reason, agrees not, authorized by the proviso (*Alias*)the meaning of it; sometime or otherwise *&c.* though she never afore at any time called by the aforesaid Name belonging to another Tribe or Family; *He that calls the Stars by their Names* (as it were) Male and Female, those lights: where joyns names, no such Bills of Divorce tolerates neither what Antiquity or Custom either occasions, as referred to those judicious, the Sequel of what concernment.

Lastly wherwith even whose additionals *Abraham* & *Sarahs*, consists but of a letter both alike old and new consenting in one. Also *Paul* for *Saul*, one so cautious that way, witness in mentioning the said Patriarks Blessing as well

well obſerves, ſaying, *Not Seeds, as of many*, &c. *but Seed*, &c.

And ſo much for that, *They would have ſaid*, &c. in ſtead of *Alius*: All they can alledge or ſay for themſelves ſo contradictory to Senſe and Verity, better to be juſtified by ſome blinde ſlow Belly *Cretians* ſuch Vipers, then by thoſe intereſted in the Name of Chriſtians, who would be unwilling to Subſcribe to any other.

And hereupon of her falſe Impriſonment undergone ; ſo many years, *If when the cauſe of the Law ceaſes, then ceaſes the Law it ſelf*: wherefore when the Adverſary detains the work, for which the Bond was entred into, occaſioned it, why ſhould he keep it, and her perſon in hold both : or by what Juſtice and Equity

ſtands

ſtands ſuch an Execution any longer afoot or in force, ſhe having been ſince put to the charge for Imprinting the ſame all over, for which was acknowledged the ſaid Obligation of Sixty pounds, no benefit whereby accrewing to her, by a certain Printer, one *Pain*, upon whoſe importunity and proteſtation 'twas obtained.

Another *Quære* thus, ſince Scandalous Names bear Action to be termed Bankrupt, *&c.* why unjuſt Cut-Throat Actions ſo many as the Adverſary pleaſes, no Redreſs in that caſe; as amounting to Hundreds no few by this Broken Printer and his Conſorts, the Burthen of them, no ſhort furrows plowed, *&c.* By City unmerciful *Adonizebeks*, unmindeful of his Confeſsion, *as he had done, God*

B *had*

had requited him, Threescore and ten had dismembred them, &c. And *Abimelech* how rewarded, *doing execution on his Seventy Brethren,* a woman his Executioner (*Judges* 9.) laying on himself (as it were) violent hands, *caused one to slay him,* not impertinent here.

The Milstones lighting on his Head, unominous either to the Press, with *those several Tables under which so many fed by him, sealed wi h his Thumbs and Great-Toes,* to unmerciful Executions of all kindes which extends.

And what Figs and Grapes such Thistles and Thorns produces, proceeding therewith the plot of this Cut-Throat Fellow ; which aforesaid Arrest in his own House, who to draw her thither fain'd had lost the

Copy,

Copy, &c. The ready way for compaſsing their deſperate Ends, ſuppoſed in having her life at mercy, being ſent to the Compter, lock'd into her Chamber by the Keeper: Not long after (ſhe all unready, &c.) between two of them carried down thence, inſtantly ſhut and bolted was into the Dungeon-Hole, Hells Epitomy, in the dark out of call or cry, ſearching firſt her Coats pockets, at leaſt expecting ſhe ſhould have made ſome proffer, &c. Fruſtrate that way, with the Key took away the Candle, there left on the wet floor to take up her lodging, beyond any draught, by ſo many poyſonous Vermin harbored: Like diſquieted Spirits ſetting up fearful ſeveral Notes, courſing about, &c.

B2 About

About an hour after, when as no need of Sun, Moon or other (*Anno* 1646. *July* 17.) whereof notice Extraordinary taken about the City, they brought her again to a Chamber, That Night till day break, the Heavens without intermiſsion flaſhing out Lightnings, as Noonday; The Element like a Caſemate ſtanding open, without Thunder at all, or any Rain, thoſe continued fireworks notwithſtanding.

VVhich time Twelve-Moneth that *Adonizebek* the Lord Major was committed to the Tower, and his Brethren (*Anno* 47.) when the Armies unexpected arrival at the *Whitſontide*, &c.

As for the perfideous Printer how hapned with him, ſoon ſpued out of Houſe and Home, his VVife within few

few days dead, in whose Brothers unhappy Name the Bond taken, he dead also.

And so when the smoaky Bottomless Pit to be opened, oppressed Captives, when seasonable for Elevating their Heads, not to despair longer, *Signs in Heaven and Earth, Sea and Waters* as recommended, contribute their testimony, no obscure Tokens, like *the floods voice uttering theirs*, unbound as it were, *clapping their hands for company*; perplexed people at their VVits end (*Luke* 21.) on all sides in that unparalleld Thraldom, That *better unborn*, then the Uncircumcised their Commissions date expired.

Of which shortned Days for the Elects cause thus, not unparalleld with

with the ten *Persecutions*, *Ten days shall have Tribulation*; The Mysterious Beasts Reign, Crown'd or Mitre'd with *his Ten Horns*, no less then charged with *open Blasphemy, against the Tabernacle*, the presence of God (to wit) &c. *opening no narrow Throat*, repaid *Lex talionis*, that *leads into Captivity*, &c. *Rev*.13.

And so much for the year of Redemption, *lifting up your heads*, &c. Tokens of it likened to the Springs infallible Messengers of Summers approach, *the Fig-tree and the rest*, proclaimed to be by Heavenly Heralds, higher Powers that bids beware the Tree, shaken like those Boughs, *&c.* so to expect fruit forbids it, of the Nations unspeakable travel, until those wonders, *&c.*

VVhere

VVhere not to be drowned in Forgetfulneſs, our New Star in *Caſſiopei*, the French taking eſſay of its influence, that *Herodian* Maſſacre not long after it, ſeen 74 years before the year 1644. our day of Reckonings forerunner; of which Great-Seal day *John heard the number* (*Rev.* 7.) even ſealed the year of God *Anno Dom.* 44. obſerving the motion of the former, that in the Eaſt 74 years afore *Jeruſalems* Iudgment, *ſworn in his wrath* as it were *By Heaven*, &c. the numbred Time of our Captivity or coming out of *Heathen Babylon*, of whoſe *Habeas Corpus* VVrit out of the ſmoky *Abyſs*, (Rev. 9.) commanded *not to harm any, but thoſe not ſealed* (viz.) *marked as for Murther and Theft*, ver. 20. And for myſteries thoſe *Oracles* however grown out of requeſt among our *Rabbies*,

Shewing they have a King over them, &c. (of the Roman Faction) where thoſe cald Cavaleers or Royaliſts, and coyn Dollors and Half Crown Pieces adored (*Dæmoniæ*) (he heard the Number of them) with Pieces of Ordnance, the Fleet or Navies preparation by thoſe hideous Hieroglyphicks ſignified, &c.

Rabbies, prefixt or ſet times ſaid to be but a certain time for an uncertain, & the like, queſtionleſs, of higheſt concernment thoſe undervalued moſt, becauſe flatters not or torments them, termed *wilde notions and brainſick*, &c. as much attentive and grateful *for precious things caſt before ſuch*: ſuffices theſe, and like that Diſpute about *her having five* (Ioh.) Bidden *Go call her Husband*: whence follows, if *Davers* one, then (*Alias*) otherwiſe called *Douglas*, he none of hers either. As farthermore for their farewel, tedious Apprentiſhips canceld forthwith; together with that granted, *What is not true is falſe*; *Ergo*, Libel baſtard ſlips, and ſiniſter actions impoſed on his people, unlawful to be fathered on Gods VVord, his Law thereon either erring not in a tittle.

Eaſter 1651. FINIS.

Mat: 25

54. *Of Times and Seasons Their Mystery* (1651; Wing D 2000) is reprinted, by permission of the Folger Shakespeare Library, from the clear copy held at the Folger (shelfmark D2000 bd. w. D2010). This copy contains some handwritten notes that may be in Lady Eleanor's hand. The text block of the original measures 140 × 89 mm.

Hard-to-read words and handwritten annotations:

3.5	(as testifies)
3.7	diversly
3.10	as though present
3.11	*Tyrant*
3.13	the *Revolted Nations* subdues
3.14	taking
3.15	consent
4.2	for as much as no few having taken
4.17	arrived
5.8	not so proper for them [transcription]
6.5	parts; she pained
6.7	appears,
6.8	perspicu
6.14	points
6.20	displayes about the fall *September*,
7.8	persons
7.11	B [transcription]
7.17	as
9.11	12.
9.16	containd [transcription]
10.14	*Cauda Draconis*
10.20	*Character*
12.7	battering *piece*
12.9	foes
12.10	his *footstool* for one: As *Dixit Dom-*
12.11	*inus, &c.* ,

OF
Times and Seasons
THEIR
MYSTERY.

By the Lady *Eleanor*.

DAN. 2.

And Daniel answered and said, The Name of God be praised; for Ages of Ages; for Wisdom and Strength are his; for he changeth the Times and Seasons, &c.

Printed in the Year. 1651.

OF
Times and Seasons
THEIR
MYSTERY.

By the Lady *Eleanor*.

Dan. 2.

And Daniel answered and said, The Name of God be praised; for Ages of Ages; for Wisdom and Strength are his; for he changeth the Times and Seasons, &c.

Printed in the Year. 1651.

A

PREFACE or APPEAL.

THe *Revelations Gospel*; *blessed Book*; of the Prophet *Davids Generation* cometh not (as testifies) by *flesh* onely, this *Man-childe* of the *Woman seed*, but diversly as in days of old *God* spake then; so now of his *Sons* coming after *one* and the *same way*; by *things* past, as though present, as follows of that *Tyrant Herod* again and his followers; who with an *Iron Scepter*, the *Revolted Nations* subdues, whose *Rod* instead of *Kissing*, to depose *him*, taking *Counsel* with one consented *Thus*.

A 2 Touch-

Touching which *Sacred Oracles*, for as much as no few having taken upon them, unacquainted with ſuch *Pedigrees Myſtery*, untimely to gather of this *Paradiſe Tree*, this hidden *Manna*, conſiſting of *Times Myſtery* and *Seaſons*; breathed by the *Father* the *breath of life*. Therewith *Miracles* and *Gifts of Tongues* not Equivalent.

Have here conceived not amiſs concerning this *Conception* by the *Holy Ghoſt*, the *Fathers* proper *Darling*, by a *touch* to thee *Reader*: VVhich *living Tree* to unfold what *date it bears*. *Off-ſpring* of *David* arrived its *Maturity* or *Period* attained. Thoſe *Olive Leaves* preſcribed for healing the *Nations malady* or *evil*, to his ſervants the *Prophets*

phets for whoſe cure aforehand being *revealed*, by him *ſtiled* his *friends*; *ſervants*, not being of their *Maſters Privy Counſel*, even things ſhortly to be done, attends or waits no longer; as ſhews, for the time is at hand (*Rev. 1. cap.*)

Notwithſtanding his then *reply*, (not so pro- for them it is not for you to know *times* and *ſeaſons*, *precious reſerves* in the *Fathers* own *hand*, or diſpoſe for after *ages*; which *Key* of *David* pretended to be in their *pocket*, a *Legacy* left onely to them and their *aſsigns*, a *ſtrain* or *note* too high for vulgar *ſpirits*. His *eye-ſalve anointed* with *Balaams*.

And thus of *Jew* and *Gentile*, born under one *Planet* or *Sign*, on this wiſe ſignified, no obſcure *Characters*, (*Rev.12.*) *And there appeared a great ſign*

sign in Heaven, *a woman clothed or arayed with the Sun*; *inthroned above the Moon*, *Crowned with twelve Stars*, no other the Golden Zodiacks signs, assigned to those parts, she pained to be *delivered*; the party otherwise called a *prisoner*: At such a time appears, *&c.* not any thing more perspicuous and clear. VVhere inlarged thus. And there appeared another sign in Heaven, *Behold a great Red Dragon*, *having seven Heads*, *&c. And he stood before the Woman*; even points to the sign *Virgo*, by the word *Virga*, *Arad*; where *Scorpio* follows. The *Dragons Tail* imparts no less, the third part of Stars drawing after him, with *Michaels* alarm, the *Arch-angels*. The *Suns* appointed *progress*, displayes about the fall *September*, *&c.*

&c. Day and Night, when going to *halfs* for the *hours* : with the Serpents loosing his place then, by the *flaming sword* expelled, wherewith proceeding *sufferings* of this her *seed*, no *new Gospel* but that from the beginning, as he wrote to that *Lady*. So of this *Deified persons* description; adorned with those *Celestials innocence* in its colours, she in travel, *&c.* That *Ostetrix* where imbrew'd, stood before her in his proper colours also with open mouth, drawn from *head* to *tail*, the *Episcopal Antichristian Order* (attended with his *Train*) stiled *The old Serpent the Devil, that Father rather*, as much to say, *Anno Dom. Octobris Michaelis, Coram Patri totius Angliæ, &c.* Such a one she appeared, *personally* to receive their

judge-

judgement, thence even to be carried away by water *close prisoner* to the *Gatehouse*, witness. And the *Serpent* cast out of his *mouth* water after the *Woman*, as a flood, that he might cause her to be carried away of the flood; wherewith he in the seventeenth *Century* shut up in the *Ark Noah*. Those days cast into the *account*. As *Item*, Against them his waging VVar; those keeping the *Commandments*: *Idolatry* for questioning it: Incensed that remnant that had not bowed the *knee* to *Baals* Altar.

All with one voice. How marvellous are thy works: VVitness *Babes*, *Sucklings*, *Heavens*, *Moon* and *Stars*, ordained to praise his *Name*, whilst others as faln into a *Lithargy*, snoring

or

or with a dumb Spirit poſſeſt. And of whoſe lying in *Childbed*, mounted on *Eagles* wings, there fed; ſo much ſuffices, together with an *Armies* large diſplayed wings, *Aquila* pointing *Northward*, where weekly intelligence none then theſe more faithful from *Patmos* Iſle; bearing date for a time, and times, and part of time, Sevens moyety. Alſo *Dan.* 12. Directed even to *Elias* days: That gracious refreſhing *ſhowre*: the unſpeakable thirſty *Earth*; for which three years and a half had waited. *Daniel* bidden go his way and reſt. (*Apoc.* 5.) As in his right hand, by the ſeven ſeal'd Book, farther expreſſes the time: where five hundred years fulfilling a *period*, amounts to the preſent *Century*, *Sions* Rod of

B deliverance,

Deliverance, when maugre the *old Serpent*: His *Sabbatical* | ominous *heads* crowned; from *An*. 33. when mounted above his *fellow Angels*; as extends unto *An*. 40. took up his lodging in the *Bottomless pit*. Also emblemed by the *ten Horns*, points *An*. 1644. Lost his *Head*: paid that *Tithe*, after bound, space of three years and a half so fast.

And so much for these, A *Woman in Heaven*; no mention of any *Man*, Calls the *Stars* by their name: namely *Virgo*, | *Cauda Draconis*, &c. VVith that *Champion Michaels* shadowing forth Saint *George*; this *Nations* Patron: his rescuing a *Lady* from a *Monster*: where the late *Luciferian Order*, inserted in the *List*, that *Character* or *Badge* of of thoſe faln Stars ; with Courts ſtiled, *Star-Chamber* and *High Commiſsion*. By whom Statutes ordered like a Noſe of *Wax*, their *actings*.

And thus how a like *bleſſed* ſhe that hears the *Word of God*, and does it : Even as the *Womb* and *Paps*, *&c*. That skirmiſh in *Heaven*, as farther that *boute* informs between them. The diſpute about *Moſes* Body ; on occaſions ſuch *Bars* ſo much as bold *Language* from the *Archangels* temper , referring the *tempter* unto the *Lord*. (*Jude*)

VVhere for their deferring, alſo likened to a *Potters* brittle Veſſel ; whoſe diſolved *Leagues* and *Unions* ſuppoſed knit ſo faſt and linked. But *Slime* and *Brick* like his great *Image*, ſuddenly became as the *Summers*

B 2 *mers*

mers threshing floor: Great *Britains* revealed downfull aforehand. The invincible *Stone* seals it; cut out without hands: *Revelations Pearl* more to be desired, then their *Elixir* admired, or *Golden Fleece*: to this battering *piece* but mire in comparison: The never failing *Rod*: His insulting *foes* deposing their *necks* his *footstool* for one: As *Dixit Dominus*, &c. Even wounding *Kings*, &c.

Concluding with her *Jubilate*, who saw this day and rejoyced; disregards not the low estate of his prisoners, fills them: *Whose mercy is on them that fear him throughout all Generations.*

June 24. John Bapt.

FINIS.

55. *The Serpents Excommunication* (1651; Wing D2012A) is reprinted, by permission of Harvard University's Houghton Library, from the unique copy held at the Houghton (shelfmark EC 65.D7455.B652t). The text block of the original measures 164 × 110 mm.

Hard-to-read words:

3.4	Sea
3.5	word damaged appears as "Tr…s"
4.4	Belt:
5.5	t'explain,
5.17	deferr'd
5.19	affront,
5.20	their
6.11	But
6.12	compared with the true,
6.15	Thy
6.16	releas'd 6.18: henceforth
6.21	Types
7.2	*PERGE*
7.7	bold.

THE SERPENTS Excommunication.

In ESSEX where cutting down a Wood, divers of these Sprouts of the Warlike Ash, or Branches grew.

John 3. *And this is the condemnation, that light is come into the World, and men loved darkness more then light.*

Printed in the Year, 1651.

THE

SERPENTS

Examination.

in [illegible] where cutting down a Wood,
[illegible] Walke [illegible]
[illegible] branches grew.

John [illegible] the world, [illegible] light.

Printed in the Year, 1671.

Cæli Jubilate, &c. *July*, *Anno* 1651.
Their Sealed Pardon.

ALl joyn in Consort him to praise,
 ye roaring Sea and Earth:
Not silent, lo with Tr[illegible]s wilde,
 yield lowd extolling mirth.
Yea all his works in places all,
 whose goodness hath no end,
Diverts his presence not, which doth
 from age to age descend.

Magnificat, a Song full New,
 who hath his wonders shown:
Vipers afore visible such,
 Witness, the like unknown.
Firy Serpents in likeness whose.
 a Generation fresh:
Fuel a Judgement bids beware
 the Rod: betokens no less.

To stiff Necks all, stopping the Ear,
 more *Pharaohs* Sirs then one:

Extol him then ye Tokens and Signs,
a ſecond *Egypt* grown.
Afreſh as though him Crucifi'd :
bound with the heavy Belt :
Pierced with Males : The Milſtone like-
as much ; ſuch Hearts do melt.

Poor folk, inform'd though *Moſes* were
and *Chriſt* on Earth again :
No want of Faith ; ſuch *Manna* now
but froath, worth not a Grain.
The Tree (reſerv'd) of Life 'tis dead,
poyſon'd, thus cold and yong :
Enſign of Peace, a Brazen O N E,
figur'd to look upon.

The ſecond Part.

LO on a pole, a living Tree,
Moſes as made for them :
Like Mutineers erected for,
or Age of grateful Men.
The Doctrine of refreſhing Times,
bids not to day deſpiſe,
When creeping things his Miniſters,
bidden Serpents like, be wiſe.

Pointing thus unto him who had
decreed *Moſes* to drown'd :

About

About his neck in Cradle whoſe
afore was ever crown'd.
Far better hang'd a Cable then,
as needleſs now to whom:
Was *Stonage* commended t'explain,
or whoſe that thundring doom.

So vertue of this *Edens* Plant,
what *Daphneys* ſuch Divine:
Apollo's Leaches bitten by,
diſmiſſed from this time.
Preſcrib'd their Swellings to abate,
Antidotes in ſeaſon:
No more the Dragon Red t'adore,
in time awakens Reaſon.

The everlaſting Rod when buds,
Contrition where the Bayl:
Neither to be deferr'd: Submit,
none other will avail.
Set in array his to affront,
their Manhoods then brings down
Such ſucklings by, driven to their heels,
doſt them Victorious crown.

Tongues Satans two edg'd Swords with-
Serpents no more appear: (drawn,
The

The Ax behold, laid to the Root,
  no nesting for you here.
His Cities waste he will repair,
  Vine-dressers other choose,
Fruits in due season to forecast,
  do not their Trusts abuse.

Sing unto him; so to him sing,
  his acts let blocks display,
Who hatching theirs, Cockatrice Balms,
  all one do him obey.
But Frogs and Lice, corrupting Flies
  compared with the true,
Feeds itching Ears; with flying News,
  Egypts Spells bidden adieu.
The Twelve alloted years expir'd,
  so *Woman* releas'd here.
Stancht tedious Issues thine; Peace too,
  be henceforth of good cheer.
Thou *Rulers Daughter* LOE arise,
  Friends return to your Rest:
Types both, how long of *Iuries* such,
  until be dispossest.

By the Lady ELEANOR.

Respice Finem.

DROIT & AVANT.

RECTE & PERGE.

He that doth bear three Lyons, or Passant,
Must Lyon like pass on, *Droit & Avant.*

Aliter,

Are thy ways right? let not thy spirits faint,
Start not aside, be bold, if *Droit Avant.*

PSALMUS DAVISI

Madam,

Y*Our Rod indeed hath swallowed mine,*
Hermes *may now turn* Hermit; *& the Nine*
Virgins turn Vestals to attend that fire,
Which in your Altars Incense moveth higher
Than e're Apollo*'s Harp was heard: Your Brass*
Doth far my Caducæan Staff *surpass.*
As Arch-Types do Types: Whilest I *look on*
Your Streams, I *loath the Lake of* Helicon.

The most Devoted to Honor You, and
unworthiest to be Honored by You
as a Kinsman,

M: Tuke.

Je Le tien.

Hold fast thy Right, that no man take thy Crown:
Unto the Death, give Fortune leave to frown.

AND thou, O *Tuke* Tipysi'd! Loe
in that one grateful Man,
Whose fellow Lepers hast out-lept,
with that *Samaritan.*
Then Favorit Irish *Bryon Tuke,*
Gifts those to thine but lame,
Conferr'd on thy Grandsir: to these
of thy Returns again.

E: Do:

FINIS.

56. *The Benidiction* (1651; Wing D1975) is reprinted, by permission of the Folger Shakespeare Library, from the clear copy held at the Folger (shelfmark D1975 bd. w. D2010). This text also appears as *The Benidiction. I have an errand* (1651; Wing D1977) and as *The Benediction. I have an errand.* (1651; Wing D1976). The text block of the original measures 135 × 89 mm. This text has no page numbers.

Hard-to-read words:

title page.7	in the
[1].7	*no Inferior Honor that Name of*
[1].17	*at an*
[2].11	*forth.*

40

THE
BENIDICTION.

FROM THE

A: lmighty O: mnipotent.

I have an Errand to thee O: Captain.
2 Kings 9. 5.

Printed in the Year, 1651.

For the Armies GENERAL, His EXCELLENCY.

MY LORD,

Y*Our Interest in the Nations unparaleld Troublesom Times: The Flaming Sword for* expelling the Man *in your hand, which Crowns with no Inferior Honor that Name of Yours: Hereof by her Hand a touch presented. Derived from his own, namely,* A. & O. *Letters of no mean Latitude: Armed beside with his Sword: Sun and Moon when as stood in Admiration, witness* ⊙☾ *their Golden Characters, stiled Eyes and Horns of the Lamb,*&c. Their voice gone out into all Lands, *Psal.* (*Rev.* 5.) *Like theirs here, every one when the fifty days at an end, heard in his proper Language,* &c. (Acts 2.)

(Acts 2.) *The Prophet* Ioel *as foresaw and others: By whom Decyphr'd his Thundring Donative of the Crown and Bended Bowe* (Rev. 6.) *as much to say,* O: Cromwel, *Renowned be Victorious so long as Sun Moon continues or liveuer.*

Anagram, Howl Rome: *And thus with one voice,* come and see, O: C: *Conquering and to Conquer went forth.*

My Lord,

OCtob. 28. 1651. *Your Humble Servant,*

ELEANOR.

57. *Given to the Elector Prince Charls of the Rhyne from the Lady Eleanor, Anno. 1633* (1651; Wing D1993) is apparently an edition of a text that is no longer extant, first printed in 1633. This text is bound together with *The Dragons Blasphemous Charge against Her* (1651), itself a later edition of *The Blasphemous Charge* [36, above]. Both texts are separately paginated and are reprinted by permission of The British Library from the clear copies held at The British Library (shelfmark Tab. 603.a.38. [1,2]). The text block of the original of *Given to the Elector* measures 160 × 107 mm, and the text block of the original of *The Dragons Blasphemous Charge* measures 165 × 106 mm.

Given to the Elector
Hard-to-read words and printed marginalia:

title page.7	Witness, how washt the late Cup; that of *Noahs*, &c. [printed marginalia]
3.1–5	Essay [printed marginalia]
3.16–19	As when *Prague* lost, he feasting [printed marginalia]
5.21	(*Sabbaths*.) [printed marginalia]
9.3	stiffned

The Dragons Blasphemous Charge
Hard-to-read words and printed marginalia:

2. 9	sence of so many.
2.10	(c) *Rev*. 17. accomplished on both
2.15	Metropolitanship
3.12–13	*Making war seven years, hath overcome*
4.1–2	H. [printed marginalia]
4.2	Beast
4.10	*Canterburies*
4.17	*Mountague*.
8.1–5	and so with the highest. My Lord of *Canterbury*, Three thousand pounds, close Imprisonment, and to continue till His Majesties pleasure be further known.
8.9–15	The Councel for the Offence insisteth on her Answers, she to appear this day and place by Bond, to hear and receive the final Order and Iudgement of the Court. At which day and place the said Lady *Eleanor Douglas* being called
9.9	written

Given to the

ELECTOR

Prince CHARLS of the *Rhyne*

from the Lady ELEANOR,

Anno 1633.

At Her being in *Holland* or *Belgia*.

Lamentation, Mourning and Wo.

Witness, how washt the late Cup; that of *Noahs*, &c.

AMSTERDAM:

Printed by *Frederick Stam.* 1633.

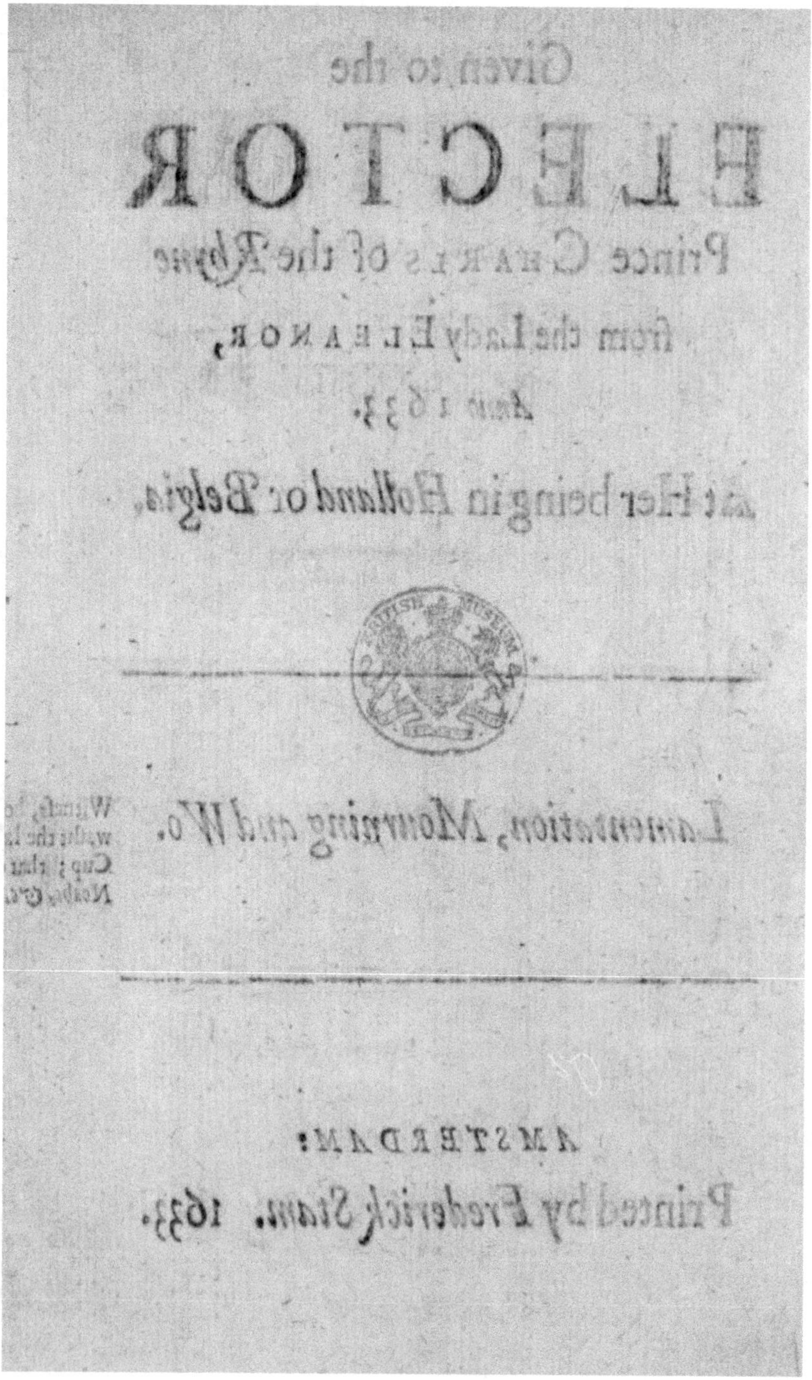

Given to the

ELECTOR

Prince CHARLES of the Rhyne

from the Lady ELEANOR,

Anno 1633.

At Her being in Holland or Belgia.

Lamentation, Mourning and Wo.

AMSTERDAM:

Printed by Frederick Stam. 1633.

To the PALSGRAVE of the *Rhyne*, Charls Prince Elector:

Took Essay of the Cup, 1635. miserably imprisoned by the French House of *Medicis* those *Medes*. Cup Bearer to the Emperor.

The Palm of the Hand, *Dan. Cap.* 5.

The Tune to, *Who list a Soldiers life, &c.*

Psal. *I will utter my grave matter on the Harp.*

By the Lady *Eleanor*, *Anno* 1633.

Babylon or Confusion.

TO *Sion* most belov'd I sing
of *Babylon* a Song,
Concerns you more full well I wot
then ye do think upon.
Belshazzar, lo, behold the King
feasting his thousand Lords:
Phœbus and *Mars* prais'd on each string,
every day records.

2.
The Golden Vessels of Gods House
boldly in drank about:
His own ('tis like) were made away,
bids holy things bring out;
Praising of Gold and Brass the gods,
of Iron, Wood and Stone,
See, hear, nor know not, out alas,
praised in Court alone.

As when *Prague* lost, he feasting with Ambassadors was betray'd, *&c.*

A 2 A hand

3. *Daniel* signifying judgement of God. Execution place.

A hand appears, lo, in his sight,
as he did drink the Wine,
Upon the Wall against the light
it wrote about a line

Stiled *Charls Stuart.*

In presence of his numerous Peers,
not set an hour full,
In Loyns nor Knees had he no might,
chang'd as a ghastly skull.

4. Pleaded hard.

Who might it read, alas, the thing,
Belshazzar loud doth shout;
Calls for Magicians all with speed,
came in, as wise went out.
Caldeans and Southsayers sage,
the meaning who so can

Judgement Parliament. The President in Scarlet.

Of *Mene Mene* third Realms Peer
in Scarlet-Robe the Man.

5. Supt not, drank a glass of wine.

His Majesty forgets to Sup,
Nobles astonish'd all;
Musicians may their Pipes put up,
stood gazing on the wall.
The pleasant Wine at length as sharp
too late, till thought upon

Sentenced his Head to be severed, *&c.*

Division of another strain
unfolds the Fingers long.

When

6.

When to the Banqueting-houſe ſo wide,
where hoſts of Lords did ring, Soldiers alarm.
So wiſely came the Graceful Queen,
ſaid, *Ever live, O King.*
Lo trouble, O King, thy thoughts no more A handmaid that followed him.
forthwith ſhall it be read;
Daniel *there is, who heretofore* Alſo one Mrs *Grace Cary*, *Anno* 1639. A Propheteſs.
like doubts did over ſpread.

7.

Could all interpretating ſhew
which profound man ſoon brought,
On whom confer the King needs would Gave his Order to B. *Juxston*, &c. not permitted to ſend it to his ſon.
his Orders ſight unſought.
Needleſs preferments yours reſerve,
Sir, keep your gifts in ſtore:
High Offices let others gain,
there's given too much afore.

8.

Yet unto thee ſhall here make known,
reſolve this Oracle true,
Sure as in thy Banqueting-houſe, The fatal place.
where all that comes may view:
The Veſſels of my God are brought, (*Sabbaths.*)
the Palm ſalutes thee know
Herewith; for theſe profan'd by thee
threatneth the fatal blow.

O King,

9\. O King, even thou, the most high God
unto thy Grandsire bold,
Caldean Land, a Nation fell
gave them to have and hold.
The Royal Scepter and the Crown
advanc'd whom he would have,
And whom he would he pulled down,
could put to death and save:

Caldeans signifying union mingling, or as Devils, Witches, *Scotland* of old, called *Caledonia*.

10\. Till walking at the Twelve moneth end,
subject full Tides to fall:
Excellent Majesty how gone,
Court exchang'd for the Stall.
Thy Grandsire on as came to pass,
at all yet minded not,
As if a feigned Story, but
his miserable Lot.

January 30. marched from *S. James* Park.

Nebuchadnezzar, a Father and Grandfather, both signifying Bewailing of the Kinred.

11\. Expelled was, whose lofty words
memory can speak well,
Hardned in pride, unheard of such,
the wilde Ass with did dwell:
Sent to the Ox it owner knows,
undreamt of this his Doom:
Fowls their appointed time observe,
wots not the Night from Noon.

By whom termed *Round dealing Gentlemen of Westminster*.

As multitudes grazing at *S. James* of late; which forenoon the Ducks, *viz*. *Duces*, &c. mounted, or flew over the Scaffold.

Even

Even that *Assyrians* haughty heart 12.
droven out with ſuch as bray,
The Diadem fits thee as well,
Aſſe go as much to ſay.
Earth that of late made ſeem to dance,
with Songs of Triumph high
All overgrown, abas'd as much,
among the Herd doth lie.

Diſguiſed Himſelf. Common Soldiers.

Bewail'd alas, dejected thus, 13.
fed, grazing now full low,
Whileſt they bedew the Earth with tears,
diſcerns not friend from foe.
Fields, Woods, for wo ring out as well
as Men, and Ecchoes call,
Mercy this Savage King upon
in holy Temples all.

By Star-light for device who gave, 14.
as graven on his Shield,
An Eagle mounted on the Creſt,
a Hart in ſilver field.
Extold again his God as high,
bleſſed him all his days:
Others reputes them as nothing,
alone proclaims his praiſe.

Threatens Entrails.

His Prayer Book.

Whoſe

Aged ſeven times ſeven, in 49. King and Queen of *Scots* both put to death of late. Render Himſelf a priſoner to the *Scots*. Promiſed or pretended.

15. Whoſe ſeven times till ſerved forth,
in vain for reſt to crave;
Whom Devils Legions do poſſeſs,
a Monarch turn'd a Slave.
Depoſed thus thou kneweſt well,
Belſhazzar, O his Son,
And renown'd ſo deliverance
voiced by every one.

Beſide 1605. *November* the fifth, *&c.*

16. A day a Trumpet made to ſound
for Generations all;
And with a Feaſt ſolemnized,
that no time might recal:
The memory of ſuch an act,
yet as it had not been,
Thy Favorites who are more this day,
or marched to thy Kin.

The *Stuarts* matcht with *Arundel* and *Weſton*, *&c.*

17. Then they adoring Wood and Stone,
Statutes forſake Divine;
Meditate carved Statutes on
in Faction do combine
With Enemies of God moſt high,
to thruſt him from his Throne,
And thus haſt lifted up thy ſelf
ſo facile and ſo prone.

Againſt

Against the Lord of Heaven thy King, 18.
not humbling of thine heart,
But stiffned hast with pride thy neck
unto thy future smart.
Behold polluting holy things
with Sabbath so Divine,
Idolatry and Revels in
that day and night made thine.

He last of those *Caldean Belchaser.* (Anagr.) *Charles Beheaded*, given him, *Anno* 33.

Altars again adored.

But he in whose hands rests thy life, 19.
even breath, and thy ways all,
Thou hast not glorified him
sent this wrote on the Wall.
God numbered thy Kingdom hath
ended; the Hand points here,
In Ballance his weighed thee too,
the set hour drawing neer.

Transported from *Babylon* the Great, to Great *Britain*, *Mene, Mene Laus*, The power of the People.

How light soever set by thee, 20.
thou as thy weightless Gold,
His Image wanting found much more
lighter then can be told.
Parted, divided thine Estate,
given to the *Medes* is;
At hand as these bids it adieu,
finish'd thy Majesties.

Crowned and married 1625. was defeated 1645.

Reveal O Daniel. (Anagr.) *Eleanor Audley.*

B Shews

WHich in ſeveral Courts by her anſwered, *anno* 33. As then *October* 23, ſhe committed to the Gate houſe cloſe Priſoner, by the ſpace of about two years, for theſe (a teſtimony to all Nations) Printed beyond Sea; ſo again the Three and twentieth of *October* was the Iriſh Maſſacre; and likewiſe *Kenton* fight, *October* 23, ſince when Reprinted *anno* 48. *Septembr.* the enſuing Moneth, were given to the then Lord General, with her own hand ſuperſcribed, THE ARMIES COMMISSION: *Behold he cometh with ten thouſand of his Saints to execute judgement on all,* (Jude, &c.) replied by him, *But we are not all Saints.* The Army at St. *Albons* then, when unexpected, came up neverthelesſ doing thereafter that, *January* 30. At her return thence, ſhe taking up at *Whitehal* her Lodging, where attending their coming, to be a beholder of the Prophetical Tragedy, &c.

FINIS.

THE DRAGONS

Blasphemous Charge against Her.

Matth. 10.

And ye shall be brought before Governnors and Kings for my sake, against them and the Gentiles.

Isaiah (63) of the year Iubile compleat, &c.

Thus will I tread down mine Enemies, for the day of Vengeance is assigned, and the year when my people shall be delivered.

Printed in the Year, 1651.

(*a*) *Englefield* Houſe, *July* 28. 1625. the voice from Heaven in theſe words, ſaying, *There is nineteen years and an half to the Judgement day, be you as the meek Virgin.*

Since when Engliſh. The Angelical Language. Its Prerogative Witneſs. All Writs, Reports, Judgements, *&c.* Enacted to be Printed in the Engliſh Tongue onely.

(*b*) And 1644. he on a Friday morning (his day of judgement) *Janu.* 10. beheaded or killed, who burnt that Teſtimony with his own hand at *Lambeth* in the preſence of ſo many.

(*c*) *Rev.* 17. accompliſhed on both, the King aged 48. Beheaded *anno* 1648. current, *January* alſo; the other ſeven years compleat, and eight current Archbiſhop before his going into priſon, tranſlated 1633. *Septembr.* 19. to his Metropolitanſhip, including the very ſeventh and eight moneth: And *Hen.* 7. and *Hen.* 8. their Character.

So again the aforeſaid 19 of *September*, whoſe Coach and Horſe with the Ferry-Boat, going (as it were) into the Abyſs, ſunk down, aſcended again.

To

To the Kings most Excellent Majesty:

The humble Petition of the Lady Eleanor. 1633.

Shews to Your Majesty,

THat the Word of God spoken (a) in the first year of your happy Reign to the Petitioner, upon Friday last early in the morning did suffer: The B: Beast ascended out of the Bottomless Pit, the Bishop (b) of Lambeth, horned like the Lamb, hearted like a Wolf, having seven Heads; viz. Making war seven years, hath overcome and killed them: Certain Books condemned to be burnt, their Bodies shrowded in loose sheets of Paper (by the Prophets being authorized:) This is the third day; if Your Highness please to speak the word, the Spirit of Life will enter into them, and stand on their feet, &c.

Beheaded.

As *Rev.* 11. those two sacred Ambassadors slain then, *Doroslaus* and *Ascham* of more concernment.

So craving no other pardon, praying, *&c.*

(c) *Shall*

Executed He, aged 48, &c.

(c) *Shall go on the Word of God to the King*, (*Rev.* 17.) The Beast that was, and is not, even he is Eight, and is of the Seven, and goes into perdition.

At the Court of Whitehal, Octob. 8. 1633.

HIs Majesty doth expresly command the Lord Archbishop of *Canterburies* Grace, and His Highness Commissioners for Causes Ecclesiastical, That the Petitioner be forthwith called before them, to answer for presuming to Imprint the said Books, and for preferring this detestable Petition.

Sidney Mountague.

Concordat cum, &c. Tho. Maydwel.

Registro

Regiſtro Curiæ Dominorum Regiorum Commiſsionariorum ad Cauſas Eccleſiaſticas. *Extract.*

Tertia Seſsio Termini Michaelis. 1633.

D*Ie Jovis viceſimo tertia, viz. Die menſis Octobris An. Dom. milleſimo ſexcenteſimo triceſimotertio Coram Reverendiſsimo in Chriſto Patre & Domino, Domino* Gulielmo *provi-denc' Divina* Cantuar' *Archiepiſcopo totius* Angliæ *Primate & Metropolitano,* Richardo *eadem providenc'* Angliæ *Primate & Metropolitano Archiepiſcopo Eboracenſi, Honorandis & prænobilibus Comitibus* Portland, Dorſet, & Carliſle, *Epiſcopis* Elien', & Roffen', & Oxon', *Dominis* Iohanne Lamb, & Nathanaele Brent, *militibus legum Doctoribus,* Matthæo VVren *de Windſor* Montford, &

And as *Apocal cap.* 12. By that ſign in Heaven the Woman, *&c.* pointing to the Suns courſe in *Virgo* then, and *Scorpio* about *Michael*-tide. The half year, A Time, and Times, and Half: ſo the Order of S. *George*, or the Dragon rather: Their Lordſhips fall includes, thoſe ſtars.

& VVorral *Sacræ Theologiæ professoribus Commissionariis Regiis ad Causas Ecclesiasticas apud* Lambeth, *Judiciarum seden' presente* Thomâ Mottershed *Regnerarii Regii, Deputato.*

Con' Eleanoram Audeley.

Dr. *Worral*: She appeared, and the Articles and Answers were publiquely read: She was Fined in Three thousand pounds, Imprisonment till she enter Bond with sufficient Security to write no more.

Mr. Dr. *Wren*, Dean of *Windsor*, he consenteth to that which is already said.

Dr. *Montford, Similitèr* with Dr. *Worral*.

Sir *Nathanael Brent*, *Similitèr* with

with Dr. *Worral*; and payment of Costs.

Sir *John Lamb*, and my Lord of *Oxford*, Agreeth with the highest, and to acknowledge her Offence at *Pauls* Cross.

Pauls though thrice as large, unable to contain the tenth part of themselves distracted. Their place found no more there.

My Lord of *Rochester*, with the highest; and if the Court will bear it, he would send her to *Bedlam*.

My Lord of *Ely*, Three thousand pounds, Excommunication, condemned in Costs, and committed *ut prius*, till she give, *&c.*

My Lord of *Portland*, and my Lord of *Carlisle*, desired to be spared from their Sentence.

To whom not unknown the Duke of *B.* Moneth of *August* foreshewed, and other like, *&c.*

My Lord of *Dorset* agreeth with the highest.

My Lords Grace of *York*, imprisonment, and not to have Pen, Ink

C and

and Paper, and so with the highest.

Not a little wrath or wilde, because foretold his fatal Friday to, 1644. his day of judgement.

My Lord of *Canterbury*, Three thousand pounds, close Imprisonment, and to continue till His Majesties pleasure be further known.

She was committed to the *Gatehouse*.

Officium Dominorum con' Eleanoram Tichet, *alias* Davyes, *alias* Douglas.

THe Councel for the Offence insisteth on her Answers, she to appear this day and place by Bond, to hear and receive the final Order and Iudgement of the Court.

Her own Answers, *&c.* by reason Dr. *Reeves*, His Majesties Advocate, so soon as but opened his mouth, saying, My Lords, I am sorry, I could not utter one word more, seemed strucken with amazement.

At which day and place the said Lady *Eleanor Douglas* being called for, appeared personally; In whose presence the Articles objected against her, and her Answers made thereunto, were publiquely read, with certain Printed Schedules and Exhibits

Exhibits thereunto annexed, which ſhe acknowledged to be of her own penning and publiſhing in Print; and the ſaid Anſwers to be her true Anſwers, and to be ſubſcribed with her own hand: By all which it evidently appeared to the Court, by her own confeſsion, That ſhe had lately compiled and written, and cauſed to be printed and publiſhed, the three ſeveral Schedules annexed to the ſaid Articles, ſome containing Expoſitions of divers parts of the Chapters of the Prophet *Daniel*, ſome other ſcandalous matter, by way of *Anagram* or otherwiſe, againſt Eccleſiaſtical perſons and Iudges of eminent place, and ſome others, both derogatory to His Majeſty and the State. And firſt as touching thoſe

He laſt of thoſe *Caldeans.* *Belchaſer.* (Anagr.) *Charls* beheaded.

 matters

matters of high Nature, which concerned His Majeſty, the Court did not any ways proceed againſt her, as holding them of too high a nature for this Court to meddle withal. But foraſmuch as ſhe took upon her (which much unbeſeemed her Sex) not onely to interpret the Scriptures, and withal the moſt intricate and hard places of the Prophet *Daniel*, but alſo to be a Propheteſs, falſly pretending to have received certain Revelations from God, and had compiled certain Books of ſuch her Fictions and falſe Propheſies or Revelations, which ſhe had in perſon carried with her beyond the Seas, and had there procured them to be Printed without Licenſe, and after

Dan. 11. interpreted thus: And at the end of years they ſhall joyn themſelves, *&c.* Late Marriages, to wit, Between *France* and *Spain*, and Great *Britain*, concluding, He ſhall come to this end, and none ſhall help Him, though He of the *Medicis* come, *&c.* Alſo *Dan.* 12. *England* deriving its name from the Angel; and at that time *Michael* ſhall ſtand up, *&c.* And there ſhall be a time of trouble: Such never, *&c.* Where a Thouſand two hundred and ninety, Three hundred thirty and five, amounts to 1625. Theſe ſuch a eye-ſore held to hear of a change then.

brought

brought them over here into *England*, and here without License, vented and dispersed them, or some of them, contrary to the Decree of Star-Chamber, made in the xxviii. year of Queen *Eliz*. of famous Memory; for the restraining of unlawful printing & publishing of Books, and to the manifest contempt and breach thereof, and to the great scandal of our Church and State, and the reproach of the true Christian Religion here professed, and established within this Realm. And forasmuch as by vertue of the Statute of *Primo Eliz*. and by vertue of Letters Patents under the Great Seal of *England*, this Court hath full power and authority to punish as well all transgressors and offenders against the said Decree of Star-

Chamber,

Chamber, touching the printing and publiſhing of unlicenſed Books, as ſuch bold attempts as thoſe of hers, in taking upon her to interpret and expound the holy Scriptures, yea, and the moſt intricate and hard places therein, ſuch as the graveſt and moſt learned Divines would not ſlightly or eaſily undertake, without much ſtudy and deliberation. For theſe her ſaid bold attempts and impoſtures, tending to the diſhonor of God, and ſcandal of Religion, wherof ſhe was found and adjudged guilty by the Court, ſhe was thought well worthy to be ſeverely puniſhed; and was firſt fined the ſum of 3000 l. to His Majeſties uſe, ordered to make a publike Submiſſion *in conceptis verbis*, at ſo many times, and in ſuch places as this Court

He fined His three Kingdoms.

Court ſhall appoint, and as ſhall be delivered her under the Regiſters Hand of this Court; And ſhe was further committed cloſe Priſoner to the Gatehouſe, and ordered there to remain during His Majeſties pleaſure, who had taken ſpecial notice of her and her Cauſe, and referred the Examination and Cenſuring thereof into this Court. And laſtly, ſhe was condemned in Expences and Coſts of Suit, which are to be paid before her enlargement: And the Keeper of the ſaid priſon was required and commanded not to ſuffer her to have any pen, ink or paper to write any thing, in reſpect that ſhe hath ſo much abuſed her liberty in that kinde already.

Aquila weeks. The Woman in that Eagles cuſtody: Not allowed a woman-ſervant, or to have a Bible; totally ſeparated from her husband, and ſo ſtript of all her Means, *Englefield* Manor for one, where the Lord 25. years ſince from Heaven ſpake unto her, of the year, *An.* 44, *&c.*

Concordat premiſſa cum originalibus in veriâ prædictâ facta collacione fideli per me.

Jo: Donaldſon, *Nortarium Publicum*.

FINIS.

58. *The Restitution Of Prophecy; That Buried Talent to be revived* (1651; Wing D2007) is reprinted, by permission of the Folger Shakespeare Library, from the copy held at the Folger (shelfmark D2007 bd. w. D2010). This copy contains some handwritten notes and corrections that may be in Lady Eleanor's hand. The text block of the original measures 140 × 90 mm.

Hard-to-read words and handwritten annotations:

[A3].16	put [transcription]
[A3v].1	then [transcription]
1.1	containing K.C. reign from his ma ... A^{0} 25 Conc. with his arraign[ment] [transcription]
1.19	as [transcription]
4.6	*gratis*
4.19	*King*
5.20	graceless voice [transcription]
6.5	other [transcription]
6.8-9	'r' in printed word 'Farmer' changed into handwritten 'd' to make 'Farmed' [transcription]
6.9	all [transcription]
6.20	(*good Lord, good*
9.12	grandeur [transcription]
10.6–11	since [ ]ermd by late unhapie [ ]ploit of Lo:…. [transcription]
10.12	a Grand-mother.
11.3	Castlehaven [transcription]
11.8	*Fire*
12.3	dost
12.8	Son [transcription]
12.11	Great [transcription]
13.2	*vering*
13.2	*Knights*
13.10	*Tyrian*
16.18	*Judes*
17.18	*Beast*
19.10	*Cum*
20.2	*Baud*
20.10	Kelem Digby [transcription]
21.18	made *even*
21.19	-*hill*, arrived
22.1	*me*
22.18	This man
25.5	touching
26.5	the
31.11	*Grave-makers* [transcription]
31.13	property [transcription]
32.11	*thine*
32.20	*Teeth*
34.13	been
37.14	*Christo* [transcription]
38.13	*guage,*
39.1	*Law*
39.2	*sand under*
39.3	trusted
41.2	hereof
43.7	or Derbys Ale Howses [transcription]
43.13	& worcester another [transcription]
46.9	resisted
47.5	mittigating
47.20	colon following word 'Hand:' crossed out [transcription]
52.6	*Synagouges*

THE RESTITUTION OF PROPHECY;

THAT

Buried Talent to be revived.

By the Lady *Eleanor*.

John 16.

He ſhall glorifie me; for he ſhall receive of mine, and ſhall ſhew unto you.

Printed in the Year, 1651.

To the Reader:

THis *Babe*, object to their ſcorn, for ſpeaking the *truth*, informing of things future, notwithſtanding thus difficult to be *fathered* or *licenſed*. That *inciſion* to the *quick*, hath under gone; without their *Benediction*, in theſe plain *Swathe-bands*, though commended unto thy hands.

No ſpurious *off-ſpring* of *Davids*, but the *Son* of *peace*. This *Oblivions Act*, *Meſſenger* thereof. *Be of good cheer, O my people*, (Iſai.40.) *O ye Prophets*, ſaith your *God*, Tell her,

her, That her *Travel* is at an end; Her *Offence* is pardoned, our *Jubiles deliverance* : Sirs, to be plain, as in the firſt place, *His Commiſsion.* He firſt of the *new Prophet*; ſo his and hers both: She the laſt of the *old.* Confeſſeth likewiſe, or beareth record of his *preſence*, *Born in the fleſh*; of whoſe *Kingdom* no end.

Although not in a *Stable* brought forth, yet a *place* like *reſtleſs*; a hard choice between *extreams* or *ſtreits* of that kinde to diſtinguiſh. No *Inferior Priſon*, or of obſcure *Denomination*; whereof that ſtreet carrieth the *name*: not the leaſt, honored with no leſs then the *Temple* for one.

VVhere belonging to paſſages of *Inns*; The one frequented all Hours, and

and Drinking, not more free then the others darkſom *grates cloſe*; famiſhed there no few. But requiſit *Bridges*, and the like, the true *Narrow way* (by ſuffering) *that leads to life*: From him a proper *paſſage* or mention. Straits of the *Virgins-Womb* had paſſed; beſides Seafaring-perſons his followers in that way not unexperienced, afore arrive the *welcome Haven*.

And ſo far *Reader*, for theſe excluded their *Approbation*, where parallel'd the *Broad-way*, *Ebrieties* leading to deſtruction: Thoſe *Gates* [illegible] into the reckoning, and ſuch holds *chained* up, *&c.* and for this *nonplus* alſo; unwilling to tranſgreſs the bounds of a *Preface*, Shewing as by thoſe *Vigilent Shepherds* (publiſhed)

liſhed) a *Saviour*: Their *peace*: them required likewiſe a *paſs* for theſe from ours, as appears, witneſſed thus, *I give thee charge in the ſight of God, which quickneth all things*, &c. *That thou keep the Commandment until the appearing of our Lord Jeſus Chriſt*; which appearing in his time, he ſhall ſhew, *That he is King of Kings, and Lord of Lords*, (1 Tim. 6.) So in another place, *For the teſtimony of Jeſus*, is the Spirit of Prophecy, *King of Kings, and Lord of Lords*, the Holy Spirits preſence namely: But arrogancy begetting incureable *blindneſs*, theſe ſavored but as *non-ſcence*, not material. *Galio* cared for none of theſe *matters*, &c.

December 25. The *Fleet*.

Poſtſcript.

But bleſſed is he not offended, &c.

Matth.

MATT: 25.

containing K. C. reign from his ... A° 25 ... with his araign...

The Book of the Reſtitution of Propheſie: the great Account, *&c.*

THe ſecrets of the Goſpel under Allegories covered and Parables, precious Leaven, generality or ſcope whereof reflects, although on the day of Judgements ſevere account, unknown day and hours reſerve: Neverthelеſs, days preceding their proper Leſſon, a warning piece for them.

Which Unum Neceſſarium *ineſtimable Pearl, the Kingdom of Heavens purchaſe, that Manna, the unknown Bdellium likened to: who ſold all to compaſs it, requires Artificials none either, preſumes cannot be fruſtrate, or by all troden under foot: of which an eſſay as enſues tendred, to watch all*

B or

or wait: so to beware if wise, how they quench the Spirit, where not unlike his dream of good consisted and bad, both because the thing Established repealable not, then their Decree, much less to be changed, &c. Dan.

That consists not in meat and drink those Externals, unto a wedding likened so many Handmaids, his Kingdoms Epitomy at hand, or forthwith to appear Virgins, their's the priority: five perfection of Numbers: Her quickning time, till when concealed, &c. (Luke) *a prime period, alluding to the Sences.*

Five were wise, other five were foolish; *no lame similitude, ten in number, its full time (as it were) or reckoning had gone out: To whom how befel those that were out of the way, saying,* Our Lamps are out or quenched,

dreamt

dreamt not an answer that way insufficient a point of what consequence to say, They had not thought or supposed, &c. *cast in the teeth with Spiritual Chandleries an Item thereof.*

In what obscurity all without the Spirit manifesting without contradiction as appears : The Bridegroom while tarried all slumbred and slept, bidden be watchful : Therefore watch, for ye know neither the day nor hour, *&c. as that for another*, Could ye not one hour refrain: *our caveat bids*, sleep on, *who allow the Spirit not transmitted beyond the Primative bounds, what real demonstration soever, as if any thing impossible with him : and thus the blinde conducting the blinde, emblems what posture Synods and Church-men found in : How provided of the wedding*

B 2 *garment,*

garment: *when that summons*, Come now for all things are ready: *The Spirit and Bride, saying*, Come, gates of Paradice wide open, no more curse, *&c.* the Tree of Life, *attain'd its Maturity, living waters* gratis Aurum Potabile *as free, no longer to be fasting then.*

And so much for their farewel restless good night, Lord, Lord, *&c. knows their voices as much as they discern (read by them) the Prophets theirs*, &c. *unworthy of the oderiffrous Mariage-gloves, or a taste of those transcendant Confections, even departed from the faith*: Depart ye follish Galatians, who hath bewitched you: *wherewith verily, The* Kingdom *of Heaven expresly unto what Nation or Kingdom to be revealed obvious as those Solemnities*:

lemnities: under the notion of a Wedding, Revels not returnable often: Whenas ſome ſupernatural anointings or Conception, as by that Mid-nights Alarm ſhaddowed forth, in due time adminiſtred: After the way of old illuſtrated, when the Word of the Lord came unto them, Recorded in ſuch a Year of their Reign, and in what Moneth; pointed to a Jubile's moiety, Five times five. The years prime *Anniverſary Feaſt,* bleſſed throughout all Generations: her VVedding-day, faithful Handmaid the Virgin *Mary,* her Five and twentieth of the Moneth, as bears date 1625. Year of Grace: His very Proclaimed Reign, Coronation accompanied with unhappy *Nuptials*: He aged 25. ſhe Fifteen, *&c.* [redacted], Twenty four from

from the Conquests Bastared Generation (compleat *Anno* 24.) matched witha Yoak-fellow, and could not come: five Yoke of other Oxen of his *Oxford* Commons an Item, must attend on her Ladiship, roaring Sabbaths Mid-nights works: No Stranger subject to be unmaskt, and Farmed Bishopricks weekly Alarms. all.

WHile she as free with her impostures to communicate our *Heavenly Saviors* homage to Idol blocks doted on painted Popets, for whose name, wo to the House suffices the Dogs in the same place licking his Blood: Moreoveras in this Maps Circumference contained, of unappy memory, Her five years Fiery Bloody days, of the name such knows none charming Letanies (~~good Lord~~, *good Lord*) they

they know not what, *ave gratia*, &c. *Pater Noster* and Creed alike intelligible, to her ſorrow Matched in her after days.

By her *Virgin Siſter* ſucceeded, in the Five and fortieth of whoſe unmatchable Reign was Interred at the *Virgins Annunciation*, &c. thoſe plentious times farewel: The *Bridegroom Sun* and his *Virgin Spouſe*, parting the hours uſhering the *Obſequies*.

So proceeding with the ſubſequent parable, whoſe Divine Nature as deſcended to a habit of Fleſh: So by this way of Domeſtique Affairs, unto the vulgar capacity condeſcends the Kingdom of Heavens Title to coroberate, preſidents produces of the preſent the fire Talents (to wit) in what Reign.

VVhere

VVhere those three of no obscure quality: Their Lord as though returned from a far Country, had acquired some great Prize or Victory, otherwise some Merchants return.

Called in the first place a prime Peer of the Land, so highly preferred *Audeley* E: of *Castlehaven*, even to hold up his Hand at the Bar, with two of his Servants Arraigned and Eexcuted all three on this wise.

He charged with the Rape, a Page protested at the last cast, a Virgin came into his Lords Service, and went away a Virgin thence. The other an Irish Papist, a Vagrant: The Footman said, had he thought Lords of the Councel bade him speak for the King, have served him so, would otherwise been advised for his Par-

don

Pardon called on St. *Dennis,* whoſe Oath taken contrary to Law and Iuſtice, refuſing an Oath of Allegiance: As Hers not at all, upon whoſe Accuſation before the Privy Counſel; taken away her Husbands life, that in Court appeared neither that day.

Anne Strange Heretrix, of that extirpated Houſe, Iſle of *Man*: In which preferred Bill, this long Proces wherein ſhuned, Anatomized that mankinde Grandams grandeur [redacted], and hers like Daughter, *&c.*

As ſhews in the day of his wrath, wounding even Kings, *&c. Sit thou on my right,* &c. thy Sentence (as much to ſay) until upon them be accompliſhed (*Revel.* 13.) *Even the brutiſh Beaſt wounded in the head,* his mortal wound: *And Hers* (*Rev.*17.)

C *where*

where one of the ſeven Angels which had the ſeven vials (namely the laſt of them) ſaying, *Come, I will ſhew thee the Judgement of the great Whore or great bellied Harlot ſitting on many waters*: The Cities Bridge on Arches, this Map as diſplayed perſon, and place, Circumſtances none more neceſſary: And ſome Haven Town from whence derives her Title of Honor. So from the Title great infers a Grand-mother. Then that imperious Hell-hound, more Mother *Jezebels* then one.

since fermd by late unhappie ploit of fo: ... aling lodges or John.

And with the Holy Spirit moving on the waters: Thus proceeding diſpelling Miſts and Darkneſs, ſaying, *Wherefore doſt thou wonder, or marvel'ſt thou* (as it were) at this *Sea-Monſter*, not more ſtrange then

then true, *The Mother, &c.* I will ſhew thee the *Myſtery* of the *Woman.* Castlehaven And the *Beaſt* that *beareth* or *carrieth her, &c.* Expreſly *Herals* their *Myſtery* which *demonſtrates*: And preſent *Century* the ſeventeenth. *As behold whoſe Arms? And they ſhall eat her Fleſh and burn her with Fire,* beſides hers ſome four-footed rather. *Skull, palms and feet*, no Dog would touch, in reference to *Feaſts.* VVhat *Bruit* or *Fleſh* of Beaſt in moſt requeſt, *Eaten, &c.* Points to ſo many *Stags Heads* born in a *Bend,* or their *Skulls, &c.* Touching whoſe *Arms* ſuffices ſo much refer'd to *Sign Poſts*: the *Red Deer* that Scarlet *Beaſt* alſo; and *Babe* in its *ſcrimſon bearing Clothe,* a Relique to theſe days; in her cuſtody: VVho cried out as much as ſhe

(*Gen.*) him ſolicited daily: By whom his garment laid up, *&c.*

And ſo what doſt thou here *Elijahs enlightning days, founded* in whoſe, Our Capital City *LONDON*, of old called *TROY*, A compound of *Babylon* the Great : As written [illegible] in her Forehead or Frontiſpiece. VVhere from *His Greatneſs* or *Lord Mayorſhip*, not onely derived Title of *Grand Cuckold* ; but Great *Britain* its addition ; ſince exchanged *Anglia* for Br*ute*, no leſs then undone, moſt proper from him (one *change* purſuing another) embrewed in that way of his *Hounds* and reſtleſs *Hunting* to prefer the Beaſts name, accords but with his *Minions* that of *Buckingham*.

So running with him *Abimaz*, The

The way of the *Plain* or present *Wavesing Gothes, Sarazens,* and *Knights* of *Rhodes* out of date, and *Romes* scituation remote: As they to their Father. See whether this thy *sons coat, &c.* whose City on a River no slender one, with its Appurtenances (from which *Allegory* of carrying) *Ships* called *Bears* and *Tygers, Sea-Horses*, fraught with *Tyrian* in *Grain, Pearls, Precious Stones, Gold,* and *Wines* in that abundance, *&c.* VVith Her Cup of poyson arayed *Cleopatra* like, sitting on Seven Headed *Nilus*: The Beast with so many Heads and Horns.

The *Woman* and *Beast* with so many *Heads and Horns*, *&c.* *Church, Court*, and *Cities* description, with *Kings*, their obeisance to her;

her; beside in what *Century*: Also his Seventeen years Reign, until (*Anno* 41) Lead away not unknown, by what means: our *Domitians* days: in whose, this City made an open example: As behold whose Bridge fired, shunning the *fire* to cast themselves into the water, forced; Eaten by *fish*, their *flesh*. Since when others suffering, no few. The *Towers* Blow for an other, with *Lightnings* and *Thunder-claps*, like *Dooms-day*, *&c.* the *Bridge* at the same time Burnt: when she no ordinary *Whore*, charged with a *Husband*, *Blood*: worthy of no other *Cup*, *Naked* and *Burnt*. Credible *Witness* of the *Churches Apostacy*, *Figures* in her later *Days* what a faithful *Spouse*; sealed with *Sabbatical Heads* of the Scarlet coloured

Beast

Beast (*Cruelties Character*) with *Oxford* and *Cambridge*, no mean *Strumpets*, whose Denomination interrested in the *Ten Horns*: Their *Tithe* an *Assembly* sitting at *Westminster*; also carried by VVater in their *Gowns*, belongs thereto.

Furthermore, as this Cities Feastivals and Funerals all set upon this reckoning, such flocking then to behold her Pomp, stiled, *The great Whore with her Cup of Drugs*: Carried in what State, By *Cerberus* Headed Hounds, her black Steeds. She sitting on the *Waters, Her Habitation* or *Title*: By Kings at Arms and others, To give attention to *Preaching Parasites*: whereas compared to the *Block-headed Beast* going to the slaughter. *Man in Honor*, as easie

for

for a Camel to go through an Needles eye, as for ſuch to enter, &c. VVhen made notwithſtanding the Beaſts Image: Laid before them: Adored Obſequies for coſtly *Blacks* bought at ſuch a price. VVelcome *Image* of the *Beaſt, Saint,* or *Devil, Whore, &c.* Honored a like, Sackcloth when more ſeaſonable then *Muld Sack* of late. Of which Sexes more remarkables then one deceaſed.

So withal (part of the Bag and Baggage) of *Saints-days* abuſed as much by the rotten *Whore*: *Eaten, &c.* That *Miſtreſs* of miſchief, and her Servant the roaring *Beaſt* wel-matcht: *Vermillian* Livery in Grain, then *Simon* and *Judes* Commemoration: The *Floods* doings rather and *Sodoms*; crowed on both

ſides

ſides, as though never ſeen afore or heard their *Horn-pipes* attended; whoſe going by water retained to theſe very days *Trojean* Games: a world of Coaches, Belconies filling and VVindows, *Spectators* and to be ſeen; becauſe *Jacobs* Flock ſpotted, like *marks* by the foul *ſpirit* ſet on them: the *tokens* imitated, *Churches* by *Paſtors* thus prepared; a like for *Theators* and *his Temple*. *Varniſhed* with poyſonous *ſpells*, or *paint* (ſhe trodden underfoot) her accurſed *Pictures*; or ſome carted like daſht, *&c.* fit *Gueſts*, *&c.* On the other ſide *reſtleſs-ſwearing Cooks* about *Firs*, and other like *Catch-poles*; appurtenances of the *Scarlet Beaſt*, for this narrow *Table* too *voluminous*: Alſo *Chriſtmas-boles*, All-nights *Game-*

D boles;

boles ; *Dancing* and *Dicing*, ſcored on the *Horns* , with *Goldſmiths-hall* and *Skinners*, from the *Cup* of beaten *Gold* ; a *health* to them too.

Through whoſe *ſtreets* formerly carried in *ſtate* by *Scarlet Liveries*, from all parts flowing to have ſight of her *perſon* or *preſence* : Totally ſtript of *Purple array*, *Margaret Pendants*, *Bracelets* and *Chains* : ſome *Kings Daughter* as though, or *one of the* Blood : became as *deformed*, *diſpicable* and *deſolate*: Hated as formerly, followed with their *Leopard skins*, the naked *Houſe of Lords*, concerned not left ; beſide plundered Pay: *Houſes*, *Kings* and *Lords*, thoſe.

As moreover, *ſhe* none of the left, that *mother* of *Witchcrafts*, branded for a Baud, whoſe *Babel-Pyramid*

Pyramid fired. Fictions of fresh *edition*, *Universsity Excrements* daily; whereby *oppressing Shops* and *Presses* with them: overflowing too shameful, whilest *Close-Stools* set to sale, lined through with *Scriptures old* and *new*: VVhen *Turks*, lest *Gods name* therein, refrain to set their foot on a leaf of Paper, whose *Alcoran Mahomets* the false *Prophets*, *Cum Privilegio*, &c. Accursed *Jerocho's* re-edified *Gates*, in the mean while *Jerusalems VValls*, waste, &c.

So sends greeting *Pathmos* Isle, to this Islands City. He when unexperienced in those *Hieroglyphick* Demonstrations *Saints* dayes, signifying beyond *Paganism* Rites celebrated. St. *John* stricken or transported with such *admiration* and *marvel*

(*O ſtrange*) and ugly: VVhat *Strumpet, Baud, &c.* As *points* to that *fiction*: of raviſhed *Europia*, carried on the *Bull* into the *Sea*: true as the others *Rape, &c.* in *Maps* and *Tapiſtries* ordinary; ſo to another not long ſince no *fiction* on this *River*. Thoſe Brace of *Spaniels, Her Graces* ſwimming match. And *Knight* Errand,
Kelem Digby
no ſmall *Bull*: ſupported by his Hand; laid upon her, *&c.* Requiſit as any in our Cities Map to be diſplayed. That *Eſprit* Order, conjured up again, entered in them as into that *Cities Swine*: becauſe the good *Spirit* moved on the *waters* alſo *Apiſhlike* by the evil *ſpirit*, and *Witches*, thoſe, *&c.* VVith his *Venetian*, ſhe free of the aforeſaid three *Stags Heads*; the *Horns* his too, *&c.* with

her

her *Cup* of *Viper Wine*, that never awakned, whether Drunken or no, *&c.* The *Floods* days not equivolent.

All which copied out by that *Piece*, when his *butcherly birth-day* kept, bound himſelf, *&c.* Inſtructed by her *Mother Baud*, dancing her lacivious *Jigs* and *Tricks*: beheaded the *Baptiſt*; late by her, and her Ladies not onely Hermophrodite acting *mankinde*; but ſworn by his *precious*, *&c.* And *wounds* by their baſe *Players*. *Let us eat and drink, to morrow is our laſt*: More true then aware of, notwithſtanding a *Mote* in anothers Eye perceive, ſo returning to his laſt account, made *even*, or *confeſsion* on *Tower-hill*, arrived the *Haven* above. *This day be thou with me*, *me*, &c. *Enter thou into thy Lord and Masters joy*. *Easter* Term, *An.Dom*.31.

Between those twain Sacrificed, he charged but as an accessary: Had the honor neverthelesse, of first entrance. Next Term theirs *Bradway* the innocent *Page*, and the other, *&c*. VVho in those times thought full little of (*Jud.*) *Bradshaw*. VVhen thirsted after his *Vineyard*, *Mervin* Earl of *Castlehavens*. So many *Manor Houses*, to few or none inferior: This *Kingdoms* forerunner; or what should him befal: His *Enemies* likewise those of his own *house* (to his last) *swearing* at every word *cursing*, *&c*.

This man never once charged with *Oath*, other *then truly and verily*: Taxt with *injustice* neither, or owing

unto

unto any : Paid and rewarded all.

By means of alteration in his *Religion*, as much disclaimed ; and mismatching himself : scandalized by others *misdemeanor*. They who worst reproached him, was, *That he had the best things in him, of any man*, as well as the worst.

Stumbled at the *Church* upon *point* of *Antiquity* : By reason whereof stood in *Poperies* defence, or *Romes*.

That *Fathers* aspersion undergone, *Origens* , *That when he wrote well,none could do better* ; *when he wrote ill, no man so bad*.

Envied among them,*Court* Motions that ever distasted, stiled to be *Pharoahs Son*, or accounted *the Creature of Fortune* ; to whose potent *adversaries*, no *slender* or *mean advantage*.

age. Cast by a *Jury* of Peers: His unnatural *Iury* of *Brethren*, as sold him, *figure* of the *Lamb*, called the *Dreamer*: *scorned* and *stript* of his *Garment*. Also between those two, through her lust. Blood of the *Grape*, as sealed the ones *pardon* the life therein. So the other the heavy *Famins* forerunner hanged up: by Birds betokened on the *Wing*, his flight, *&c*.

In the end tasted *Egyptian slavery*, themselves *Straw-gathers*: *Types* of the scattered *Jews* not onely; but of a *spiritual Famin*, proceeding from forgetfulness, *&c*. Parables, consisting of a twofold-like *Construction*; as those aforesaid *Fellow-servants*, in one day said to have their *Heads* lifted up both, who advanced so. *All knees to*

bowe,

bowe, *&c.* Afterward biding them not be sad; for their preservation sent thither: So much for the word *throughout all ages*, and the *world* through. Also to[illegible]ing his leave taken at *Tower-hill*, so highly rewarded. *Well done good and faithful servant.*

Follows the second a Lieutenants turn next of *Ireland*, *Strafford* no *shallow Brain-piece*, over-powered by the *old Serpents* policy. *Papist* by reason in highest *Offices*, had his *quietus est*, *Easter* Term (*Anno* 41.) Sealed with no ordinary *Arms*, the *Ax*: Neither wanting after his *ability* of what *Faith* or *Belief*, *Kingdoms* slippery places, as unto her a second *Eve*; for her forwardness, ye know not what ye ask: VVhilest on the

E other

other ſide as backward. This piece interlined, as ſhews, when preſented the *Lord General* herewith, a *Manuſcript* prayed to be *priviledged*, by him referred to [illegible] *Bar*: Lodging in *Ax-Alley*, where about three *weeks* ſpace waited on.. Other *uſe* of which (as though) had not made, returned them, not vouchſafeſt the value of a word. No *Babe* in long *Coats*, though bewrayes, *barbarous* alike, not to *bleſs* where they ought, and to *contemn* or *curſe*: No leſs then *cowardize* alſo in a high degree, what ſhould be improved to *Hide*, *&c.*

In the mean time unburied *Lord Deputy Iretons*, ſad welcome rung out, landed, whoſe *Corps*.

Farther giving to underſtand, had advertiz'd him what befel immedi-

ately

ately afore, ſigned with *Whitehals Powder miſchance.* Bidden to ſhake of their duſt, that have but *ears* for a ſhew: How in the ſame moneth *October,&c.* about the ſame hour at *Night, &c.* wherein delivered to *His Excellency* by her a *Book*, Entituled, *Babylons Hand-writing*, bearing date *Anno* 1633. Printed beyond Sea;by the ſame token with *Specticles* put on, read by him. That *watch word* ſuperſcribed, *Is a Candle to be put under a Bed, &c.* (uſeleſs and unſafe) He that hath Ear hear this *Piece. Contents* of the ſaid Book (*Dan.*5.) contained in a ſheet of *Paper*, ſometime ſerved on the late K.*C.* after his return from *Scotland*, *Anno* 33. Crowned, *&c.* concluded with *Charls* Be, from his name, attended

E 2 with

with his Riotous *Lords*, *Belshazer* the last (to wit) *Beheaded*, *&c.* to beware his *Banquetting Houses salutation*; *Great Babylons* exchanged *Feast*, into such confusion, instead of *kissing hands*, stampt a *hand writing*, subscribed, Great *Britains Lamentation Mourning* and *Wo*.

VVhereupon like his *killing* and *slaying Decree*, *Dan.2.&c.* She to *appear* and *answer* forthwith, as by that *Babylonian* reference annext, Signed *Sydney*, *Mountagne*, for *presuming* to *prefer* and *imprint*, *That detestable*,&c. *An.Dom.*1633. *October*, *Whitehals* no petty Trespass.

Of which *Babylonish* Garment hidden as it were in his Tent to this day.

So much by the way for that, and of

of his *Kingdoms* no delay admitting, as by the foresaid *Advertisement* to the speechless Dr. B*a*. B*alams* madness reproved, when served or sufficed from those Ears. *Did I ever serve thee so before*: put to silence by the *dumb Ass*: all as swift that way; but *Midas* Ears, their long Hair hides not, or Perwigs either.

And thus in reference to the *premises*, from a *Wedding*, its late hour. That cry also after a long time his return, of a cried *Court-day*. Officers they called to appear, called *Thou slothful servant Dr*. Laud, as appears, He the last Arch. B. of *Canterbury*. The one Talent even buried by his hand, *Achans* graceless Scholar.

In the Earth: he buried in the

Valley

Valley of *Achor* : a heap of Stones *Dungbil*-like ; his Monument and theirs conſenting thereto : Had not alone troubled *Joſhua*, expoſtulating in *rent clothes* : VVherefore, *&c.*

Root of all Evil, filthy lucre confeſſes did covet : *Thus and thus*, *&c.* In the *Valley* of *Trouble*, took up his Lodging. Sign of the *Spade*, fitter for it.

And thus after a *verbatim* way, for our *biding days* in ſeaſon : Servants ſuch of *Mammon* or *Money*. *Weeping* and *howling* their Portion : Of the *Spiritual Calling*, or *Clergy voice*, as follows : Called *Thou ſloathful*, *&c.* One in ten theirs, reaped where *ſowed* not ; gathered where had not ſtrawed. A ſevere or hard *man*, counted every *Sheaf*, &c. *Tythe* gatherers

gatherers (to wit) far and near, with usury ten in the hundred; not wanting their *Trade*; known in others Name.

In relation to whose *Name* these, even the *Beast* out of the *Loathsome pit* ascended (*Rev.*17.) *And they shall wonder whose names not in the Book of life, &c.* (or *Church-book*) namely, That of *Canterbury* derived from some *Grave-makers* occupation, below the *Dung-hils* office. As at first every *Creature* after its property.

As hence appears how had occupied, *&c.* That *digged and interred,* shrowded it in the ominous *Napkin* to their *Napery* pointing, or *ghostly* array withal.

And one thus unfolding another, as that *farewel* of his. Bidden, the *dead*

to

to *bury the dead*. Either becauſe *rich* and concealed it, or might *allude* to his *name*: In like caſe as *Canterbury* or *Salisbury*.

The Title of *Grăce Buried*, neither in *ſilence* or *forgetfulneſs*. That *Paradox* for another, as implies.

His own bare meaſure meted or returned him; he without excuſe, knew his *Lords* ſeverneſs neverthe-leſs: Lo there, *That is thine*, &c. As from *him that hath not*, ſaying, *Even that he hath ſhall be taken away*. Of Parentage obſcure, as much to ſay, *His Graceſhip digraded ſhall be* (*Jan.* 10.) a day and hour not aware of, to Preach his own *Funeral Sermon*, not mentioned in his *Diary*. That *Fridays Chriſtmas Cup*, *gnaſhing of Teeth*: VVho hated the light, de-pended

pended upon the former days *provision*, *Star-Chamber* Decrees and Articles, was cast into the prison of utter-darkness; besides *Extortion* added to *Usury*; *Covetousness* very *Idolatry*, also with *Gluttony* charged: Emblem'd the *Napkin*, their excess and concealed *Bags*; so of which one *Talent* asigned; in short thus, saying, *Lord he hath ten*: Disputed as though some other better deserved it; answered, *He that hath, more shall be given him*, or *shall have abundance*, &c. Even *Anno Dom.* 1631. *Easter*, (to wit) had the *superabundant* honor to be *the heavenly Lamb*; ancient of days *Figure*, foreshewing by a *Harlot Spowse*, Remonstrates not onely *Romish Massacres*, that *Smoaking Clarret*; but by *Pro-*

F *testants*,

testants, how : to the *brim* filled, *&c.*

VVherewith a word of the said *Prisoners* present release, by the figure *Ironia*, recommended, *&c.* delivered by *His Majesties Chaplains*, His *gracious Message* and *royal Favor* toward him.

He whereas was to have suffered as a common person should die, now like a *Peer* of the Land, *beheaded, &c.* appointed to sift him, no others admitted, having been under *Inquisition* so long; upon their *information*, had thrice taken the *Sacrament* upon it, was innocent of those *crimes* for which adjudged to lose his life: whereupon thanks not omitted, replied, *Would esteem it a coller of precious Stones should draw him up to him,*

him, embraced the Tree, to his Feet.

And by these *Jews*, our *High Priests*, in what *Execrable* maner *Crucified* on their *Altars*, prepared for that purpose; roaring with one consent, *Sacrifice* and *Eat*, both one, or indifferent; also *Altar* and *Table*.

Like as in *Golgotha*, That fatal *Fridays* dismal day, (end of the week) *bowed then the knee*. *Chams* accursed *seed*, by whom a *Giant-crucifix Goliah* like, not the value of a *Napkin* to cover, &c. Horrible to behold, *eclipsed light*, covered the *Ten Commandments*, under colour of an *Altar Hanging*, wanting no *nailing* either: Of course *Woollen*, *Purple*, *&c.* fastned down, lest those precious *Tables* an eye sore.

F 2 VVhilest

VVhileſt mounted over the *Lords Table*, to kneel before it, with the *Centurion*: No *Dwarf* mounted on his *Courſer* or *Beaſt*, to be worſhipped to, ſuperſcribed a true *Copy*, brought over by *Father*, *&c.* in his *Holineſs* Chappel done thereby; *Lietchfield* Minſter for one, were forced afterward for fear of the *Parliament Forces*, thoſe *Clerk-Vicars*, to bury it in the *Dunghil*, not one would harbor it. As this added, the very hidden *Talent*, his *Lords buried Goods*, accords with the *Tables* of the *Law*, from no cauſeleſs jealouſie, as Extant in our *Bibles* ordered, except the Book of *Apocalyps*, and other like, leaſt edifying, may be beſt ſpared; allow others read every *Sabbath*, *&c.*

Beſides

Besides how many silenced imprisoned, other some *Crucified* on *Pillaries*, whilest he and his *Panders*, eating and drinking with the *drunken*. *Item*, *Oxfords* Roast, three hundred *Dowes* or *Deer* at a *Chancellorships* dinner, with *Spiritual Courts* abominable *Bribery* taking on both *Hands* from those stripped of their *livelihood*, *Widows*, but *Tenants* for life; no Commiseration for such, especially, present pay, or else turned out.

Unto which annext his *vow* of *Chastity*, stiled, *Pater in Christo*, &c. Verily, false *Christs* shall deceive many, *whose names not written from the foundation*, &c. (*Rev.*) Exchange *commodities*; those *Virgins* Canonized in his *Tables* admire, *Laud* his name, &c. the apprehended old *Serpent*,

Serpent, alias Satan, whose false *Keys*, as though his *succession*. Iron Gates opened of their own accord, were in their custody (*Apoc.*20.) *The Key whereas of the sealed Abbyss*, *whose proper Seal.*

And thus proceeding, a compleat *Jury*, their *Verdict* with one consent, *Prophets* and *Apostles*; Touching our *Nations story. English, Irish, Scotish* and *French*, every one as heretofore heard in their proper *Language*, fulfilling nothing so *secret* and *covered*, that shall not be revealed and made manifest.

Including withal *Times* reign or reckoning, *Five thousand five hundred years compleat since the Creation.* Secondly, *Two thousand years before the Law, and Two thousand under the Law.*

Law. Laſtly, Compleat *One thouſand under the Goſpel*, from thoſe intruſted Servants account, which would have amounted (had not he faln ſhort) to *One thouſand* years more, or had it not happened into ſlothful hands. The *Three Ages* otherwiſe equally *Two thouſand* years unto each allotted.

VVhereof thus (*Apoc.* 17.) concerning *place*, *time* and *perſons concomitants*: *Five are faln; one is, the other is not yet come*: *And when he cometh, ſhall continue a ſhort ſpace*: Namely, *the fifteenth century paſt and gone; the ſixteenth bears the name, the other not compleat to be, but ſhortned*. Here is the minde that hath *Wiſdom* (*viz.*) to number the time, *Pſal.* reflects on King *James* the Sixth.

Others

Others as weak as he wiſe, From a *Parliament* called by himſelf, to abſent *his perſon*, here ſignified, *Of one minde*, called by *write*; others by moſt *voices*, *Choſen ones*. And as rewarded for the moſt part afterward, who hate the *Whore* and make her deſolate: A *Widow*, as much to ſay, *Utterly ſtript of all*, *by the Ten Horns*, fulfilling ſuch a time, amounting to ten years ſpace. As moreover, *For God ſhall put into their hearts, to fulfil his will*, &c. repented as it were; alluding to which words, *Have mercy upon us*, *and incline our hearts*, &c. or *Write thy Laws in our hearts we beſeech thee*; where *acts* againſt *Idolatry* and *Adultery*, made death that *act*, put into the *liſt* of the aforeſaid *ten Horns*, ſo many years fulfilling.

In

And ſo proceeding with his *relation* hereof, who wrote to her ſtiled ſo highly, *The Elder, To the Lady Ele: &c.* in our *British* Language, as to the full expreſt, *Apoc.* where accompanied with inſatiable *Tyrant Times Myſtery* (*Eating all things*) his diſplayed *Arms*: alſo the *Stuarts Arms* or *Coat*; The B*ulls-head* blazoned, that ſign in *Taurus*, giving to underſtand farther of *Europes* Apoſtate Churches, returned to *wallow in the mire*, all from her ſitting on the waters of B*abylon*, with inlarged *skirts*, thoſe of *hers* as afore ſhewed; computed by the *floods* execrable *Age*, *Hearts* as *Buff*: Signed and ſealed with B*abylons* Great Seal, The Beaſts heart: That fulfilled ſeven times, not to be Cancelled either.

G How

How long afore his *reaſon* to him returned a *Jubiles* ſeven times ſeven, where included.

Laſtly, VVhat affinity between them, fixt place as ſignified from her ſitting poſture, *&c.* So *reſtleſs time* by the weary *Beaſt*. Names written on both their foreheads, That *City Miſtreſs* as upon Hers, *Myſtery Babylon* or *London*: Alſo *Mars*, *Mercury*, *Venus*, *&c.* Names of *Blaſphemy* on *his*, all *her moſt humble Servants.* The *Scarlet Beaſt*, *Anno Ætatis*, *&c.* when her downfal withal.

By perſons repreſented of no obſcure *decent*: Namely, Houſe of *Derby*, matcht with the Houſe of *Oxford*, armed on both ſides with the *Horns*: no *ſecret*, either he bearing the *Stags heads* metamorphized into

into a *Bear* : Father of him who ſuffered. On all *four* acting in their *likeneſs*; and other of that kinde on *Stages* in *Paſtorals*, tumbling to the admiration, *&c.* A *bleſsing* by the *mothers* ſide : So *wherefore wondereſt thou at ſigns, &c. Rev.*17. or Derbys Ale Houses x

And ſotiſh *Bathe*, another like *odium* of the *Beaſt*, forerunners of Great *Britains* unlucky derivation, not onely from B*rute*, but of *Cities* names their ſympathizing, called after theirs, or participating. & worcester another

And ſo far for theſe literally prefigured, The preſent *Age* ſent to *School* to the *Ox*, *Aſs*, and *Camel*; In their *Litter* knows its owner, better obſerves the time, and for *times Myſtery* and *Seaſons*. The weaker *Sex* preferred more proper for them, requisit for former days neither: To whose Disciples not a little earnest (answered) *A thing not in his dispose, he was but the Word*; but *his Fathers* where he pleased, a *Conception*; as much to say, By *special Grace*: VVitnessed to be by them though.

And shunning *Circumlocution*, where like theirs under terms *Enigniatical*, concealed by way of *Numbers* and *Figures* numberless. VVhosoever understands any one, serves for the *master Key* to that *hidden Treasure* or *Quintesence*.

Of the *third* or *last similitude*, as follows, The last days dreadful *alarm* likened unto that *Sessions* day, attended with a guard of *Angels*, by a *King* sitting on his *throne*: On the

right

right hand faithful to *him* that ſtood in defence of the *cauſe*; on the *left* that took up *Arms* againſt him: which *remarkable* days of ours compared to a *Shepherd*, *Jacobs* ſeparating the *ſheep from goats*. Our *Nations* prime Commodity, *Wool*, *Sheep*, no mean fence againſt *Hunger* and *Cold*; alſo pointing to ſuch a *year* and *ſeaſon*: *viz*. The diſtance between the *Suns* entrance into *Aries*, the crowned *Ram*; probable when as the *Worlds Creation*. And that of the Tropick *Capricorn*, the *Hoary bearded Goat*: Character of *Spring* and *Winters* approach; whereby ſlaughtered ſheep as betokens an execution day, at hand; from the *fold* to the *ſcaffold*, *&c*. So foreſhewed to be the very *year*, aforehand *revealed*.

His

His *sinister reign* shadowing forth from 1625. *March*, until his *arraignment* after *Christmas*, the late *Charls* his doleful *note*, imprisoned, harborless, not worth a House: A Stranger (to wit) of another *Nation*, where by way of retaliation as he had close imprisoned others, unresisted *The blessed Lambs voice*, and *Decembers*, &c. Made it his own case, in as much, *Had not visited the least of those his Lambs*, *Hunger*, *Starved* and *Cold*: For any *mercy* on their part, *Rebels* proclaimed to his *Kingdom*, alluding to the *flaming sword*; That *Doomsday* when they expelled thence, whose *Valediction* depart, *&c.* The never departing *sword* and *smoake* their portion. The *Righteous* on the other side, or *Round-heads*

heads pointing to *Paradice* their return to *peace* : As those *Thunderclaps* then, and *Lightnings*, *August* 23. *A°* 51.

So much for mittigating this *Mittimus* to *Hell*, exprest by way of *Terror*, his *Judgement day*, the *Scape Goat*, no *Purgatory* pardon : whose Funeral attended with those three, *Hamilton* and *Holland*, *&c.* made by them ; No private Account, Extends to oppressed Prisoners *Christmas* Cry, Verily *Sterved* and *Rotting*, so over charged those *Penfolds* ; under any *colour* or *pretence* buried quick, by accursed *Cut-throats* daily, and imprisoned *Anno* 45. VVhose Twenty three years Reign, from *Anno* 25. until *Anno* 48. The *Scepter* when resigned, the Hand ꝫ *Table of bounty*

bounty turned to a *blow*; as by the Fruitlesſs fatal *Tree Mythologiſed*, of three years ſtanding afore came under the heavy *laſh*; beſides a *Leaſe* of three years more ex-pired; Allſo a warning to *Churches*, his *Houſe*, for uſurped *Keys reſignation*. Enēmy to the *Nations cure*, the *Tree* of *Life*: *Scepter* and *Keys* both. The *Epilogue* or *End* of which *ſubject* or *excommunication*, concluded with his *voice*, The inthroned *Lamb* in *Bethlehems* Manger, concerning otherſome in this *burthenſome age*; as unto thoſe groaning reſtleſs *Companions*, overcharged by their unmerciful owners. *Come unto me alſo ye heavy laden, and* (your intolerable *Tax*) *I will eaſe you*, and inſupportable Bonds, thoſe *Yokes*, ſaying, Be-

hold

hold I come quickly: *Whose righteousness like the strong Mountains*, &c. *Judgements like the great deep*, to be manifested, &c.

Thus much for their *Analogy* or likeness, unexpectedly also come upon us unto the last great days account likened. And for this *Antichristian Beasts* sevenfold names of *blasphemy*, namely *Saturn* and *Jupiter*, &c. Days of the week *christned* in theirs, and Moneths in their *commemoration Ethnicks*; after *Julius C* and *August*, containing VIC-LVVVI. Those *Members* no inferior ones of the *Roman* breed, Hours of the Moneth *666*, whose number also pointing to the days of *Noah 1656*. By so many Moneths amounting unto 55 years and a half. Then

H *Treasure*

Treasure lyable to *Plunder* , of more consequence to count those at hand, including his reign of 55 years and odde Moneths succeeded him, wounded not least by his begotten *Brutus*.

So then how passes for current, or accords together, that such taking upon them to be qualified with *humility* and fear of *God*, do *prohibite swearing* in others and *blaspheme* themselves. Make *Laws* for strict keeping the *Sabbath*, notwithstanding so stupid and carnal, stop the *ear* against his *Word* and *Law*, *Thou shalt have no other gods*.

VVhilest the *simple* deluded by *assumed Titles* of *Saviours*, and the like; called *Defenders of the Christian Faith*, An *Antichristian* Authority other-

otherwiſe called, *The Blood thirſty devouring Beaſt*, riſing out of the *Water* in the *Lambs* Roſe coloured *Robe*; wounded (as it were) with the Crown of *Thorns*: whoſe *Baptiſm* and *Sabbaths* exerciſe, edifying as their *Bells*, *Feaſts* and *Faſts*, part of the Forty and two Moneths reckoning; and *breathing* the *Holy Ghoſt*, witneſs the three abominable *Frogs* for another; with the *gift of healing*, *Miracles* by *ſucceſsion*, the *Image* of the *Beaſt* worn, &c. So of *Elias* Alarm, *Fire* cauſing to come down, &c. (*Apoc.* 13.) in the ſight of men by *lightning* as *burnt* ſo many *Barns*, laſt *Harveſt* fulfilling; alſo the *Harveſt* great, but *Laborers* few: Put to their Heels for the Preſs then, not to be forgotten. Subſcribed I am *A*

H 2 &

& O, &c. And have the *keys, &c.* As our *Liberty* proclaims ; and the *Holy Ghosts* reign for evermore, sent in his name the *Spirit* of truth, otherwise called *The Lamb* ; likewise by their *Synagouges* how confined within *Iron gates* : VVhose *Angelical* presence signifies, as declares, *He was in prison* ; *Depart ye cursed* : *So blessed are they,* called unto ye Lambs marriage supper.

Qui se humiliaverat, ipse exaltabit.

Ele: Da. & Do.
Fleet.
Candlemas.
Her *Purification.*
1651.

Principium & Finis.

59. *Tobits Book, A Lesson Appointed for Lent* (1652; Wing D2016) is reprinted, by permission of the Folger Shakespeare Library, from the clear copy held at the Folger (shelfmark D2016 bd. w. D2010). This copy contains some handwritten comments that may be in Lady Eleanor's hand. The text block of the original measures 140 × 90 mm.

Hard-to-read words and handwritten annotations:

Front leaf:	The legible sections are as follows: 'psalm 1. That Man is Blest that Hath noT walked wronge / Ungodly counsel to depend upon / nor in the waye sinners dwelt or stay / Nor sat in scorners chayre' [transcription]
4.2	by him: Or *fatherly Instructions*
4.10	as at
4.11	by
4.18	But
5.15	not [transcription]
5.16	*cometh*
6.3	*Pen'd*
6.7	*thee*
7.8	far
7.14	*consequence,*
7.16	'of' crossed out by hand; '*those*' transformed into '*Those*' [transcription]
10.2	*Refining*
11.5	long
15.2	spared
15.5	much [transcription]
15.16	Luke *&c.* [transcription]
16.5	*friends of*

Lstoy

Ags like theire sinners bond

psalm: 1

That Man is Blest that hath not
walked wronge
Ungodly counsell to depart
nor in the waye sinners dwell
or stay
Nor sat in scorners chayre
[illegible]

41

Tobits Book,

A

LESSON

Appointed for

LENT.

Expressing, foresaw upon his being anointed. And from the seven days celebrated Nuptials success: the Churches glorious estate at last. After that order put to flight, under the conduct of Asmodeus, *or delivered up to Satan: Enemies of the Lambs Marriage-Supper.*

Printed in the Year, 1652.

CONTENTS.

Concerning the Angel his chasing away the Evil Spirit bound or confined to those remote parts. And of Tobit *restored to his sight. By a Fish made whole. Then* &c.

AND here *our Lord.* As in these troublesome days of ours shut out of doors *Excommunicated* thus. His word *Entrance* none admitted. By whom preferred *Fishermen.*

Even his words *recommended old Tobias Story* anointed with the *Fish gaul.* VVhere in short, not *impertinent* though for this present *Frozen Age.* Insisting not on that *ample*

A2 *confession*

confession of his uprightneſs related by him: Or *fatherly Inſtructions* ſuch.

But with the matter proceeding of *Raphael the Angel* (ſo called) one of no *mean deſcent* ſent for their *cure*. In that obſcure maner diſguiſed who took their *Journey* together forthwith. The *yong man Tobias* accompanied with his *Dog* as at other times probable amongſt whom. Alſo by their *Overſeers* what credit given unto *Prophets*. As in theſe *days particular Revelations* how valued, evident ſoever *held uſeful as Scaffolds*. The *Structure* being *erected*. To them ſuch *anointings* not ſuppoſed *appertains* with whom *New Lights*. But like a *candle* at *Noon* lighted to behold the *Sun*.

Such

Such an *Egyptian Ecclipse* or *blindness* of their *understanding* the *face* or *state* of the *Church* under. By all degrees of men. *undervalued*. Notwithstanding whose assurance, *Nothing so secret and reserved which should not revealed be at last*. Even *whatsoever spoken in darkness, manifested not in Cathedrals. But on the House top*. No obsure place &c. as here whether they will forbear or hear, offered these *Blessed Declarations*, whose House this left unto them, *Behold desolate*. Verily shall see him not until they say, *Blessed that cometh in his Name*.

Eliah his *Spirit* (to wit) *Even a new restoring all things first*. VVitness (Cor. 4.) *Therefore judge nothing before the time of the Lords coming, who will*

will lighten things hid in darkneſs. Namely the ſame *Spirit* by which they were *Pen'd* or *Written*, to be explained. Of which *refreſhing Times* the Spirit again pour'd out. The *Apoſtle* again thus (Tim.) *I charge thee in the ſight of God, who quickneth all things, That thou obſerve the commandment until the appearing of our Lord, which in due time he ſhall ſhew,* teſtified on this wiſe. *King of Kings and Lord of Lords. The alone Potentate and ſole Biſhop* (as much to ſay) then the aforeſaid time *&c.*

And ſo farther touching the *Church* returned to its perfection: arrived the Harbor of reſt. He foreſhewed when he was yong that girded himſelf *&c.* (*Peters*) mentioning which Myſteries

Myſteries (*ver.* 15.) *Wherefore gird up the loins of your mindes, be ſober, and truſt perfectly in that grace brought unto you in the revelation of Jeſus Chriſt,* &c.

In the mean time inhibited, doting about queſtions, begeting *ſtrife*, far from *ſobriety*, bidden prefer rather agreeable to godlineſs, *wholeſom Doctrine*, as for the other but frivolus and vanity.

And ſo much for them charged to try the Spirits, a point of ſuch *conſequence*, dreamt not of their *Tryal* ſo nigh. *And for gold their Godſlaves thereto, blinding the eyes of those innumerable Angels as though immortal* &c.

Go forward ſhall with the former that of this *Fiſhing Voyage*: where the

the dumb *Fish* for expeling the dumb *Spirit* named *Asrnodeus* from *Demon*, derived *That Grand Tempter*. He bound as declares in *Egypt*, ominous to our days miserable Slavery that Imports. The *Gaul* prefiguring *Judgement* seals it: Since no removing such *Scales* without it, or able to clear the sight together with the *heart* and *liver*, That compound *Cordial* against *Obstructions*, of that nature: where buried in the *Bride-bed* so many from poysonous infused *Spels*. Forewarned not one by anothers example, or convinced *Judgements upon Judgements* notwithstanding.

And passing on with the good *Angel*, a *Door* or *Passage* opening in *Heaven*. The *Abyss* its darksom *hold*, whenas

whenas free to and fro for *Apostate Spirits* and *Fiends* to ascend. He gotten loose taken with her. Unacquainted with *Tobias Tobacco* dryed on those *coals*, affrighted with the *smoak* and *choking scent* removed his Lodging.

Unto what time extends other *amplification* requires not. Then those twice assigned seven days, for such *Rites* solemniz'd *&c.* together with those Angelical drugs *Operation*, emblems of the *Spirit*, its *Elixir* powder er of the aforesaid *Heart* and *Liver* of the *Fish* ready to devour him, as though would have swallowed him.

VVhere the one as betokens a scourge from his immediate Flight. Thence so in what Century the other informs, without doubt about

B the

Floods age. The *Gentiles* their *Tryal* or *Refining* time. Signed with the *Fish* leaped out of the *Flood Tygris*: of which except the *Intrails* reserv'd for *Medicine*, the rest *rosted*.

Sacraments or *pledges* of *Scriptures* first their *history* part for the *Churches* present service or use. Afterward to be imparted those subtilties revealed the mystery of it. Also ominous *Prototypes* of the Age present its *Bloody actings* from his being assaulted. By the *Fish* prefiguring the escaped *Danger* of this *Encounter* with the *Diabolical spirit*. Blown up in such a moment unexpected.

VVhereupon after his short effectual *Prayer*, aluding to *Eves temptation*. *Sarah* his wife who conceived with *child* (a mystery none of the

least)

leaſt) joyning both in *Prayer*. Barren ſo long. Maugre the *Old Serpents* rage at length bound by the Angel. Sions ſtate ſhadowing forth her *Fields* unmenur'd: ſo long laid fallow. Ploughed again nevertheleſs as in *primitive days*.

Laſtly thence of their departure. The Angel *Raphael* returned ſent about the money. The ſworn days a Fortnights ſtay ſworn by *Raguel*: which time of abſence in regard of his Father ſeeming much longer, took their leave with the *Bride* and large *bleſsing*: together with the ſaid *Dog* following to his blinde *Maſter*, not a warning piece little beneficial.

In the next place: How they went afore the circumſpect *Guide* and *Tobias*, to prepare things in readineſs

B 2 for

for unexpected *Ghests* such. His Father meeting him, by whom healed forthwith: forerunner of the stumbling Age significant *dictates*; on the future of a supernatural blessing: when swallowed up in dispare, at their wits end.

According to whose express charge observed, not to take a strange woman to wife. But of his people one of a holy descent: withal above others, namely of *PRIDE* to beware: his *seed* that they might inherit the *Land*. Arrogancy (not unknown) the *Mother of want*, inseparably joyned with a servile condition. Concluding with the *beatifical Vision* the true healing *Angel*, discovering himself unto them: one of the seven *Angels* or *Spirits* in presence of the

Throne:

Throne: preſents the Prayers of the *Saints* (to wit) in reference to the *Sabbath*, alludes to the *Sabbatical Century*. *Raphael* ſignifying *The Medicine of God*.

As his vigilent parents for his return, alſo to watch all: So from whoſe ſtumbling mentioned in what obſcurity the laſt days. Dreaming of ſuch anointings as much or ſupernatural *participations*.

His *Grave* whenas prepared abroad and at home both: their ſon by whom ſhe conceived (as it were) returned into a *New World*: ſuch a change cloſed with Father *Tobias* Trumpets Alarm or Prayer: by the *Angel* preferred, withal pointing to his cloſe *Impriſonment* in the *Whales womb*, three days in *Travel* of him:

heard

heard whoſe cry out of the *Deep*, who acknowledges brings up from *Hell*, *&c.*

And *Hell* and the *Grave*, one and the ſame word *Gebenna* expreſsing both as in that ſimilitude from unlikeneſs.

And in Adam *as all died*, *ſo in Chriſt all made alive*, Cor. 15. *O the depth of the wiſdom and knowledge of God.* By the Ancients *Origin*, *Tertullian* and others: no queſtion made thereof *with whom all things poſsible*, but to be implacable abſolutely.

And ſo much for theſe, the *childrens teeth not ſet an edge for the Fathers default*. *Captive Angels* put into the *Liſt*. The word *Everlaſting*, That canſell'd alſo being determinable ſignifying *Ages*: and farther, paſsing

paſsing for *ad infinitum*. VVhen as ſpared in tender conſideration of one *Heathen City*, wherein ſo many thouſands diſcerning not the *right Hand* from the *left*. And *Eve* hers as a thouſand for one how much more ſpotleſs in that nature. Then why thus incenſed our *JONASES* againſt them *Abraham* ſtiles *Sons* worſe then annihilated a million of times, whoſe love a thouſand times ſurmounts his hate: By that *Jewiſh* envious elder Brother as figured, expoſtulating with his Father, *&c.* where in truth a *prefixt* ſpace of *time* ſignified, more proper then of place fixt, *&c.*

Prayed *O ye ſinners, therefore repent, turn and do Juſtice, ſhew mercy, who knows whether he may extend commiſeration to this ſinful City*: as in behalf

half

half of thoſe *Innocents*, whoſe *ſit-tuation* not far from *Paradice*.

As by the *Fiſh* taken in *Tygris River* of ſuch vertue, *&c. O make ye friends of the unrighteous Mammon, That they may receive you into everlaſting Habitations*: pointing to the tranſitory whereon ſet up their reſt, all *dote*. So finiſhed his magnificat *Tobias*, that *Brides* incomparable *Luſtre* or *preparation*: *New Jeruſalems* precious *Edifice* ſo raviſhed with it.

From the Lady Eleanor.

Tobias ſignifying good, for Good-Friday.

F I N I S.

---

60. *Bethlehem, Signifying The House of Bread: or War* (1652; Wing D1978) is reprinted, by permission of the Folger Shakespeare Library, from the clear copy held at the Folger (shelfmark D1978 bd. w. D2010). The text block of the original measures 140 × 90 mm.

Hard-to-read words:

4.12	Brocht
4.13	with
4.14	*Centurion*
5.3	*City*
5.9	possessing
6.4	*Prison,*
6.13	*signifying*
7.2	City
7.8	*Assessment*
7.20	*vail*
9.15	The
10.1	*Core*
10.19	*Audley*
11.1	her
11.2-3	the *Paternal*
11.4	thence
11.16	*Bulls* or other like actings:
11.18	*livion*:
12.1	*hold him*
12.2	*en him*
12.3	*Fleet*
12.15	conjured

42

BETHLEHEM

Signifying

The House of Bread: or VVar.

Whereof informs,

VVhoso takes a small Roul to taste cures forthwith Distraction in the supreamest Nature; with such vertue indu'd.

By those TORMENTERS Firy SERPENTS as they when stung, were heal'd a view by taken of the Brazen ONE.

Ezekiel 16.

Cause Jerusalem to know her Abomination, &c.

Printed in the Year, 1652.

Touching the healing of the present Evil.

SHews (as not unknown their *influence*) the better that we may judge of things to come; from Examples in vain not recorded of things past: *Achan* as his story for one *Epitomizes*: By whom the *golden Wedge* or *Tongue* hid, wch trespass until discovered of his, *thus and thus*, *&c.* no peace or presence of the *Lord* any more. So whence as follows, *Cause the city to know*, *&c.* for recovery of *health*, to have knowledge of the *disease* since the first step thereto.

Acters or consenters, know ye or be informed, of one and the same na-

ture:

ture: that of the one *Talent buried also by him or not improved, &c.* where so much for the better ordering the *Medicine* or *prescribed Rule*: shewing how in days of those late *high Priests* it came to pass *Anno Dom.* about 36. By them after what *execrable maner Crucified the Oracles of God*, their late *Altars* for that purpose prepared; to be short, over which a *Gyant Crucifix* being erected: *The value not of a Napkin to cover*, &c. exposed to the view of all to *kneel before it*: like as in *Golgatha that Fridays dismal Day bowed the knee*: Then his humble Servants also.

VVhich *Goliah portray'd with Crown of Thorns*, wanting neither its *Superscription*, done by that in his *Holyness Chappel*, a true *Copy* brought

B 2 over

over by *Father*, &c. VVhileſt that *Original* as ſhamefully covered the *Ten Commandment* at the Eaſt end plac'd : to their low *obeyſance* at every turn, leaſt an *Eye-ſore*.

Had contrived under colour of an *Altar Hanging*, faſtned down to the wall of courſe *purple Woollen*, even to *Ecclipſe that Light of Lights* : whereby to cover the *Ten Commandments* no *obſcure buſineſs* as befel : Brocht in *Litchfield Minſter* : where this *Monſter Table* appointed with the *Centurion*, armed at all points, mounted on this *Courſer* : the *Beaſt* worſhipt too.

Unſufferable to behold, the one not more *ignominiouſly expoſed*, then the other *obſcured* : to give free paſſage to whatſoever abomination.

VVhere-

VVhereupon, *O accursed*, as obliged for bringing to light the same *Court* and *City* to awaken: Their *Lord Major* that *year* a *Litchfield man*: resolved to set some *mark* upon their *purple Covering*, whereon she cast a *Confection* made but of *Tar*, mixt with *wheat Starch*, with fair *Water* heated, *&c.* Them possessing with such outrage flocking about it, some *Gunpowder Treason* as though: upon whose *fright*, post a *Sergeant at Arms* was sent down at *Candlemas* to carry her up: Carriers unable to pass after that *Summers drought*, when as much wet again: At whose *Arrival*, though *Higher Powers* certified by the *Sergeant at Arms*, of such causless *Panick Terror*: yet said, in regard *who knows what she may do in other*

Mother

Mother Churches: Held it fit to commit her to the *Cities Custody*; one as it were buried quick in *Bedlems* loathsom *Prison*, infected with those *foul Spirits* day and night *Blasphemming*: where was shut up by the space of two years sufficiently published or brūted by that time.

VVhen began, the *War* kindled in *Scotland*: And so much for that designed place *Bethlehems Hospital*, alias *Bedlem*: *Bethlehem* the *House of Bread signifying, or War, &c.* undergon in behalf of that *crying cause*, causless *Jealousie* of hers.

Never that was called to appear or *answer* whether *Guilty*, but *surprized* in that sort, or the *Adversary* against her appearing: *Conscious* of their abominable *Cause*, of whose proceedings

ings by *Luke* thus recorded: in which aforesaid City dwelt a *Judge*, saying within himself not difficult to judge when *Though I fear not God nor reverence Man*: yet least this never ceasing *Widow* by her VVriting, *&c.* inlarged thus no ordinary *Assessment* were mentioned: who by casting into their *Treasury those two mites*, from that seeming *Paradox* outstript them all, as *Englefield Manor* for one devoured, *&c.* accompanied with the unparalleld last *troublesom times Description*: when that *Famine of Faith* a fore-runner of his coming.

Return shall to the former of those *precious Tables*, able to dissolve *Millstones: Like as when rent the Temple-vail, Stones and Graves unable to contain*

tain, &c. men whileſt more *obdurat* as in the Bladder of uncircumciſed *Hearts*, which nothing *penitrates*.

Oyes, himſelf *Weſtminſters Cryer*, in the mean while much *People* gathered, ſeveral *Soils* thoſe, proclaims *Earth*, *Earth*, in relation to her *Ears* not few: how difficult to bring forth fruit in kinde, three for one miſcarrying: *He that hath ears*, &c.

VVhich *Ten Commandments* laſtly how were Reſtored; although yielded not to *pluck down* the aforeſaid *Cloth* that *Altar Ornament*, appointed nevertheleſs in an *Azure Table* the *Law engraven* to be in *gold Letters*: Hanged up in all *Churches*, bearing date, *Anno* 37.

To be buried in ſilence neither, where by accident in the *Priſoners Chamber*:

Chamber: when brought into it, beheld on the wall *the two written Tables in Moses hand coming down out of the Mount*, the onely *Ornament* or *Picture* there, hang'd up on a *Nail*: not long after rent down by the *Keeper*; because unto some shewed or as a token then what done by them in *Churches*: not calling to minde; *As visits unto the third and fourth Generation, That hates them, so mercy shews to Thousands that love his Commandments.*

And so return to their *sufferings*: As testifies (*Apocalips cap.* 11.) The *Tables* of the *Law* those *Lights* inclusive with the two invincible *Witnesses*, *Where the Lord Crucified*, &c. *Waters* converting into *Blood*: whose insulting *Enemies* rewarded there-

B after

after with *Care* and his Companions in that *Earthquake*, &c. as when *Prebends* and *clerk Vicars* forced, were afterward for fear of the *Parliament Forces* to bury it in a *Donghil*, not one would harbor it, so low obeysances had made thereto afore: And this in *Stafford*-shire their *Lord Major* aforesaid of that County, fulfilling what *honor* his *anointed ones* to expect: *If the Master of the House call'd Devil or Beelzebub*: *Bedlem* no dishonor for them, especially whilest *Grandees* in that measure their *House* infected.

As moreover for that aforesaid Shire or intire County of *Stafford*, not long since belonging to whose *Ancestors*, the house of *Audley* of no obscure *Denominations*. *Audley* of

England

England from whence derives her *Antiquity*. *Touchet* of *France*, the *Paternal Name*. *Castlehaven* in *Ireland*, thence her *Precedence* alike concerned in each. From the *Province* of *Wales* that of *Davis*: and *Douglas* of *Scotland* the *Doughty*: such a one of the several *Nations* as intimates no less: *A Prophet shall the Lord like unto me raise up unto you of your Brethren, him shall you hear, &c. And every soul which will not hear, shall be destroyed from among the People*: (Acts 3.) so a *Deliverance time*, whose word a *Law*: stoops to no *Bulls* or other like actings: *Prophets* howsoever buried in the *Land* of *Oblivion*: which *Nations*, as much to say, avenge her shall of her Adversary thus supported: *My hand shall*

hold

d him fast and my arm shall strength- *him, nor gates of Hell shall not pre-* *vail against her*: *O Hell or Fleet-Pri-* *son* (to wit *where is thy Victory* now.

And for a leading touch, these suffices for this *spreading soar*, its swellings to asswage threatning, no less then *Ears* and *Throat*: By our *Achans* for the accursed thing put among their own *stuff*, as upon his *Humiliation shewed them*: And for this Analogy between the *Times* of spiritual *Egypts* Map. And for that prophet parallel'd with *Moses*, by whom the Golden Calf conjured down by his *Serpent Rod*: *Those first and last of Prophets*. Containing a Brief of a like Dispute as between them about *Moses* Body. *Jude*.

June. *Elea: Aud: Touch: Castleha: Da: & Do:*

9781032918044